CHENG & TSU

"Bringing Asia to the World"

变化中的中国
Reading Into a New China

Deciphering a Changing Society

Volume 1

Second Edition

Duanduan Li ▪ Irene Liu

CHENG & TSUI

"Bringing Asia to the World"™

Copyright © 2017, 2010, 1998, 1992 by
Cheng & Tsui Company, Inc.

Second Edition 2017
First Edition 2010
A New Text for a Modern China 1998
A Chinese Text for a Changing China 1992

5th Printing, 2023

27 26 25 24 23   5 6 7 8 9

ISBN 978-1-62291-125-7 [Second Edition]

Library of Congress Cataloging-in-Publication Data:

Liu, Ruinian.

[New text for a modern China]

Reading into a new China: integrated skills for advanced Chinese = [Bian hua zhong de Zhongguo] / Duanduan Li, Irene Liu.

p. cm.

Originally published: A new text for a modern China, 1998.

Parallel title in Chinese characters.

Includes index.

Chinese and English.

ISBN 978-0-88727-627-9 (v.1 pbk.) – ISBN 978-0-88727-693-4 (v.2 pbk.)

1. Chinese language –Textbooks for foreign speakers—English. I. Li, Duanduan. II. Title. III. Title: Bian hua zhong de Zhongguo.

PL 1129.E5L585 2009

495.1'82421--dc22

2009075154

The *Reading into a New China* series encompasses a digital edition on Cheng & Tsui FluencyLink™. Visit cheng-tsui.com for more information on the other components of *Reading into a New China*.

Printed in the United States of America

Publisher
JILL CHENG

Editorial Manager
BEN SHRAGGE

Editors
RANDY TELFER with LIJIE QIN

Creative Director
CHRISTIAN SABOGAL

Illustrator
KATE PAPADAKI

Photographs
© Adobe Stock
© Cheng & Tsui

Cheng & Tsui Co.
Phone (617) 988-2400 / (800) 554-1963
Fax (617) 426-3669
25 West Street
Boston, MA 02111-1213 USA
cheng-tsui.com

This Second Edition of *Reading Into a New China* is dedicated
to the memory of an inspirational teacher, author, and friend, Dr. Irene Liu.

Contents (Volume 1)
目录（上册）

Preface to the Second Edition

It has been six years since *Reading Into a New China* was first published. The enormous changes taking place in China, which have occurred at a breathtaking pace, call for a new edition to update information and discussion topics regarding this remarkable country. The Second Edition's subtitle, *Deciphering a Changing Society*, conveys the complexity of contemporary China; while the completely revamped layout adds new clarity to our instructional design. In this new edition, we have made the following changes and additions:

1 Updated lesson content to reflect recent changes and developments in Chinese society.

2 Substantially revised several lessons (e.g., Lessons 1 and 9) and made technical corrections and clarifications in the rest.

3 Added more communicative exercises to further bolster the textbook's pedagogical approach (outlined in the Preface to the First Edition) and for students to apply their language skills to practical tasks, enabling them to "read into a new China" more effectively.

4 Provided the main readings in each lesson in both simplified and traditional characters.

5 Removed the HSK column from the vocabulary lists due to the change (in 2010) from four levels to six levels and the realization that this information was not frequently referenced by many students.

6 Added a host of images, including lively photos and infographics, to further engage students and complement the Second Edition's contemporary new design.

Volume One of the new edition contains ten lessons, which are now organized as follows:

Section	Objective(s)
Pre-Reading Activities Pre-Reading Discussion Lesson Overview	To activate students' existing knowledge about the theme To provide visual clues about the lesson and stimulate discussion To provide cultural, social, and historical background
Vocabulary Vocabulary-Building Skills Idioms and Common Phrases Main Vocabulary	To broaden students' knowledge and use of words, idioms, and phrases To develop vocabulary-building skills to increase speed and effectiveness in vocabulary acquisition
Reading First Reading: Skimming for the Main Idea Second Reading: Scanning for Details and Comprehension Reading Skills	To present high-interest topics that develop students' reading skills and stimulate discussion
Word Usage and Sentence Patterns	To explain and model new words and sentence patterns
Grammar	To introduce new structures and grammar items To summarize previously learned structures and grammar items To illustrate how previously learned structures and grammar items can be used in more complex ways
Practice Pronunciation Word Usage and Sentence Patterns Grammar Comprehensive Exercises Reading Speaking Writing	To provide contextualized exercises for integrated language skills development

I would like to thank the teachers and students at the University of British Columbia who have used the textbooks during the past several years for their helpful comments and suggestions. Working with the Cheng & Tsui staff was once again a great pleasure. I thank, in particular, Jill Cheng and her excellent editors for their ongoing encouragement and help.

I am also grateful to Dr. Patricia Duff of the Centre for Research in Chinese Language and Literacy Education (CRCLLE) at UBC for her constant advice and generous support. Her graduate student, Hui Li, has been a wonderful assistant with the revisions to this textbook.

I hope that students and instructors will find the new edition to be both inspirational and instrumental in tackling challenges at the advanced level of Chinese language learning and teaching.

Finally, it was with deep gratitude and affection for my co-author, Dr. Irene Liu, that I completed the revised version of this book. Sadly, Irene passed away in June 2015, before she could see the final version. However, it was her vision and passion for Chinese language education that laid the foundation for this book, and I therefore dedicate it to her.

Duanduan Li
Vancouver, Canada
September 2016

Preface to the First Edition (Abridged)

It has been a decade since the publication of the advanced reading textbook *A New Text for a Modern China*. Since then, many things related to the book have changed. First, the social and economic situation in China has undergone a tremendous transformation. Second, in recent years, research in the field of second-language reading pedagogy has produced a rich pool of findings on how people process texts when reading. This knowledge has enabled teachers to develop approaches to teach reading more effectively. Third, the linguistic theory of Chinese discourse grammar is now more developed. A functional, discourse-based grammar, according to many experts, is more suitable than a less contextualized sentence-based grammar to explain how the Chinese language works. All this new information has continuously reshaped our teaching philosophy over the years. We felt it was time to revise and re-envision *A New Text for a Modern China*, transforming it into a timely, updated textbook that takes into account all of these developments, reflecting new conditions and contemporary issues in the "New China."

Before revising this textbook, we went about a series of tasks to ensure that the new edition would meet the needs of students and teachers. We first carefully re-examined *A New Text for a Modern China* in order to understand the areas that needed changes. Next, we reflected on our own teaching experiences and studied the most current research findings in reading pedagogy and discourse grammar. We also asked our students who were using that textbook for comments and suggestions. Based on that review process and the information that emerged, we developed a group of guiding principles that we have used to write the new textbook, now titled *Reading Into a New China*《变化中的中国》. Apart from the many improvements in content, this book also features a completely new design, tailored for maximum ease of use for students and teachers. The textbook is now divided into two volumes, with each volume including practice exercises as well as instructional material.

The Target Learners

Reading Into a New China is designed mainly for students of Chinese as a foreign language at an advanced low to advanced high level of proficiency, as designated by ACTFL standards (or third-year Chinese language courses at most North American universities and colleges). Heritage students at the intermediate level can also take advantage of the many new features of this textbook to advance their language and especially literacy skills.

Our Guiding Philosophy: Skills Integration with a Special Focus on Reading

Reading Into a New China aims to develop both fluency and accuracy in Chinese through a topic-based syllabus. The topics are of high interest to students and provide maximum opportunities for thinking and discussion, promoting the development of both linguistic and communication skills. While we have adopted an integrated approach to teach all language skills coherently, it is on reading and building reading skills that we place our special focus.

The reason for this focus is that in beginning and intermediate levels of Chinese study, oral communication skills are usually stressed in order to build a strong foundation in spoken Chinese. However, at the advanced level, it is not enough to be proficient only in oral communication skills. Students must also have well-developed written communication skills to meet the challenges of potential employment and increased engagement in Chinese-speaking communities. Third-year students, with their sound foundation of first- and second-year Chinese, are at the ideal stage to begin to learn formal written Chinese.

One of the unique features of this reading-focused textbook is that the reading is supported by other skills. Students are encouraged and helped to further advance their oral proficiency while developing reading and writing skills. Third-year students should learn to expand their speaking repertoire from topics of everyday routines and interests to more intellectually and linguistically challenging topics, such as social issues and current events. The combination of writing exercises and discussion questions in this book provides ample opportunities for students to go beyond the text and put all their integrated skills to work.

Some Pedagogical Considerations on the Use of English in Instructions

In language teaching, we take the position that an effective language classroom should be one where active student participation in Chinese is the norm. It should not be a place where the instructor lectures and students passively listen. The instructor's role in the class is to create an environment in which students can actively discuss the content of the lessons, to reinforce and build upon previous learning, and to clarify specific difficult or confusing points in the lessons. This ideal situation cannot happen unless the students are well prepared before class. In order to help students prepare effectively, we have written all explanations about grammar and reading skills, and general instructions, in both Chinese and English for easy comprehension. Chinese sentences used as examples are provided with English translations. However, simple instructions (especially repeated ones) are only given in Chinese to increase the target language input and reduce over-reliance on English by learners.

About the Lessons

One of the keys to teaching a language effectively is to present high-interest, provocative material that will engage readers. The readings in this book have been carefully chosen to include a variety of viewpoints on current issues of population, education, family, gender, environment, business, and technology in a rapidly changing China. Vocabulary and concepts related to these issues are recycled throughout the text, building up a basic core of knowledge.

The transition from dealing with spoken-style materials to written-style materials can be a demanding but gratifying process for learners. Well-chosen materials at an appropriately challenging level can maintain learners' interest and inspire them to continue to develop their language and literacy skills, as well as their knowledge of Chinese culture and current social issues and events. Texts that are well beyond students' linguistic competence might cause anxiety and frustration. For this reason, we have chosen to use mostly modified materials written specifically to suit the literacy level and linguistic needs of third-year students, rather than purely "authentic" materials taken directly from magazines or newspapers, which might be too difficult for learners at this level.

The genres of writing presented and developed in this book are of three kinds: narrative, expository, and news features. These lessons can help students build up their knowledge and skills concerning general writing styles normally used in Chinese works of literature, official documents, essays, and news, and thus are a good source for understanding twenty-first-century Chinese society. This serves as good preparation for learners' future reading of unmodified authentic written materials in real life.

Features

Pre-Reading Activities

Each lesson starts with a brief overview in English to introduce the thematic content. Visual stimuli (photos or illustrations) related to the theme, followed by discussion questions, are also provided. The intention is to help activate students' prior knowledge and prepare them mentally for the main text. In addition, the overview also provides information about the text's organization and genre of the main reading. The information in this section can benefit students in three major ways:

- by enhancing students' opportunities to make sense of the information they will encounter in the text;
- by increasing students' interest and confidence in the topic and thus motivating them to read the text; and
- by establishing realistic reading expectations about the lesson and the skills required to read the material effectively.

Vocabulary

In addition to the lesson's main vocabulary list, this section includes a new feature called "Vocabulary-Building Skills." Designed for self-study, this part presents ten to fifteen new words composed of characters known to the students. Students are asked to guess the meaning of the compound words based on the meaning of the known characters. This activity encourages students to make intelligent guesses and helps build students' knowledge of Chinese morphology in order to increase their speed and effectiveness in vocabulary acquisition. Another advantage of this practice is to let students get used to seeing new words without anxiety. Students in the habit of reading word for word tend to stop at every unfamiliar word to look up the meaning in a dictionary. If the pauses are long and frequent, comprehension will suffer because the train of thought is interrupted. The ability to make intelligent guesses from context can help students take the risk of tolerating some ambiguity or uncertainty while reading, and thus improve their reading fluency.

Approaches to Teaching Reading

The most common method of teaching reading in Chinese at present typically involves decoding, or "bottom-up" information processing through word-by-word translation of the text for comprehension. This is inefficient and often leads to slow, inaccurate reading. Our position is that both top-down (activating readers' background and expectations for comprehension) and bottom-up (decoding words, phrases, and sentences for comprehension) processes are necessary to tackle the complexity of reading. Thus, in *Reading Into a New China*, we emphasize both strategies by asking students to use their prior knowledge to understand the main idea of the text, and relate it to their own worldview and opinion. At the same time, they should also pay close attention to detailed information and deeper meaning by decoding important vocabulary, phrases, and sentences. Skill-focused activities that highlight the thinking process of proficient Chinese readers are carefully designed. For example:

First Reading: Skimming for the Main Idea

This activity requires students to read the whole text without stopping and then select the main idea of the text from three provided statements. This is the goal of the first read-through of each lesson.

Second Reading: Scanning for Details and Comprehension

This activity requires students to look for specific information in each text. Typically, students respond to true/false and multiple-choice questions, link specific solutions to problems, and locate technical terms and definitions.

Other specific skills of the reading process are articulated for the students in each lesson. They include guessing meaning from context, understanding written structures, identifying text organization, making inferences, distinguishing facts from speculation, and many others. The objective is to gradually build up students' ability to read Chinese independently in the future.

Word Usage and Sentence Patterns

This section uses contexts provided by the text to focus students' attention on the usage/function of ten to fifteen target items of vocabulary and sentence patterns. These target items have been selected for their usefulness in communication, especially in formal and written styles. Extra examples are provided to illustrate varied usages and functions in different contexts beyond the text.

Grammar

To reach the goal of developing integrated language skills, *Reading Into a New China* gives systematic attention to grammar for both fluency and accuracy in Chinese. Each lesson not only introduces new grammar features or rules (e.g., word formation rules, idiomatic expressions, topic chains, rhetorical devices, formal and informal styles, etc.), but also reviews and summarizes previously learned fragmentary grammatical items in a more systematic and functional way (e.g., categorizing functions of connectives for cohesion and coherence in reading and writing in discourse-level communication). Grammar is explained in clear and plain language, from a pedagogical perspective, without unnecessary technical terms or jargon.

Contextualized and Communicative Exercises for Integrated Language Skills

Reading Into a New China provides students with ample exercises for learning and practicing the integrated skills of reading, speaking, and writing, in addition to vocabulary and grammar. We have significantly increased the number and variety of exercises in the textbook, eliminating the need for a separate workbook. These contextualized exercises offer students opportunities to carry out communicative tasks that require exchanging information and negotiating meaning. For example, vocabulary exercises are always provided at an extended discourse level so that students can use the newly acquired language for comprehension and communication. Grammar exercises provide both controlled practice and communicative activities. Reading skills covered in the text are practiced in interesting and relevant supplementary reading tasks to reinforce the training. In the speaking activity, students are given a chance to make connections between the readings and their own lives and opinions, to recycle newly learned vocabulary and structures, to develop their oral communication skills, to approach the readings more critically, and to share their opinions with their classmates. The final exercise is always writing, which provides another chance for vocabulary recycling, writing skill practice, and closure for each lesson.

Acknowledgments

Writing this book has been a wonderful experience. During this period of time we have received a great deal of help, encouragement, and support from our dear friends and colleagues, for which we are grateful. We wish to acknowledge their contributions to this book project and express our appreciation and gratitude to them.

First of all, we would like to thank John Meskill and Patricia Duff, who offered us their professional advice, scholarly feedback on second language learning, particularly for Chinese language learning, and expert help in English editing throughout the writing process. This book would not have been possible without their sustained support and encouragement.

In addition, we would like to thank the following graduate and undergraduate students at the University of British Columbia who contributed in various ways to the creation of this book, from technical help to content editing, proofreading, and audio recording. They are: Pan Luo, Jingchan Liu, Rachel Wang, Hui Yu, Elliot Yates, and Wanhui Qing. We also acknowledge, with thanks, practical and financial support received from the University of British Columbia Centre for Research in Chinese Language and Literacy Education and from the Social Sciences and Humanities Research Council of Canada that enabled us to remunerate these assistants.

The preparation and completion of this book were greatly facilitated by the editors and staff at Cheng & Tsui Company, whose assistance and professional work on the manuscript was superb. We are particularly grateful to Jill Cheng, for her great confidence and support in this project, and our excellent editor, Laurel Damashek, for her sharp mind, keen eye, and guiding hand in helping to bring this project to closure.

Finally, we thank the Chinese language learners in the United States, Canada, and elsewhere who have provided so much inspiration to us over the years and who have been the impetus for this new textbook. We hope you will enjoy it!

We hope this new textbook can help our students develop language proficiency that can live up to the name of "advanced Chinese." We are also aware of the fact that, despite our best efforts, it will have its shortcomings. We welcome your ideas and hope that teachers and students who use it will provide us with any feedback or suggestions for improvement by contacting the publisher at editor@cheng-tsui.com.

The Authors
March 2009

Introduction to the Basics of Written Chinese

After studying the language for two or more years, you will have learned the fundamental system of everyday spoken Chinese and informal written Chinese. Having acquired this knowledge, you are now ready to advance to formal written Chinese. In order to smooth this transition, we will outline some important aspects of written Chinese: punctuation, sentence boundaries, topic chains, zero-pronouns (unstated/implied pronouns), and classical words used in the modern language. You will learn about and practice these topics in more detail in the lessons, but a basic familiarity with them at the outset will help you become comfortable with written Chinese.

Punctuation

Fourteen types of punctuation marks are used in written Chinese. Many of them look and function like those used in English. However, there are subtle differences. For example, due to the language's syntactic flexibility, commas are used much more frequently in Chinese than in English. There are also differences in the appearance of some punctuation marks, such as periods (a small circle in Chinese vs. a small dot in English) and ellipses (six dots in Chinese but three dots in English). Finally, a few punctuation marks (such as 顿号 and 书名号) are only used in Chinese. (See Lesson 9 for details.)

Sentence Boundaries

As in English, a period is used to end a sentence in Chinese. However, guidelines as to what constitutes a Chinese sentence differ from the rules in English. An English sentence is defined by syntactic rules alone. A Chinese sentence, besides syntax, must also take semantic factors (i.e., meaning) into consideration.

Syntactically, a Chinese sentence consists of one or more clauses; semantically, each clause provides one piece of information about the subject or the topic of discussion. There are no specific rules to limit the number of clauses that can be included in a sentence. The author decides the number of clauses, based on how much information he or she intends to provide. For example:

> 她是法国人，汉语说得很好，在北京住过多年，现在在上海工作。
> She is French but speaks Chinese very well. She lived in Beijing for many years and now works in Shanghai.

The Chinese example above is one sentence in which the writer tells the reader that the topic 她 has four distinct features: 1) she is French; 2) she speaks Chinese well; 3) she has lived in Beijing; and 4) she now works in Shanghai. It would normally require more than one sentence (or additional conjunctions) in English to express the same ideas.

Additionally, the underlying relationship between subject and predicate in the two languages is not the same. In English, it is often an actor-action relationship, in which the actor (subject) initiates the action (predicate). However, in a Chinese sentence, the subject is not typically the actor who carries out the action. For example, in 饭吃完了 (The meal is consumed), 饭, rather than the doer of the action 吃, is the topic of the sentence. (See "Topic-Comment Sentence" in Lesson 1.) This type of sentence construction is much more important and frequent in Chinese than in English.

Topic Chains

The topic-chain structure appears frequently in written Chinese. This type of sentence follows several syntactic rules:

- The sentence must consist of two or more clauses. The clauses are separated by commas and the sentence ends with a period. The clauses can be of various syntactical structures, including V + NP, NP + Adj., and preposition + NP + VP.
- The topic is often a noun phrase (NP) that occurs in the subject or object position in one of the clauses (generally the first clause.) This topic is stated only once in the entire chain. Subsequent mentions of the same topic within the chain (usually represented by a pronoun in English) are omitted. The omitted pronouns are referred to as "zero-pronouns," which function as a cohesive device tying all the clauses together to form a topic-chain structure.
- Different kinds of temporal and logical connectives, such as 就…, 再…, 因为…, and 虽然…, may be used to show the relationships among the clauses.

Semantically, a topic chain is like a network of information with the topic as its nucleus. The clauses provide various kinds of information about the topic. The information can concern an act, a mental or physical state, or an intention. As an analogy, a topic chain in Chinese is like an English run-on sentence that expresses many ideas. A run-on sentence is ungrammatical in formal English, but completely acceptable in written Chinese. Here is an example of a simple topic chain structure. It consists of only one topic of discussion, 赵英 (Zhao Ying):

赵英是一个聪明的女孩, 但是有一个问题, 看见认识的人很热情, 看见不认识的人就很不客气,
所以朋友不多。

Zhao Ying is a smart girl. However, she has a problem. She is warm when she meets someone she knows, but she is rude to people she doesn't know. Therefore, she doesn't have many friends.

This topic chain consists of five clauses providing five pieces of information about the topic, Zhao Ying. (See Lesson 5 for details.)

Zero-Pronouns

Zero-pronouns are important for understanding connected discourse in both spoken and written Chinese. They are commonly used as a cohesive device.

A zero-pronoun represents a noun phrase (or pronoun) that is deliberately omitted from its legitimate position in a clause or sentence because it has been mentioned in previous sentences within the chain (as in the above example sentence about Zhao Ying). It is usually the subject or topic of a clause; it is less frequently the object of a clause. Zero-pronouns, as previously shown, are especially important in topic-chain sentences. They are used to show topic continuity in the chain.

Zero-pronouns may also be used across paragraphs. The zero-pronoun often occurs as the subject or topic of the first sentence in a paragraph, with its referent in either the previous or subsequent paragraph.

Generally, if an item has been mentioned in a previous context, or the referent is in the immediate environment, a zero-pronoun may occur because it is assumed the reader knows what is being discussed. (See Lesson 5 for details.)

Classical Words in Formal Written Chinese

One of the important differences between informal/spoken and formal written Chinese is that formal written language may include many classical words. This is especially true in expository and journalistic writing of the sort included in this book. Unlike modern Chinese, which often uses compound words to express one meaning, classical Chinese uses more single-character words. In order to relate as much information as possible in a limited space, journalistic writing uses more classical words.

Classical words do not necessarily have exact modern counterparts, especially those used as function words. They have their own grammatical features. For instance, 而 (ér) is a classical function word. It has no independent meaning of its own, and thus no definite counterpart in modern Chinese. The interpretation of 而 depends on its context. Grammatically, 而 is a linking word that links two words or phrases together. It can be interpreted as "and" if the two words or phrases are complementary in meaning; however, it can be interpreted as "but" if the two words/phrases have opposite meanings (see Lesson 1, "Word Usage and Sentence Patterns").

Furthermore, classical words are important components in many idiomatic expressions and set phrases such as 成语, which are frequently used in written Chinese. Therefore, a mastery of classical words can help you better understand formal writing. (See Lessons 1, 9, and 10 for details.)

We hope that this preliminary information will provide a conceptual framework to help you gain literacy in formal written Chinese. As you work through the readings and exercises in this book, you will find that your understanding of these important language structures will deepen. You will be able to understand them when they occur in your reading, and even employ them successfully in your own writing.

Abbreviations
缩略语表

adj.	adjective
adv.	adverb
attr.	attributive
conj.	conjunction
i.e.	idiomatic expression
intj.	interjection
m.o	measure word
n.	noun
num.	numeral
ono.	onomatopoeia
part.	particle
p.n.	proper noun
prep.	preposition
pron.	pronoun
v.	verb
v.o.	verb-object

Audio Information

Readers have access to free audio files that correspond to sections of the text marked with this icon: 🔊. To access the audio, simply visit www.chengtsui.co/resources and follow the instructions.

For technical support, please contact support@cheng-tsui.com or call (800) 554-1963 (toll-free) or (617) 988-2400.

人口大爆炸

- 这张照片大概是在什么地方照的？
  你从这张照片里看到了什么？

- 你对中国的人口问题有些什么了解？

- 如果你去过中国，请介绍一下你看到过的
  中国人口情况。

- 你知道哪些跟"人口"有关的词汇？

People in modern China are greatly concerned with population density, which is reflected in widespread media coverage. This lesson's reading is a news feature reporting the effects of overpopulation in three different Chinese cities. The stories describe issues that touch on city dwellers' daily lives, including traffic congestion and overcrowding in railway stations and hospitals. Each story is stylistically similar. Data is used to illustrate the problem, while metaphor and simile evoke the immense size of the population.

1

第一课

生词

自学生词

Match each new word with its English translation by deducing the word's meaning from its characters.
(The first one is done for you.)

无车(無車)日　　　通行　　　绿灯(綠燈)　　　人民币(幣)　　　候车(車)室

大厅(廳)　　　高峰　　　好不容易　　　人次　　　超时(時)

1　大厅＿＿＿＿＿＿ lobby, hall
2　＿＿＿＿＿＿ go overtime
3　＿＿＿＿＿＿ with great difficulty, finally
4　＿＿＿＿＿＿ Car-Free Day
5　＿＿＿＿＿＿ pass through

6　＿＿＿＿＿＿ person-time
7　＿＿＿＿＿＿ waiting room, waiting lounge
8　＿＿＿＿＿＿ peak
9　＿＿＿＿＿＿ RMB, Chinese currency
10　＿＿＿＿＿＿ green light

成语和惯用语 Idioms and Set Phrases

	成语／惯用语	单字解释	意思
1	难上加难 *nán shàng jiā nán* 现在找工作非常不容易。要找好工作那更是难上加难了。	难(難) difficult 加 add, increase 增加	Make a difficult situation even more difficult
2	成千上万 *chéng qiān shàng wàn* 成千上万的人群涌上街头庆祝节日。	万(萬) ten thousand	Thousands of, millions of
3	人山人海 *rén shān rén hǎi* 国庆节那天, 广场上人山人海。		Mountains and seas of people

	简体	繁体	拼音	词性	英文
1	爆炸		*bàozhà*	v./n.	explode; blast, explosion
2	未		*wèi*	adv.	not
3	交通		*jiāotōng*	n.	traffic
4	拥堵	擁	*yōngdǔ*	adj.	crowded, jammed
5	不堪		*bùkān*	v./adv.	cannot stand; extremely
6	蜗牛	蝸	*wōniú*	n.	snail
7	堵		*dǔ*	v.	block, suffocate
8	爬行		*páxíng*	v.	crawl
9	与	與	*yǔ*	conj.	and
10	统计	統計	*tǒngjì*	n./v.	statistics, census; gather statistics
11	损失	損	*sǔnshī*	n./v.	loss; damage
12	超过	過	*chāoguò*	v.	surpass, exceed
13	亿	億	*yì*	num.	hundred million
14	期间	間	*qījiān*	n.	period, duration
15	将近	將	*jiāngjìn*	adv.	close to, almost
16	聚集		*jùjí*	v.	gather, get together
17	最终	終	*zuìzhōng*	adv.	finally, at last
18	挤	擠	*jǐ*	v./adj.	shove, push; crowded
19	提前		*tíqián*	v.	shift to an earlier time
20	排队	隊	*páiduì*	v.	line up
21	检票	檢	*jiǎnpiào*	v.o.	check tickets
22	临时	臨時	*línshí*	adj.	temporary
23	车厢	車廂	*chēxiāng*	n.	carriage, compartment
24	拥挤	擁擠	*yōngjǐ*	adj.	crowded, packed
25	走道		*zǒudào*	n.	aisle
26	春运	運	*chūnyùn*	attr.	Spring Festival travel season
27	流量		*liúliàng*	n.	volume of flow, rate of flow
28	挂号	掛號	*guàhào*	v.	register (at a hospital)
29	门诊	門診	*ménzhěn*	n.	outpatient service
30	打仗		*dǎzhàng*	v.o.	fight a war
31	如此		*rúcǐ*	pron.	so, such, like this
32	重庆	慶	*Chóngqìng*	p.n.	a large city in Sichuan Province

第一读：掌握课文大意
First Reading: Skimming for the Main Idea

Skim the reading; then select the option below that best captures its main idea.

a 北京、上海的人口报道

b 车站和医院客流量统计

c 从不同城市看人口问题对中国人生活的影响

第二读：细节和理解
Second Reading: Scanning for Details and Comprehension

Read the text again carefully and answer the following questions.

1 为什么记者选择"世界无车日"来做北京交通的报道？

_____

_____

2 北京2014年有多少人？

_____

_____

3 根据这篇报道，北京交通拥堵的原因是什么？

_____

_____

4 重庆火车站怎么解决旅客太多的问题？他们的方法有没有效果？

_____

_____

5 为什么春节期间坐火车"难上加难"？

_____

_____

6 请说说火车上"拥挤不堪"的情况。

_____

_____

7 为什么说去医院"看病像打仗，挂号像春运"？

_____

_____

8 在中国看病和在你的国家看病有什么相似的地方？有什么不同的地方？

_____

_____

人口大爆炸

北京

2014年9月22日是"世界无车日"，然而北京城内汽车并未减少，交通仍然拥堵不堪。尤其是早晚高峰时期，成千上万的汽车如蜗牛一般堵在道路上慢慢爬行，或根本无法通行。有人说："世界上最遥远的距离不是生与死，而是看见绿灯你却过不去。"

2014年的北京，总人口达到2114万，汽车数量超过500万辆。据统计，北京一年因堵车造成的损失就超过60亿人民币。

重庆

春节期间，重庆火车站旅客流量再上高峰。昨天，将近20万人聚集在车站周围，最终有4.5万人挤上火车。从大年初二开始，售票厅提前从早上7点开始售票，42个售票窗口外都排满了长长的队，所有的检票厅都改成了临时候车室，而车站大厅前的广场上仍然是人山人海。等到人们好不容易挤上火车，却发现车厢里也是拥挤不堪，不但座位上坐满了人，走道上挤满了人，连厕所里都站满了人，上厕所比上火车还难！

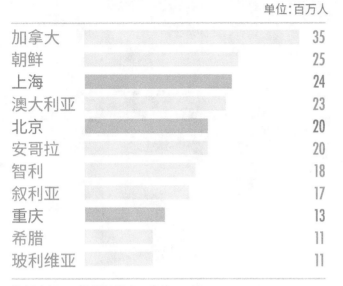

中国大城市与其它国家人口比较

单位：百万人

加拿大	35
朝鲜	25
上海	24
澳大利亚	23
北京	20
安哥拉	20
智利	18
叙利亚	17
重庆	13
希腊	11
玻利维亚	11

数据来源：CIA世界概况（2015年）

世界上最遥远的距离不是生与死，而是看见绿灯你却过不去。

在过去10年内，春运旅客流量每年增加近1亿人次。火车站平时就十分拥挤，春节期间坐火车就更是难上加难了。

上海

昨天，上海儿童医院内挤满了病孩和家长。挂号[1]要排队，候诊要排队，化验检查、交费取药也要排队。好不容易拿到132号的李奶奶抱着发烧的孙子说，"早上7点就从家里出发，大概要到下午3点才能回家"。据医院统计，昨天门诊量高达6000多人次。而夏季高温期更是天天爆满。即使医生们超时工作，每个病人也只能得到几分钟的看病时间。

看个病像打仗，挂个号像春运，这句话描述的是很多医院的情形。但春运的紧张和拥挤仅为一年一次，而在医院却是天天如此。◆

---

[1] In China, people don't have family doctors. Patients need to go to the hospital and "register" (挂号) *(guà hào)* at the front desk before they can see a doctor. Because the demand for appointments far outstrips supply, patients have to line up very early and for a long time to fill one of the limited slots available. Below is the common process for seeing a doctor in a Chinese hospital. (There may be more steps if the illness is serious or complicated.)

挂号 Register
候诊 Wait for treatment
门诊／看病 Outpatient service / visit doctor

检查 Receive medical examination
开药 Have medicine prescribed
交费 Make payment
取药 Pick up medicine

人口大爆炸

北京

2014年9月22日是"世界無車日",然而北京城內汽車並未減少,交通仍然擁堵不堪。尤其是早晚高峰時期,成千上萬的汽車如蝸牛一般堵在道路上慢慢爬行,或根本無法通行。有人說:"世界上最遙遠的距離不是生與死,而是看見綠燈你卻過不去。"

2014年的北京,總人口達到2114萬,汽車數量超過500萬輛。據統計,北京一年因堵車造成的損失就超過60億人民幣。

重慶

春節期間,重慶火車站旅客流量再上高峰。昨天,將近20萬人聚集在車站周圍,最終有4.5萬人擠上火車。從大年初二開始,售票廳提前從早上7點開始售票,42個售票窗口外都排滿了長長的隊,所有的檢票廳都改成了臨時候車室,而車站大廳前的廣場上仍然是人山人海。等到人們好不容易擠上火車，卻發現車廂裡也是擁擠不堪，不但座位上坐滿了人，走道上擠滿了人，連廁所裡都站滿了人，上廁所比上火車還難！

在過去10年內，春運旅客流量每年增加近1億人次。火車站平時就十分擁擠，春節期間坐火車就更是難上加難了。

上海

昨天，上海兒童醫院內擠滿了病孩和家長。掛號要排隊，候診要排隊，化驗檢查、交費取藥也要排隊。好不容易拿到132號的李奶奶抱著發燒的孫子說，"早上7點就從家裡出發，大概要到下午3點才能回家"。據醫院統計，昨天門診量高達6000多人次。而夏季高溫期更是天天爆滿。即使醫生們超時工作，每個病人也只能得到幾分鐘的看病時間。

看個病像打仗，挂個號像春運，這句話描述的是很多醫院的情形。但春運的緊張和擁擠僅為一年一次，而在醫院卻是天天如此。◆

阅读技巧

A 略读与寻读 Skimming and Scanning

Skimming means reading quickly in order to absorb the overall theme, tone, or general meaning of the text. It is often used as a precursor to a more detailed search for specific information. When you skim, you read across each line of text rapidly, ignoring punctuation and minor words, but taking in the main words and phrases that are related to the theme of the text.

When you do a close reading of the text after skimming it, you will find that you read more fluently and accurately. In this book, you will practice skimming for the first read-through of every lesson.

Scanning involves looking quickly through the text to find a specific detail, such as a key word, date, name, or time, as when you are trying to find a specific departure time on a train timetable, or locate a particular name in a contact list.

In this book, you will practice scanning for the second read-through of every lesson. When practicing scanning, read the questions listed under "First Reading," then go over the text quickly, with a pen in hand and the questions in mind. Write down the answers as soon as you find them.

There are more reading comprehension questions listed under "Second Reading." You may need to read the text more carefully to answer these questions.

B 书面语：报刊阅读 Learning the Style of Formal Writing: News Article Reading

This lesson introduces a feature news article. Generally speaking, news articles in Chinese have three characteristics. First, the language is more formal than casual speech, and classical or literary words are often used. The following table compares formal and colloquial expressions used in this lesson. (For more detailed information concerning formal vs. informal Chinese language, see the Grammar section in this lesson.)

Formal (正式)	Informal (非正式)
内	里
与	跟、和
售	卖
而	而且、可是
（将）近	差不多
仍然	还是
最终	最后
如…一般	像…一样

Secondly, news articles customarily use abbreviated terms, e.g., 文革 for 文化大革命 (the Cultural Revolution), 春运 for 春节期间旅客运输 (Spring Festival travel season), 候诊 for 等候诊治 (waiting for treatment by a doctor), and 病孩 for 生病的孩子 (sick children).

Finally, the style of news features is different from that of hard news. Hard news articles normally start with a full summary, which should incorporate as many of the "Five Ws" (Who, What, Where, When, and Why) as possible. Although feature articles also attempt to include the Five Ws, they are more literary. Moreover, news features are typically less time-sensitive than hard news, though no less newsworthy. They can be good tools for discussing complex issues that are too extensive for the terse style of hard news items. The body of a news feature may include the author's opinions and provide visual details to bring the story to life.

词汇与句型

A 如 + N + (一)般 + V/adj.:
to V like N (as adj. as N)

如 + N + 般 introduces a simile as a description of the action indicated by the verb or adjective. The adverbial marker 地 is optional. This expression is more often used in descriptive and literary writing than in daily speech.

1 成千上万的汽车如蜗牛一般堵在道路上慢慢爬行。

   Hundreds and thousands of cars are crawling slowly like snails on the roads.

2 她的微笑如阳光般灿烂。

   Her smile is as brilliant as the sunshine.

B 在……内 within a duration of time

The duration of time can be minutes, days, months, or years. The focus is "within," which means "no more than this interval of time." (在 can be omitted.)

1 在过去10年内，春运旅客流量每年增加近1亿人次。

   Within the past ten years, the passenger flow during the Spring Festival travel rush has increased by nearly one hundred million person-times per year.

2 他三年内就学完了四年的课程。

   He finished four years of courses in three years.

3 这本新书很受欢迎，我们书店在几个小时内就卖了500册。

   This newly published book is very popular. Our bookstore sold five hundred copies within hours.

C 在 X 期间 during a specific period of time

This pattern indicates that a specific event took place or will take place during a specific period of time. "X" (i.e., the period of time) may take the form of a noun phrase or a verb + object construction. The preposition 在 must be included when the time phrase follows the subject, but may be dropped when the time phrase precedes the subject.

1 我在读研究生期间认识了许多学者。

   During my graduate studies, I became acquainted with many scholars.

2 春节期间你打算做什么？

   What are you going to do during the Spring Festival?

3 他在上海开会期间去看了几位老同学。

   While attending the conference in Shanghai, he visited several of his old classmates.

D PW + V + 满了 + N:
a place is/was filled with or full of something/people

This can be regarded as a kind of "topic-comment" sentence (see Grammar note B). The verb in the verb phrase V + 满 explains what exact action (e.g., 放, 坐, 挤, 开) has been involved in filling the place (with things/people).

1 不但座位上坐满了人，走道上挤满了人，连厕所里都站满了人。

   Not only are the seats jam-packed with people (sitting), the aisles are congested with people (squeezing); even the restrooms are crammed full of people (standing).

2 抽屉里放满了文具。

   The drawer is filled with stationery (by putting).

3 留学生宿舍已经住满了。

   The dorms for foreign students are full (by occupying).

4 树上开满了花。

   The tree is in full blossom (by blooming).

E 好（不）容易
it was after great difficulty/trouble…

Interestingly, 好不容易 and 好容易 mean the same thing. Functioning as an adverb, 好（不）容易 is used to express something that someone has achieved only after great difficulty. 好（不）容易 is often used with 才, which indicates the delayed attainment of the result.

1　回家的人太多，他们好（不）容易才
　　挤上火车。

　　There were too many people trying to return home. They had to really push their way onto the train.

2　我们好（不）容易才找到了这个机会。
　　一定会尽力而为！

　　It was with great effort that we got this opportunity. We'll definitely try our best!

3　我好（不）容易才说服他陪你去晚会，
　　你为什么又不要他去了？

　　It was with great difficulty that I convinced him to go to the party with you. Why don't you want him to go now?

F 如此 so, such, like this
(informal: 这么，这样)

1　但愿如此。（口语：希望能这样。）

　　I hope so.

2　她从未见过如此自私的人！（口语：她
　　从来没有见过这么自私的人！）

　　She has never seen such a selfish person!

3　情况本该如此。（口语：情况本来应该
　　是这样的。）

　　This is how it should have been.

G 比较"内"与"里"

内 and 里 both mean "inside, within." Their differences are:

1　内 is more formal, and tends to be used in written language and fixed phrases such as 成语, while 里 is much more colloquial and more widely used.

　　Fixed phrase: 内外有别 (Differentiate between the insiders and outsiders.)

　　Public sign: 请勿入内 (Please do not enter.)

2　内 is generally used after monosyllabic words, while 里 can be used with either monosyllabic or polysyllabic words. (Note: The symbol ⊗ is used throughout this book to indicate incorrect or ungrammatical usage.)

　　校内　　室内　　国内　　　门内
　　学校里　教室里　联合国里　大门里　家里　手里
　　⊗ 校里　⊗ 室里　⊗国里

3　When expressing "within a period of time," use 内, not 里.

　　年内　　　　本周内　　　　一小时内
　　⊗年里　　　⊗本周里　　　⊗一小时里

4　They have different collocations when forming complex place words:

里 + 边、面、头			以、之 + 内	
～边	～面	～头	以～	之～
教室里边	车站里面	屋子里头	长城以内	十年之内

语法

A 多音字
Characters with multiple pronunciations

In English, some words have different pronunciations due to differences in meaning or part of speech. For example, "lead" is pronounced differently depending on its usage as a noun (a kind of metal) or a verb (to guide or direct). The stress patterns of words like "import" and "record" vary depending on whether they function as verbs or nouns.

In a similar way, some Chinese characters also have more than one pronunciation, each representing a difference in meaning and/or grammatical category (e.g., noun or verb). Most of them involve only a change in tone, but some of them involve a change in both tone and pronunciation. The table below shows the types of changes.

语音变化	字例	语音	语义变化	词例
声调 Tone only	数	shǔ shù	count (v.) number (n.)	数一数 数学
声母 Initial only	校	xiào jiào	school (n.) proofread (v.)	学校 校对
韵母 Final only	还	hái huán	still (adv.) return (v.)	还要 还书
声调与声母 Tone and initial	长	zhǎng cháng	grow (v.) long (adj.)	长高 很长
声调与韵母 Tone and final	得	dé děi de	obtain (v.) must (v.) (particle)	得到 得用功 学得好
声母与韵母 Initial and final	行	xíng háng	go, walk, do (v.) line, trade (n.)	行动 银行

More than half of these multi-pronunciation characters belong to the first group (tone change–only). For example: 好 (hǎo, hào), 为 (wéi, wèi), 教 (jiāo, jiào), 量 (liàng, liáng), 少 (shǎo, shào), 兴 (xìng, xīng), 难 (nán, nàn), 看 (kàn, kān).

The correct pronunciation is normally evident from the context and the characters it is in combination with. Therefore, when you learn a character's different pronunciations, you must remember their difference in meaning and function, the combination of other characters, and the context in which the character is used. Exercises for such characters will be provided in each lesson to reinforce mastery of these "tricky" pronunciations.

B 话题说明句 Topic-comment sentences

One of the distinctive features of Chinese is the existence of topic-comment sentences. In English, almost every sentence requires a subject and a predicate; this is not necessarily the case in Chinese, however. Chinese grammar relies more on "idea-joining" than "form agreement" (e.g., subject-verb agreement), due to its topic-prominent features. Therefore, in addition to subject-predicate sentences that follow a format familiar to English speakers, Chinese also has sentences based on a topic and a comment. There is a semantic or logical relationship between the topic and the comment, but usually only a relatively loose grammatical connection between the two.

B1 Subject-predicate sentences

A subject refers to the doer of an action or the entity in a state of being, and a predicate describes the action the subject engages in or the state the subject is in.

1 人们好不容易挤上了火车。

With great difficulty, people finally squeezed their way onto the train.

(Subject as the doer of the action "to squeeze")

2 北京是中国的首都。

Beijing is the capital of China.

(Subject as the entity in a state of "being")

B2 Topic-comment sentences

A topic is what the sentence is about, and a comment is what is said about the topic. The topic can optionally be followed by a pause in speech or a comma in writing. Unlike the direct semantic relationship between the subject and the predicate, the relationship between the topic and the comment can be rather loose, as demonstrated in the following sentences:

1 2014年的北京，总人口达到2114万，汽车数量超过500万辆。

Regarding Beijing in 2014, its total population reached 21.14 million, with more than five million cars.

2 重庆火车站旅客流量再上高峰。

As for Chongqing Train Station, its passenger flow rate has hit another peak.

3 这个计划，大家都不喜欢。

As for this plan, nobody likes it.

4 所有的检票厅都改成了临时候车室。

All the ticket-checking halls were converted to temporary waiting rooms.

5 春节期间坐火车就更是难上加难了。

It is even more difficult to travel by train during the Spring Festival season.

6 火车上挤满了人。

The train was crowded with people.

You can see from the above examples that all the topics do not have direct semantic relationships with the verb phrases (i.e., they are not the "actors" of the "actions").

B3 The function of topic-comment sentences

The topic-comment sentence is a very productive structure in Chinese. It enables the speaker to focus on the topic of the conversation and communicate effectively and coherently in discourse, with great flexibility. Any structure—words, phrases, and sentences—can be used as a comment in a topic-comment sentence.

Recognizing the function that topics play in Chinese sentences (and discourse) can also help learners better understand some distinctive grammar structures of the language. For example, you may have noticed that Chinese doesn't mark passive voice as strictly as in English. Why? Since the main function of passivization is to turn an object into a subject, it is not necessary in a "topic-prominent" language to explicitly mark it. In fact, many passive sentences in English are realized as topic-comment sentences in Chinese, like Sentence 6 above.

For the same reason, Chinese does not use "dummy subjects" like the English "it" in "It is exciting that our team won the last game" or "there" in "There is a big tree in front of the house." In Chinese, the topic is the most important part of the sentence, so it doesn't matter if there is no apparent subject. (See Sentences 5 and 6.)

C 中文的正式语体与非正式语体 Formal vs. informal Chinese

As in any language, Chinese uses different styles of expression, ranging from the formal to the informal (or the written/literary to the spoken/colloquial), in different situations. The formal style is usually used in official or serious situations, while the informal style is used in ordinary or relaxed situations. Although there are informal forms of written Chinese (notably in fiction and in the popular press), and formal styles of spoken Chinese (particularly in professional discourse, or prepared public speech), written Chinese is usually more formal than spoken Chinese.

Formal Chinese is signaled by complex, complete sentences; impersonality; avoidance of colloquial or slang vocabulary; and a consistent preference for learned words, often derived from classical Chinese. Just as in English, where one can use "but," "however," "nevertheless," or "nonetheless" to express the same meaning in different situations, one can also use 可是, 但是, 然而, or 而 in Chinese in accordance with such factors as the type of occasion (private vs. public), the size of the audience, and the relationship of the speaker/writer with the audience. The ability to use the formal language style, especially the ability to vary one's style according to the situation, is often considered a mark of higher mastery of the language.

This lesson's reading uses the expository style, which is commonly found in journalistic writing. A feature that indicates the formality of this article is the use of certain words from classical Chinese such as 及, 与, 则, 而, 之, 据, 达, 为, and 此, and some other formal expressions used in literary style writing such as 将近, 仍然, and 如……一般. These expressions are usually not used in everyday spoken language, except in idiomatic expressions. The following tables compare these formal words and their informal counterparts, which you have previously learned:

NOUNS

Formal	Informal
本	这／我
此	这个
当前／目前	现在
何	什么
内	里
春季	春天
许多	很多
父亲	爸爸

VERBS

Formal	Informal
为	是
将	要
达	达到
饮	喝
禁止	不准
认为	觉得
允许	准
指出	说

CONJUNCTIONS

Formal	Informal
及	和
与	和、跟
则	却
而	而且／可是
却	可是
据	根据
由于	因为
因此	所以

OTHERS

Formal	Informal
之	的
为	为了
于	在
仍然	还是
如果…就	要是…就
即使…也	就是…也
立刻	马上
比如	比方说

Metaphor 隐喻 and simile 明喻 are literary devices with which language can be made more vivid. Metaphor and simile compare seemingly unrelated things to show readers the likeness between them. Their function is to describe the appearance, characteristics, or behavior of certain things. Simile is easier to detect than metaphor because it uses explicit signals, such as 像……一样 and 如……般. This lesson includes one metaphor and two similes. They are used to evoke mental images so as to engage the readers more closely with the subject. Note that although both of the following expressions are associated with huge crowds of people, they bring out different feelings.

人山人海
"mountains and seas of people" (a metaphor)

如蜗牛般慢慢爬行
"crawl slowly like snails" (a simile)

These two images can also create different conceptual effects in readers' minds. While 人山人海 emphasizes the size of a crowd that is static, 蜗牛 suggests slow movement.

看个病像打仗，挂个号像春运。
"Going to a hospital is like going to war, while getting a hospital registration is like trying to get on a train at Spring Festival."
(a simile)

A 语音 Pronunciation

Write the following underlined Chinese characters in *pinyin*. Pay special attention to their different pronunciations in different contexts.

流<u>量</u>　（　　）　　测<u>量</u>（　　）

<u>好</u>不容易（　　）　　喜<u>好</u>（　　）

<u>重</u>要　（　　）　　<u>重</u>庆（　　）

延<u>长</u>　（　　）　　增<u>长</u>（　　）

自<u>行</u>车　（　　）　　银<u>行</u>（　　）

<u>难</u>以忍受（　　）　　困<u>难</u>（　　）

<u>看</u>见　（　　）　　<u>看</u>家（　　）

<u>为</u>了　（　　）　　认<u>为</u>（　　）

B 词汇与句型

B1 词语搭配 There are two groups of words below. In each group, match the words on the left with those on the right to form meaningful phrases by considering their appropriate collocations. (Each word can be used only once.)

Group One (Verb + Object)	Group Two (Noun + Noun)
1 堵 ＿＿＿ 时间	1 高峰 ＿＿＿ 高温
2 延长 ＿＿＿ 队	2 车站 ＿＿＿ 流量
3 报道 ＿＿＿ 车	3 夏季 ＿＿＿ 期间
4 造成 ＿＿＿ 新闻	4 旅客 ＿＿＿ 时期
5 排 ＿＿＿ 损失	5 春节 ＿＿＿ 大厅

B2 用括号内的词语或句型改写句子 Rewrite the following sentences using the expressions provided in parentheses.

1 她非常关心她的学生，就像母亲关心自己的孩子一样。（如……一般）

＿＿＿＿＿＿＿＿＿＿＿＿＿＿＿＿＿＿

＿＿＿＿＿＿＿＿＿＿＿＿＿＿＿＿＿＿

2 昨天重庆火车站从10点到12点就卖出了2000张票。（在……内）

＿＿＿＿＿＿＿＿＿＿＿＿＿＿＿＿＿＿

＿＿＿＿＿＿＿＿＿＿＿＿＿＿＿＿＿＿

3 他在法国工作的时候参观了不少博物馆。（在……期间）

＿＿＿＿＿＿＿＿＿＿＿＿＿＿＿＿＿＿

＿＿＿＿＿＿＿＿＿＿＿＿＿＿＿＿＿＿

4 飞往南京的飞机上每个座位都坐着乘客。（坐满）

＿＿＿＿＿＿＿＿＿＿＿＿＿＿＿＿＿＿

＿＿＿＿＿＿＿＿＿＿＿＿＿＿＿＿＿＿

5 去上海的火车票真难买，我花了好几天功夫才买到一张。（好不容易）

＿＿＿＿＿＿＿＿＿＿＿＿＿＿＿＿＿＿

＿＿＿＿＿＿＿＿＿＿＿＿＿＿＿＿＿＿

B3 选择填空 Choose the most appropriate words from the list to fill in the blanks. (Note: Not every word will be used.)

a	损失	g	通行
b	如此	h	排队
c	爆炸	i	临时
d	超时	j	增加
e	超过	k	爆满
f	提前	l	拥挤不堪

1 我们公司上个月的业务大量增加，只好_____ 雇用了30个工作人员。

2 昨天是假日，街上到处都是人，电影院和商店也都_____。

3 飞往香港的旅客请注意，请准备好登机牌，_____登机。

4 今天老师有事，_____一个钟头下课，学生们兴高采烈地跑出教室。

5 他看起来很高兴，原来是老板把他的年薪从4万元_____到了5万元。

6 要学好外语，每个班的人数最好不_____15名。

7 有人担心要是中国不控制人口，将来会发生人口_____。

8 他的错误使公司受到了巨大的_____。

9 人们都不能相信小狗竟然_____聪明。

10 工会发出指示，不准让工人_____工作。

C 语法

C1 From the right column, find the items that can most appropriately comment on the topics in the left column. (Each item can be used only once.)

Topic		Comment
1 这次考试，……	____	我们都没钱买。
2 这件事，……	____	挂着一幅画。
3 我那辆旧车，……	____	能力很强，脾气不太好。
4 这个人，……	____	幸亏我昨天晚上复习了。
5 这些东西，……	____	那是个美丽的城市。
6 墙上……	____	写完了吗？
7 门外……	____	恐怕你们都想不到是谁。
8 王先生……	____	你想清楚了没有？
9 北京，……	____	人口太多。
10 第二篇文章……	____	很不容易。
11 中国……	____	站着一个人。
12 中国要把人口减下来……	____	前天卖了。

C2 用话题说明句回答问题 Answer the questions with topic-comment sentences.

1 问：你觉得昨天的考试怎么样？

答：昨天的考试，_____

_____

2 问：你觉得学中文难吗？

答：学中文，_____

3 问：你的假期过得怎么样？

答：这个假期，_____

_____

4 问：怎样才能解决中国的人口问题？

答：解决中国的人口问题，_____

_____

C3 用"内"和"里"填空 Fill in the blanks with 内 or 里.

1 室_____禁止吸烟。

2 我喜欢在教室_____看书。

3 在过去的三个星期_____他一直在忙着写这篇论文。

4 你们一定要在三个星期＿＿＿＿把这篇论文写好。

5 这种商品国＿＿＿＿也能买到。

6 今天开学，学校＿＿＿＿一下子热闹起来了。

7 车厢＿＿＿＿面拥挤不堪，到处都站满了人。

8 政府计划将每年增长人口控制在1000万之＿＿＿＿。

C4 下面的句子用口语怎么说？ How would you restate the following sentences in informal style, as if you were in a conversation with a friend? Make sure to pay special attention to the underlined parts.

例：北京城内汽车并未减少，交通仍然拥堵不堪。

口语：北京城里的汽车并没有减少，交通还是非常拥堵。

1 昨天，重庆火车站旅客流量再上高峰。

＿＿＿＿＿＿＿＿＿＿＿＿＿＿＿＿

＿＿＿＿＿＿＿＿＿＿＿＿＿＿＿＿

2 将近20万人聚集在车站周围，最终有4.5万人挤上火车。

＿＿＿＿＿＿＿＿＿＿＿＿＿＿＿＿

＿＿＿＿＿＿＿＿＿＿＿＿＿＿＿＿

3 夜深了，街上行人稀少，而车站大厅前的广场上仍然是人山人海。

＿＿＿＿＿＿＿＿＿＿＿＿＿＿＿＿

＿＿＿＿＿＿＿＿＿＿＿＿＿＿＿＿

4 等到人们好不容易挤上火车，却发现车厢里也是拥挤不堪。

＿＿＿＿＿＿＿＿＿＿＿＿＿＿＿＿

＿＿＿＿＿＿＿＿＿＿＿＿＿＿＿＿

5 春运的紧张和拥挤仅为一年一次，而在医院却是天天如此。

＿＿＿＿＿＿＿＿＿＿＿＿＿＿＿＿

＿＿＿＿＿＿＿＿＿＿＿＿＿＿＿＿

C5 英译汉 Translate the following sentences into Chinese.

1 She completed all her university courses within three years. Everybody thinks that she is very intelligent.

＿＿＿＿＿＿＿＿＿＿＿＿＿＿＿＿

＿＿＿＿＿＿＿＿＿＿＿＿＿＿＿＿

2 There are too many books in his room. His bookshelf is full of books, his desk is laden with books, and even his bed is piled up with books. (Use the verbs 放, 摆, and 堆.)

＿＿＿＿＿＿＿＿＿＿＿＿＿＿＿＿

＿＿＿＿＿＿＿＿＿＿＿＿＿＿＿＿

3 There were many people waiting for that bus. It was with great difficulty that I finally squeezed myself in.

＿＿＿＿＿＿＿＿＿＿＿＿＿＿＿＿

＿＿＿＿＿＿＿＿＿＿＿＿＿＿＿＿

4 My salary is too low to afford a car. To buy a house is even more difficult.

＿＿＿＿＿＿＿＿＿＿＿＿＿＿＿＿

＿＿＿＿＿＿＿＿＿＿＿＿＿＿＿＿

5 Before Christmas, so many people went shopping that many of stores extended their opening hours.

＿＿＿＿＿＿＿＿＿＿＿＿＿＿＿＿

＿＿＿＿＿＿＿＿＿＿＿＿＿＿＿＿

D 综合 Comprehensive

D1 选词填空 Choose the most appropriate words from the list below to fill in the blanks in the passage. (Not every word will be used.)

a 难上加难　　g 拥挤不堪

b 如此　　　　h 流量

c 堵　　　　　i 将近

d 人山人海　　j 成千上万

e 交通　　　　k 爆满

f 期间　　　　l 高峰

黄金周旅游

从1999年第一个国庆"黄金周"(National Day Golden Week holiday) 开始，国庆长假给旅游市场创造了不错的经济效益，但是也带来了不少问题。比方说：火车上_____、高速公路_____成停车场、各地景区游客_____等等。仅北京故宫每天游客_____就高达17万。游客多得看不到地面。杭州著名的西湖每天要接待_____60万游客，结果是"只见人，不见湖！"人们说，黄金周_____出游，行路难、住宿难、用餐难、购票更是_____。别人旅游去看高山大海，我们旅游却是看_____！旅游本来是为了放松心情，但_____旅游让人太紧张，太难受。

最近，越来越多的人选择在国庆长假出国旅游。_____的中国游客来到日本、韩国、泰国。连欧美各国也迎来了不少中国游客。

Tiananmen Square (天安门广场) in Beijing

D2 按照这篇文章的意思，下面的说法对不对？ Based on the passage, are the following statements true (T) or false (F)?

1 _____ "黄金周"是国庆节时一个星期的长假期。

2 _____ 黄金周给旅游行业造成了很大的经济损失。

3 _____ 黄金周的集中出游方式给游客带来了很多麻烦。

4 _____ 为了解决交通拥堵问题，中国在高速公路上建了很多停车场。

5 _____ 黄金周让很多中国人有时间出门旅游。

6 _____ 旅游应该让人觉得心情轻松。

7 _____ 人们在杭州的问题是找不到西湖。

8 _____ 出国游可能没有在国内旅游那么拥挤。

When you practice "scanning" the following readings, you don't need to read every sentence, and you don't need to know every word. Instead, first read the three questions listed before the passages, then go over the passages quickly, with a pen in hand and the questions in mind. Write down the answers as soon as you find them.

There are more reading comprehension questions (multiple choice) after the passages. You may need to read the passages more carefully to answer these questions.

English is provided for a few difficult words. There may be some other words that you do not know. Don't look them up. Try to guess their meanings from the context, or ignore them if they are not related to the information you are looking for.

E1 带着问题扫描 Scanning with questions

1 什么是计划生育政策？

_____

_____

2 1990年中国总人口是多少？

_____

_____

3 中国的土地总面积是不是世界上最大的？

_____

_____

短文（一）
中国需要实行计划生育

70年代末，中国开始实行计划生育 (family planning) 政策：一个家庭只能生一个孩子。从那时起，中国大约少生了2亿多人。这个数字说明中国的计划生育工作使人口增长得到了一定控制。但是据中国第四次人口调查，到1990年7月1日，中国

总人口仍然高达11.6亿，并且每年增长超过1500万人，这个数字等于加拿大总人口的一半。

中国的土地总面积 (miànji) (surface area) 位于世界第三，但是人均 (rénjūn) (per person) 土地面积还不到世界人均值的三分之一。中国有无数的河流湖泊，而人均水量却是世界第88位。虽然近年来经济发展很快，但是因为人口太多，坐车难、看病难、住房难等问题还是解决不了。专家们说，中国需要继续实行计划生育。

E2 回答问题

1 如果中国没有实行计划生育政策，到1990年7月1日，中国总人口可能是：

a 13 亿   c 14 亿

b 9 亿   d 11.6 亿

2 加拿大总人口大约是：

a 3000 万   c 750 万

b 1500 万   d 1000 万

3 中国的人均土地面积是：

a 世界第三位

b 世界第88位

c 世界人均土地的三分之一

d 比世界人均土地的三分之一还少

4 根据这位作者的看法，中国人坐车难、看病难、住房难等问题的原因是：

a 经济发展不够快

b 人口太多

c 人均土地面积太少

d 人均水量太低

1 中国跟日本，哪个国家人口密度更大？

_____

2 西欧跟非洲，哪个地区人口密度更大？

_____

3 非洲的自然资源怎么样？

_____

短文（二）
中国人口太多了吗？

常常有人把"中国人口太多"作为中国贫穷落后的原因。真的是这样吗？

首先，从人口密度 (mìdù) (density) 来看，中国为每平方 (square) 公里134人，日本为每平方公里336人，德国为每平方公里232人，英国为每平方公里245人。为什么很少有人说"日本、德国、英国的人口太多了"？

中国与其它国家的人口密度比较
单位：人／平方公里

印度	436
日本	349
英国	267
德国	232
中国	145
肯尼亚	79

数据来源：世界银行（2014年）

再说，人口越少就越有利于经济的发展吗？西欧是世界上人口密度最高的地区之一，同时又是经济最发达的地区之一；非洲的人口密度比西欧低多了，自然资源又非常丰富，而非洲却是世界上经济最落后的地区。

可见，把"中国人口太多"作为中国贫穷落后的原因是没有什么道理的。

E4 回答问题

1 根据这篇短文，哪个国家的人口密度比中国的高？
a 英国
b 日本
c 德国
d 英国、日本、德国

2 非洲
a 人口密度比西欧高
b 人口密度比西欧低
c 自然资源比西欧丰富
d 自然资源不如西欧丰富

3 根据这位作者的看法，
a 中国人口太多是没有什么道理的。
b 人口越少就越有利于经济的发展。
c 人口密度高不应该是一个国家贫穷落后的原因。
d 日本、德国、英国的人口太多了。

F 口语

F1 Discussion Topics

1 如果你去过中国，你对中国人口现状有什么印象？

2 计划生育政策有什么好处？有什么坏处？

F2 Presentation Topic: 人口对于社会的影响

Research one issue (traffic, travel, hospital service, etc.) presented in this lesson. Consider the following questions and prepare a short presentation in Chinese for the class.

1 这些问题（堵车，旅游拥挤，看病难，等等）是不是由于人口问题造成的？

2 这些问题可以怎样解决？

F3 Debate Topics

本课阅读练习的两篇短文表达了两种很不同的看法。他们都用数据与事实来支持自己的观点。你同意哪种观点？为什么？请你在网上或图书馆查找有关中国人口的最新资料，就下面的题目（或自选的题目）跟同学辩论。

The two reading passages in the Practice section express two different opinions. They both use statistics and examples to support their ideas. Which opinion do you agree with? Why? Find the most up-to-date information on China's population issue, and debate with your classmates on a topic below (or choose your own topic).

人类应该对生育率进行控制 vs.
人类不应该对生育率进行控制

F4 Extended Group Research Project

In a small group, choose one of the following topics to research. Prepare a presentation in Chinese with a visual component. Each member of the group should take turns presenting. Include a list of new vocabulary words for your classmates.

a 教育资源问题
   Population and Educational Resources

b 人口与住房问题
   Population and Housing Problems

c 人口与环境问题
   Population and the Environment

d 人口与就业问题
   Population and Employment

G 写作

作文题：我对中国人口问题的看法
(400-500字)

Use the information from your research to write an essay of 400–500 characters on China's population issue. Cite at least two facts or statistics to support your arguments.

Use at least five of the following words and expressions from this lesson:

PW + V + 满了 + N	好不容易	影响
在……期间	而	如……（一）般
在……内	增长	使

中国第 13 亿个小公民

阅读前讨论

- 你从这张照片里看到了什么？
- 根据课文题目，猜猜这张照片上的小孩是谁。
- 这个小孩的出生有什么特别的意义？

Whereas Lesson 1 focused on the effects of overpopulation in China, this lesson looks at the Chinese policy to address population growth. The reading begins by describing an important historical moment—the birth of China's 1.3 billionth citizen—before delving into its wider implications. Writers commonly use anecdotes to begin expository articles, as interesting stories can attract readers' curiosity and engage them in further reading.

In order to highlight the complexity of the Chinese population problem, this reading contrasts 1) the differing views of parents and population specialists on this momentous occasion, and 2) the accomplishments of China's birth control policy and the new problems it has introduced. The issues are mainly presented in terms of facts and statistics, which make the arguments very persuasive.

生词

自学生词

Match each new word with its English translation by deducing the word's meaning from its characters.
(The first one is done for you.)

证书(證書)　　出生　　人口　　祝福　　上升　　下降

数(數)量　　老龄(齡)　　重男轻(輕)女　　谈论(談論)　　公民　　达(達)到

1　人口_____ population

2　_____ old age

3　_____ talk about, discuss; discussion

4　_____ value male more than female

5　_____ wish happiness to; blessing, benediction

6　_____ quantity, amount

7　_____ reach, achieve, attain

8　_____ descend, drop, fall, decline

9　_____ citizen

10　_____ be born

11　_____ certificate, diploma

12　_____ rise, ascend

主要生词

	简体	繁体	拼音	词性	英文
1	随着	隨著	*suízhe*	prep.	along with, in the wake of
2	婴	嬰	*yīng*	n.	infant, baby
3	正式		*zhèngshì*	adj.	formal, official
4	接受		*jiēshòu*	v.	accept, take on, undertake
5	颁发	頒發	*bānfā*	v.	issue, award (certificate, medal)
6	荣誉	榮譽	*róngyù*	n.	honor, glory, credit
7	无比	無	*wúbǐ*	adv.	incomparably, unparalleled
8	喜悦		*xǐyuè*	adj./n.	happy, joyous; happiness
9	忧	憂	*yōu*	v.	be worried, be concerned, worry
10	对	對	*duì*	m.	pair, couple

	简体	繁体	拼音	词性	英文
11	值得		zhídé	v.	be worth, deserve
12	实行	實	shíxíng	v.	carry out, implement
13	生育		shēngyù	v./n.	give birth to; childbearing
14	政策		zhèngcè	n.	policy
15	世纪	紀	shìjì	n.	century
16	年代		niándài	n.	decade, time, era
17	预期	預	yùqī	v.	expect, anticipate, predict
18	敲		qiāo	v.	knock, strike, beat
19	警钟	鐘	jǐngzhōng	n.	alarm bell
20	面临	臨	miànlín	v.	be faced with
21	挑战	戰	tiǎozhàn	v./n.	challenge
22	预计	預計	yùjì	v.	estimate, calculate in advance
23	素质	質	sùzhì	n.	innate quality
24	年限		niánxiàn	n.	a fixed number of years
25	结构	結構	jiégòu	n.	structure, composition
26	首先		shǒuxiān	adv.	first, first of all
27	率		lǜ	n.	rate, proportion, ratio
28	比例		bǐlì	n.	ratio, proportion
29	幅度		fúdù	n.	range, scope, extent
30	超过	過	chāoguò	v.	surpass, exceed, outstrip
31	此外		cǐwài	conj.	besides, in addition, furthermore
32	传统	傳統	chuántǒng	n./adj.	tradition; traditional
33	观念	觀	guānniàn	n.	notion, thought, concept
34	性别	別	xìngbié	n.	gender
35	失调	調	shītiáo	v./adj.	lose balance; unbalanced
36	抽样	樣	chōuyàng	v./n.	sample
37	调查	調查	diàochá	v./n.	investigate; investigation, survey
38	关注	關	guānzhù	v.	pay close attention to
39	焦点	點	jiāodiǎn	n.	focus, focal point, central issue

课文

Skim the reading; then select the option below that best captures its main idea.

a 中国的人口问题

b 一个小男婴出生的故事

c 中国人口的新问题

Read the text again carefully and answer the following questions.

1 中国第13亿个公民的到来有什么特殊意义？

_____

_____

2 人口专家和孩子的父母的心情有什么不同？为什么？

_____

_____

3 如果没有计划生育政策，中国的第13亿个公民本来应该在哪一年到来？

_____

_____

4 现在中国人口面临着哪三大新挑战？为什么？

_____

_____

5 "人口老龄化"与"出生性别比例失调"对中国的将来会有什么影响？

_____

_____

2005年1月6日0点2分，随着一个胖乎乎的男婴在北京出生，中国人口正式达到13亿。孩子的父母高兴地接受了中国政府颁发的"中国第13亿个公民"荣誉证书及人们送上的鲜花和祝福。与孩子父母无比喜悦的心情相比，中国的人口专家对这第13亿个小公民的到来则是半喜半忧。

值得高兴的是，由于实行计划生育政策，每对夫妻的平均育儿数从上世纪70年代初的5.8下降到现在的1.8，全国在过去30年中少生了3亿多人。而中国的13亿人口日也比预期的晚到了4年。

然而，专家指出："13亿人口日的到来，再一次敲响了人口问题的警钟。"现在中国人口问题面临着三大挑战。挑战之一还是人口数量问题。未来十几年中国人口每年预计还要增加1000万人左右。挑战之二是人口素质问题。据2012年联合国《人文发展报告》，中国25岁以上人口平均受教育年限为7.5年，还不到美国100年前的水平。挑战之三是人口结构问题。结构问题首先是人口老龄化，随着出生率下降，老年人口比例大幅度上升。2014年中国60岁以上老人已经超过了全国人口的15%。专家预计，到2050年左右，老年人口将占中国人口的三分之一。此外，中国文化中重男轻女的传统观念，也使出生人口的性别结构出现失调。2014年全国抽样调查结果表明，中国人口中男性数量比女性多了3400万人。

如果说以前谈论中国的人口问题，主要是说"人太多"，那么，近年来，"人口素质"、"人口老龄化"及"出生性别比例失调"等问题已经成为人们关注的新焦点。随着人口形势的变化，中国政府也在调整政策。从2015年10月起，实行了30多年的"独生子女政策"成为了历史。新的"二孩政策"让中国夫妇终于可以生两个孩子了。◆

> **13亿人口日的到来，再一次敲响了人口问题的警钟。**

中国大陆总人口及出生率
1954年—2014年

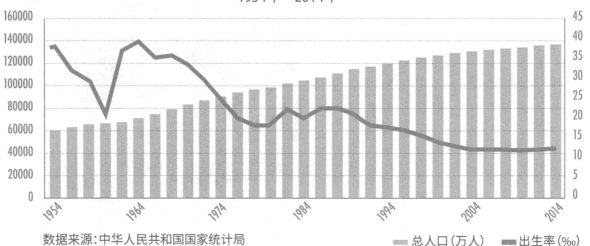

数据来源：中华人民共和国国家统计局　　　■ 总人口(万人)　■ 出生率(‰)

中國第13億個小公民

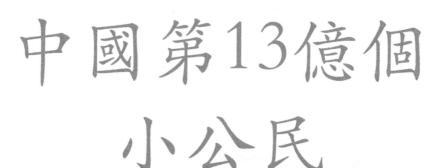

　　2005年1月6日0點2分，隨著一個胖乎乎的男嬰在北京出生，中國人口正式達到13億。孩子的父母高興地接受了中國政府頒發的"中國第13億個公民"榮譽証書及人們送上的鮮花和祝福。與孩子父母無比喜悅的心情相比，中國的人口專家對這第13億個小公民的到來則是半喜半憂。

　　值得高興的是，由於實行計劃生育政策，每對夫妻的平均育兒數從上世紀70年代初的5.8下降到現在的1.8，全國在過去30年中少生了3億多人。而中國的13億人口日也比預期的晚到了4年。

　　然而，專家指出："13億人口日的到來，再一次敲響了人口問題的警鐘。"現在中國人口問題面臨著三大挑戰。挑戰之一還是人口數量問題。未來十幾年中國人口每年預計還要增加1000萬人左右。挑戰之二是人口素質問題。據2012年聯合國《人文發展報告》，中國25歲以上人口平均受教育年限為7.5年，還不到美國100年前的水平。挑戰之三是人口結構問題。結構問題首先是人口老齡化，隨著出生率下降，老年人口比例大幅度上升。2014年中國60歲以上老人已經超過了全國人口的15%。專家預計，到2050年左右，老年人口將佔中國人口的三分之一。此外，中國文化中重男輕女的傳統觀念，也使出生人口的性別結構出現失調。2014年全國抽樣調查結果表明，中國人口中男性數量比女性多了3400萬人。

如果說以前談論中國的人口問題，主要是說"人太多"；那麼，近年來，"人口素質"、"人口老齡化"及"出生性別比例失調"等問題已經成為人們關注的新焦點。隨著人口形勢的變化，中國政府也在調整政策。從2015年10月起，實行了30多年的"獨生子女政策"成為了歷史。新的"二孩政策"讓中國夫婦終於可以生兩個孩子了。◆

阅读技巧

A 说明文的特点 The Features of Expository Writing

This lesson introduces an expository essay. The purpose of expository writing is to explain or interpret a point of view, a theory, or a plan. In general, this type of writing has three components: the introductory paragraph, which states the subject of interest; the second part of the essay, which expounds upon or interprets the subject in detail; and the final component, which is usually the conclusion. Techniques that structure the presentation of information and ideas in the process of explanation include cause and effect, comparison and contrast, time order, problem and solution, and simple listing or categorizing. Of course, not every essay includes all of these techniques. Therefore, they will be presented to you gradually as the lessons progress. This lesson introduces ways to compare and contrast.

B 篇章关联词：比较和对比 Discourse Connectives: Comparison and Contrast

Comparisons and contrasts are used to present similarities and differences between two entities. There are specific connectives or words that signal comparative/contrasting ideas in discourse. Being able to recognize and use words that signal comparison and contrast is a very useful reading (and writing) skill. You can use them as cues to pull ideas out of a passage or to compare, contrast, and express your own opinions.

Comparison words signal that the author is pointing out a similarity between two subjects. Review the following commonly used comparison words:

Comparison Words	Example Sentences
跟(和、与)…一样(相同、相似)	我家乡的天气跟这儿完全一样。夏天热冬天冷。
如……一般	成千上万的汽车如蜗牛一般堵在道路上慢慢爬行。
(好)像……似的	他们好像发现了新大陆似的，涌向窗口。
同样	连云港市新出生婴儿性别比例严重失调，同样面临这个问题还有海南、河南、广东和安徽。

Contrast words signal a change in the direction of the writer's thought. They tell you that the author is pointing out a difference between two subjects or statements. Review the following commonly used contrast words:

Contrast Words	Example Sentences
但是、可是、而、然而……	所有的检票厅都改成了临时候车室，而车站大厅前的广场上仍然是人山人海。
则、却	等到人们挤上火车，却发现车厢里也是拥挤不堪。
不同，相反，不一样	张太太性格开朗，喜欢跟人交朋友。而张先生的性格却完全相反，他不爱说话，常常一个人呆在家里。
与／跟……不同的是	与专家看法不同的是，他认为人口多并不是中国落后的原因。
另一方面……	计划生育政策减少了中国出生人口，但另一方面，也带来了人口老化，出生性别比例失调的新问题。

C 阅读技巧练习 Reading Skill Practice

Circle the connectives or words that signal contrast or comparison in these passages from the reading:

1 孩子的父母高兴地接受了中国政府颁发的"中国第13亿个小公民"荣誉证书及人们送上的鲜花和祝福。与孩子父母无比喜悦的心情相比，中国的人口专家对这第13亿个小公民的到来则是半喜半忧。

2 值得高兴的是，由于实行计划生育政策，每对夫妻的平均育儿数从上世纪70年代初的5.8下降到现在的1.8，全国在过去30年中少生了3亿多人。而中国的13亿人口日也比预期的晚到了4年。然而，专家指出："13亿人口日的到来，再一次敲响了人口问题的警钟"。

There are two contrasts in the above passages. What are they?

_____

_____

_____

Do these passages focus on similarities or differences?

_____

What words helped you answer the question?

_____

_____

D 怎样读长句子 How to Read Long Sentences

Deciphering long and complicated sentences is one of the key difficulties in reading texts such as this one. This lesson provides the opportunity to practice tackling long sentences in order to grasp the gist of an idea. It is best to find the "kernel" parts of the sentence by deleting such "peripheral" elements as modifiers, adverbs, time phrases, prepositional phrases, and examples or illustrations. Complete the following task as practice, following the example below.

1 孩子的父母高兴地接受了中国政府颁发的"中国第13亿个公民"荣誉证书及人们送上的鲜花和祝福。(N1 接受了N2)

Kernel sentence:

父母接受了荣誉证书及鲜花和祝福。

2 70年代末开始实行的一家只能生一个孩子的计划生育政策使中国过去30年来少生了3亿多人。(N1使N2…)

Kernel sentence:

_____

_____

3 由于实行计划生育政策，每对夫妻的平均育儿数从上世纪70年代初的5.8下降到现在的1.8。(由于…，N 下降到)

Kernel sentence:

_____

_____

词汇与句型

A 随着 along with...

Pattern: N + (随着 + X) + V + O or (随着 + X), + N + V + O

This pattern indicates that the main event (N + V + O) develops/developed along with another event (X). It often implies that X is/was the cause of the main event or action. The phrase 随着 + X may occur either before or after the subject.

1 中国人的思想，随着经济的发展，得到了很大的解放。

Chinese people's thinking has greatly opened up with the development of the economy.

2 随着这个胖乎乎的男婴在北京出生，中国人口正式达到13亿。

With the birth of this chubby baby boy in Beijing, the Chinese population has officially reached 1.3 billion.

3 随着人口迅速增加，住房成了一个严重的问题。

As the population increased rapidly (or, with the rapid growth of population), housing has become a serious problem.

4 树叶随着季节的更换而改变颜色。

Leaves change their colors along with the changing seasons.

B 然而 however, yet, nevertheless, nonetheless

然而 is similar to 可是 and 但是, but is usually used in more formal contexts. It is often followed by 又／却／还／仍然 to indicate a contrast with, or opposition to, the previous clause. The emphasis of the sentence is usually after 然而.

1 中国的人口出生率下降了。然而人口老龄化、婴儿性别比例失调等新问题又出现了。

The birthrate in China has slowed down. Nevertheless, new problems such as the aging population and the gender imbalance among new babies have emerged.

2 这家公司的设备都是一流的，然而产品质量却不太好。

This company has the best equipment. However, the quality of their products is not very good.

3 虽然中国经济发展得很快，然而跟世界发达国家比起来仍然差得很远。

Even though China is developing its economy very rapidly, it's still far behind many of the world's developed countries.

4 谁都想得第一名，然而第一名却只有一个。

Everyone wants to win first prize, but there is only one first prize.

C 此外（除此以外，除了这个／这些以外）besides, in addition

此 means "this," which refers to the previously mentioned subject matter. 此外 means "besides (what has been mentioned)," or "in addition (to what has been mentioned)."

1 随着出生率下降，老年人口比例大幅度上升，此外，中国文化中重男轻女的传统观念，也使出生人口性别结构失去平衡。

With the decline of the birthrate, the proportion of the elderly population has risen dramatically. In addition, the traditional male-centered view in Chinese culture has caused an imbalanced gender distribution among newborn babies.

2 小王会说英文、法文，此外，还会一点日文。

Xiao Wang can speak English and French. What's more, he also knows some Japanese.

3 他喜欢看书、听音乐，此外，就没有什么别的爱好了。

He enjoys reading and listening to music. Besides these, he has no other hobbies.

4 她一生只写过两本书，此外，就没有别的作品了。

She only wrote two books in her life. Besides these, she has no other publications.

D 与……相比 compared with...

与……相比 is a prepositional phrase that can be used before or after the subject to introduce the target of comparison. It is more formal than 跟……相比.

1 <u>与</u>那所大学<u>相比</u>，我们的条件好多了。

Compared with that university, our conditions are much better.

2 <u>与</u>他们公司的产品<u>相比</u>，这种电脑质量高多了，价钱也便宜多了。

Compared with the products of their company, these computers are much better in quality, and much lower in price.

3 中国的出生率<u>与</u>三十年前<u>相比</u>下降了很多，然而人口还在继续增长。

The birthrate in China, compared to thirty years ago, has dropped considerably. But the population is still increasing.

E 由于 owing to, thanks to, due to, because of, on account of

1 <u>由于</u>实行了计划生育政策，中国人口出生率下降了很多。

Thanks to (owing to) the birth control policy, the birthrate in China has slowed down greatly.

2 <u>由于</u>健康原因，他父亲提前退休了。

Due to health reasons, his father retired early.

3 运动会<u>由于</u>天气关系而改期举行。

The sports game has been rescheduled due to bad weather.

Note: Both 由于 and 因为 can be used to introduce reason and cause, and are sometimes interchangeable. The word 由于 in all three previous sentences can be replaced by 因为. However, 由于 is usually used in more formal situations. Also, while 因为 can be used in the second clause, 由于 cannot. Therefore, one can say "他父亲提前退休了，因为他近年来身体越来越不好," but not ✖ "他父亲提前退休了，由于他近年来身体越来越不好。"

语法

A 形容词重叠 Adjective reduplication

Adjective reduplication, which typically denotes liveliness or intensity, is common in Chinese. There are generally four forms: AA, AABB, A 里 AB, and ABB.

1 大大的眼睛、胖胖的孩子、冷冷地说、暖暖的阳光 (AA)

   Big, big eyes; chubby kids; say coldly; cozy warm sunshine

2 高高兴兴地走了、干干净净的房间、认认真真的态度 (AABB)

   Leave happily; nice and clean room; serious attitude

3 糊里糊涂地过日子、小里小气的人 (A 里 AB)

   Muddle along; a stingy guy

4 胖乎乎的婴孩、红彤彤的玫瑰、绿油油的草地、慢吞吞地走路 (ABB)

   Chubby baby; red, red rose; green lawn; walk slowly

Note: Forms 2 and 3 can be simplified to AB (e.g., 高高兴兴 can be 高兴, 糊里糊涂 can be 糊涂), but ABB cannot be reduced to AB. (There are no such words as ⊗ 胖乎 or ⊗ 红彤 in Chinese.)

B 说数字 Saying numbers

When reading a fraction, use the formula ···分之···. The denominator always precedes the numerator. The order is the opposite of that in English:

- ⅓（三分之一）
- 1⅜（一又八分之三）
- 20%（百分之二十）
- 5/1000（千分之五）

When reading a decimal, use the formula ···点···. The number before 点 is the whole number and the figures after 点 are the decimal places, as in English:

- 1.2（一点二）
- 45.68（四十五点六八）
- 3.141592（三点一四一五九二）

C 中文数字和阿拉伯数字的用法 Usage of Chinese and Arabic numerals

In general, Arabic numerals are widely used:

- 21.35元　¥21.35
- 270美元　$270 (US)
- 48岁　　48 years old
- 11个月　11 months
- 1480人　1,480 people

For idiomatic or conventionalized expressions and abbreviations, Chinese numbers must be used:

- 一心一意 put one's whole heart into
- 星期五　Friday
- 十几岁　teenage
- 五四运动 May 4th Movement

For dates, either system can be used. However, consistency should be maintained throughout a piece of writing, e.g., "1998年5月1日10时30分" or "一九九八年五月一日十时三十分."

D 多、少、早、晚 as adverbials in comparative sentences

When 多, 少, 早, and 晚 are used as verb-adverbials in comparative sentences, they must occur before the verbs. Such verbs must be followed by complements of quantity to indicate the concrete difference of the result of comparison. (Note the differences in the English translations.)

1 计划生育政策让中国在过去30年内少生了3亿多人。

   The birth control policy in China resulted in three hundred million fewer births.

2 由于公司业务发展很快，我们比去年多聘了十位员工。

   Due to the company's fast-growing business, we hired ten more employees than last year.

3 他们比我们早出发一个小时，却比我们晚到二十分钟。

   They left one hour earlier than us, but arrived twenty minutes later.

E 半……半…… half...half...

This phrase uses antonyms to express the coexistence of two opposite states (e.g., 半喜半忧, part joy part worry). Similar examples are:

1 尽管他说这件事是他亲眼看见的，我对他的话仍然半信半疑。

   Even though he said he saw it with his own eyes, I still can't believe it completely.

2 网上看到的新闻，恐怕有一些是半真半假的东西。

   I am afraid that some online news is not reliable.

3 人们都知道这个国家存在着半明半暗的童工现象。

   Everyone knows there is child labor in this country, although it is half hidden.

F ……化 ...ize

化, originally meaning "change, transform," can be used as a suffix. It can be added to a noun or an adjective to convert it into a verb, indicating "to change (or transform) into the state of the noun (or the adjective)." Its function is very close to that of the English suffixes "-ize," "-ify," and "-ing."

- 住房商业化 to commercialize housing
- 美化环境   to beautify the environment
- 人口老龄化 population aging
- 中国现在需要工业现代化。

   At present, China needs to modernize its industry.

练习

A 语音

Write the following underlined Chinese characters in *pinyin*.
Pay special attention to their different pronunciations in different contexts.

<u>数</u>清楚（　　）　　　人<u>数</u>　　（　　）

<u>着</u>急　　（　　）　　　看<u>着</u>　　（　　）

<u>重</u>要　　（　　）　　　<u>重</u>新　　（　　）

<u>调</u>查　　（　　）　　　失<u>调</u>　　（　　）

<u>为</u>了　　（　　）　　　成<u>为</u>　　（　　）

<u>教</u>书　　（　　）　　　<u>教</u>育　　（　　）

<u>还</u>是　　（　　）　　　<u>还</u>钱　　（　　）

数<u>量</u>　　（　　）　　　商<u>量</u>　　（　　）

<u>少</u>年　　（　　）　　　<u>少</u>数　　（　　）

高<u>兴</u>　　（　　）　　　<u>兴</u>奋　　（　　）

B 词汇与句型

B1 词语搭配 Match the following words by considering their appropriate collocations.

Group One (Verb + Object)	Group Two (Noun + Noun)
1 敲响 _____ 目的	1 自然 _____ 证书
2 颁发 _____ 政策	2 二十一 _____ 资源
3 实行 _____ 挑战	3 新年 _____ 素质
4 值得 _____ 警钟	4 受教育 _____ 世纪
5 面临 _____ 证书	5 荣誉 _____ 年限
6 达到 _____ 高兴	6 国民 _____ 祝福

B2 选词填空 Fill in the blanks by choosing the most appropriate words from the list below. (Note: not every word will be used.)

a 达到	g 政策	m 资源
b 接受	h 下降	n 年限
c 荣誉	i 上升	o 以
d 半喜半忧	j 由于	p 无比
e 值得	k 预计	q 预期
f 实行	l 素质	r 面临

1 _____情况变化，我们现在_____的困难比_____的多。

2 在本公司服务_____为三十年_____上的员工才能得到这个荣誉证书。

3 最近的房价_____得很快，一所房子比去年贵了20%。但专家认为这是一种不正常的现象，他们_____房价不久就会_____的。

4 你觉得聘用新员工时，是应该看他的经验还是看他的_____？

5 实行这项环境保护_____，是为了不让那些工厂浪费国家的自然_____。

6 _____我们注意的是，旧的问题还没有解决，新的问题又出现了。

7 快毕业了，同学们都_____。毕业当然是好事，可是找不到工作怎么办？

8 不管你能不能_____这个事实，我看我们是无法_____这个标准的。

9 下星期的毕业晚会_____有三千人参加。

10 她为祖国争得了_____，心中感到_____骄傲。

B3 完成句子

1 中国的人口出生率下降了，然而

   _____

2 虽然我们在一起工作十年了，然而

   _____

3 与十年前相比，

   _____

4 跟第三世界国家的人比起来，

   _____

5 这次去北京，主要是参加一个会议，
此外，_____

6 由于情况比较复杂，

   _____

7 随着秋天的到来，

   _____

8 中国的经济发展这么快，主要是由于

   _____

9 随着经济的发展，

   _____

10 他这一生只去过一次日本，此外

   _____

C 语法

C1 这些数字用中文怎么说？ How do you state the following numbers in Chinese?

1 2/3	_____	2.7	_____
5/8	_____	36.54	_____
55%	_____	108.1	_____
43/1000	_____	99.99	_____

C2 把下面句子中标出的书面语改写成相应的口语 Replace the underlined formal words with their informal counterparts.

1 <u>与</u>三十年前<u>相比</u>，中国人现在的生活好多了。_____

2 <u>据</u>专家研究，人口太多会带来很多社会问题。_____

3 <u>除此以外</u>，他没有别的意见了。

   _____

4 很多人喜欢在大城市生活，<u>而</u>我却觉得小城市更有意思。_____

5 我这点中文对付简单的会话还可以，教书<u>则</u>还差得太远。_____

6 这种药的有效期限<u>为</u>两年。_____

7 世界上有四大河流，长江是<u>其中</u>之一。_____

8 来听演讲的有<u>本</u>校师生，外校师生，<u>及</u>社会上的文学爱好者。_____

C3 汉译英 Translate the following words into English:

标准化 _____

全球化 _____

西化 _____

私有化 _____

简化 _____

丑化 _____

数字化 _____

国际化 _____

C4 英译汉 Translate the following sentences into Chinese, paying special attention to the underlined words.

1 Due to bad weather, we arrived three hours <u>later</u> than expected.

_____

2 To prepare for the work, he went one month <u>earlier</u> than the others.

_____

3 I was very tired, so I slept one hour <u>more</u> than usual.

_____

4 I only studied five months <u>less</u> than my sister, but her Chinese is much better than mine.

_____

_____

5 According to the current speed of economic development, the Chinese government <u>predicts</u> that China will realize industrial modernization within twenty years.

_____

_____

6 The result is completely different from what they <u>predicted</u>.

_____

D 阅读

短文（一）
不该出生的女婴

　　刘云本来应该有三个女儿，但是因为想生一个男孩，她把二女儿[1]给了别人，并且在知道怀 (huái) (conceive) 的第三个孩子也是女儿时，又做了堕胎 (duòtāi) (abortion) 手术。

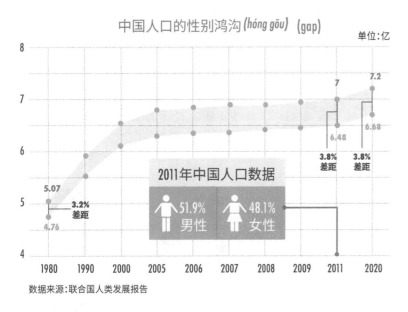

中国人口的性别鸿沟 (hóng gōu) (gap)
单位：亿

数据来源：联合国人类发展报告

2011年中国人口数据
51.9% 男性　48.1% 女性

　　经过多年的努力之后，刘云终于生了一个儿子。她丈夫花了很多钱请客，庆祝这件大喜事。他们希望将来儿子能上大学，已经开始打算送儿子上一所很贵的幼儿园。但对九岁的女儿，他们没有什么计划。然而，当刘云回忆起七年前的那个冬夜，她让亲戚抱走她二女儿的情景时，她的眼睛红了。"我只听她哭了一次。我甚至都没看到她的小脸。后来我哭了又哭，真的非常想她。但是

我没法不那样做，我先生家一定要我生个男孩。"

　　近年来仍有一些父母因认为女婴不该出生而堕胎或将女婴遗弃 (yíqì) (abandon) 甚至杀害 (shāhài) (kill)。据UNICEF报告，中国每年大约有10万弃婴，其中大多数是女婴。

D1 回答问题

1　刘云为什么一定要生个儿子？

_____

2　刘云和她丈夫对孩子们的将来有些什么计划？现在在做什么准备？

_____

_____

3　他们对儿子和女儿有什么不一样？

_____

_____

4　刘云到底爱不爱她的女儿？请举例说明。

_____

_____

_____

5　这篇文章的题目为什么叫"不该出生的女婴"？

_____

6　弃婴问题是由于什么原因产生的？怎样才能解决？

_____

_____

---

[1] When the one-child policy was in place (1978-2015), having one child was promoted as ideal and the limit was strongly enforced in urban areas, but actual implementation varied according to location. In most rural areas, families were allowed to have two children if the first child was female or disabled.

D2 阅读技巧练习 Reading Skill Practice: Complete the following chart according to the previous short article.

刘云夫妇对孩子的态度	男孩	女孩
出生后		
教育计划		
刘云对女婴的态度	（行为）	（内心）

短文（二）

新闻一则

这是一条未经改写的新闻。读新闻时，你不必认识每一个字。请快速读完后根据你的理解回答后面的问题。

Read this news item (you don't need to know every word) and answer the questions after the reading.

2007年8月24日，新华社报道[2]

　　江苏省连云港市新出生婴儿性别比例严重失调，男女性别比为163.5比100。同样面临幼儿性别严重失调的还有海南、河南、广东和安徽，其中海南的男女比例为136比100。中国计生协会公布报告，呼吁应对中国人口面临的新挑战。协会会长姜春云说，新出生婴儿男女性别比日趋升高，全国已达119（正常出生人口性别比为103至107）。

---

[2] "Zhongguo nannü xingbie bili shiheng chuang xin gao" 中国男女性别比例失衡创新高 [China's Male-to-Female Ratio Imbalance Reaches New High], *Xinhua she* 新华社, Aug. 24, 2007, at *BBC Zhongwen wang* BBC中文网, available at <http://news.bbc.co.uk/chinese/simp/hi/news-id_6960000/newsid_6963000/6963005.stm>.

D3 根据短文内容，选择最佳答案

1　这条新闻的主要意思是：
　a　江苏省连云港市新出生婴儿性别比例失调
　b　海南、河南、广东、安徽幼儿性别比例失调
　c　海南幼儿性别比例失调
　d　中国新出生婴儿性别比例失调

D4 根据这条新闻，

1　江苏省新出生婴儿性别比是_____比100。
2　海南幼儿性别比是_____比100。
3　中国总人口新出生婴儿性别比是_____比100。
4　正常出生人口性别比应该是_____比100。
5　为什么新闻说江苏省连云港市0-4岁幼儿性别比例"严重失调"？

_____

E 口语

E1 Discussion Topics

1　人口太多会给社会带来什么影响？
2　人口太少会给社会带来什么影响？
3　人口老龄化又会给社会带来什么影响？

E2 Presentation Topic: 人口对于社会的影响

Pick a city or country that you are interested in and research its population issues. Consider the following questions and prepare a short presentation in Chinese for the class.

1　这个国家有什么人口问题？
2　这些问题是怎么造成的？
3　你认为怎么样才能解决这个国家的人口问题？

E3 Debate Topics

Research both sides of the following topics. The class will be divided into two sides. Each side will take turns presenting arguments.

1 中国现在仍然需要实行计划生育 vs.
   中国现在不需要实行计划生育

2 家里只有一个小孩会
   对孩子的成长不利 vs.
   家里只有一个小孩不会
   对孩子的成长不利

E4 Extended Group Research Project

In a small group, choose one of the following issues in China to research. Prepare a presentation in Chinese with a visual component. Each member of the group should take turns presenting. Include a list of new vocabulary words.

1 城市农民工 Migrant Workers

2 户口制度 The Hukou System

3 男女比例失衡 Gender Imbalance

4 人口老龄化 Aging Population

F 写作

作文题：任选一题（400-500字）

a 我对中国人口政策的看法

b 解决中国人口问题最好的办法

Select one of the two topics listed above. Then write an essay of 400–500 characters using the vocabulary and grammar patterns you learned from this lesson. Create an outline before writing.

The structure of your essay should be arranged in three parts, in the following order:

1 Statement of opinion

2 Elaboration

3 Conclusion

Try to do the following:

1 Start the article with a story or anecdote.

2 Illustrate your point with comparison and contrast.

3 Support your point with statistics.

Exchange rough drafts of your essays with a classmate and edit each other's work. Incorporate these revisions into your final draft.

Use at least ten of the following vocabulary words from this lesson:

随着	世纪	结构	失调
正式	预期	首先	调查
无比	警钟	率	年代
值得	面临	比例	关注
实行	挑战	超过	焦点
生育	预计	传统	
政策	素质	观念	

Use at least three of the following sentence patterns from this lesson:

随着……

然而……

此外……

与……相比

由于

住房

- 上面这张照片中的房子，你愿意住哪一种？为什么？
- 住房的基本条件是什么？
- 买房子好还是租房子好？为什么？
- 如果你去过别的国家／地方，那里的住房情况跟你现在的居住环境有什么不同？
- 你知道哪些跟"住房"有关的词汇？

阅读前讨论

Due to government policy and recent rapid economic growth, housing conditions in China have changed drastically over the past sixty years. The expository essay in this lesson expounds upon the housing situation in detail, describing China's past and present policies, their effects on housing conditions, and the causes and consequences of the policy change.

3

第三课

生词

自学生词

Match each new word with its English translation by deducing the word's meaning from its characters. (The first one is done for you.)

公房　　私房　　居民　　　　房地产(產)　　实(實)在　　　　新建

人均　　户(戶)均　飞涨(飛漲)　上涨(漲)　　开发(開發)商

1 实在　　　 indeed, as a matter of fact

2 ＿＿＿＿＿ real estate, realty

3 ＿＿＿＿＿ shoot up, rise dramatically

4 ＿＿＿＿＿ state-owned housing

5 ＿＿＿＿＿ developer

6 ＿＿＿＿＿ resident, inhabitant

7 ＿＿＿＿＿ privately owned house

8 ＿＿＿＿＿ newly built

9 ＿＿＿＿＿ per capita, per person

10 ＿＿＿＿＿ per household

11 ＿＿＿＿＿ rise, go up

成语和惯用语

成语／惯用语	单字解释	意思
1　应运而生 *yìng yùn ér shēng* 世界上学汉语的人越来越多，各类汉语学校也<u>应运而生</u>。	应(應) respond to, answer 运(運) fortune, destiny, luck, opportunity 而 conjunction, used to link two verbs here. The first verb 应运 is a modifier (an adverbial indicating "the way/manner") to the second verb 生. 生 be born, emerge	Emerge in response to the proper time or opportunity

	简体	繁体	拼音	词性	英文
1	采用	採	*cǎiyòng*	v.	adopt, use
2	制度		*zhìdù*	n.	system
3	老百姓		*lǎobǎixìng*	n.	ordinary people
4	兴建	興	*xīngjiàn*	v.	build, construct
5	归	歸	*guī*	v.	belong to
6	补助	補	*bǔzhù*	v./n.	subsidize; subsidy
7	住宅		*zhùzhái*	n.	residence, dwelling
8	面积	積	*miànjī*	n.	area, square measure
9	平方		*píngfāng*	n.	square
10	米		*mǐ*	n.	meter
11	负担	負擔	*fùdān*	v./n.	burden; load
12	收入		*shōurù*	n.	income, revenue
13	维修	維	*wéixiū*	v.	maintain, repair
14	广大	廣	*guǎngdà*	adj.	broad, numerous
15	分配		*fēnpèi*	v.	distribute, allocate
16	公正		*gōngzhèng*	adj.	just, fair
17	严重	嚴	*yánzhòng*	adj.	serious
18	鼓励	勵	*gǔlì*	v.	encourage, urge
19	采取	採	*cǎiqǔ*	v.	adopt, carry out
20	措施		*cuòshī*	n.	measure, step
21	调整	調	*tiáozhěng*	v./n.	adjust; adjustment
22	贷款	貸	*dàikuǎn*	n./v.o.	loan, mortgage
23	价格	價	*jiàgé*	n.	price
24	法律		*fǎlù*	n.	law
25	权	權	*quán*	n.	power, rights

	简体	繁体	拼音	词性	英文
26	至于	於	*zhìyú*	prep.	as for
27	制		*zhì*	v./n.	make; system
28	迅速		*xùnsù*	adj.	rapid, speedy
29	宽敞	寬敞	*kuānchǎng*	adj.	spacious, roomy
30	舒适	適	*shūshì*	adj.	comfortable, cozy
31	扩大	擴	*kuòdà*	v.	broaden, expand
32	改善		*gǎishàn*	v.	improve
33	居住		*jūzhù*	v.	reside, dwell
34	公寓		*gōngyù*	n.	apartment
35	豪华	華	*háohuá*	adj.	luxurious, extravagant
36	别墅		*biéshù*	n.	villa
37	纷纷	紛	*fēnfēn*	adv.	one after another
38	统计	統計	*tǒngjì*	n.	statistics, census
39	局		*jú*	n.	bureau
40	商品		*shāngpǐn*	n.	commodity, goods
41	速度		*sùdù*	n.	speed, pace
42	造成		*zàochéng*	v.	bring about, cause
43	限制		*xiànzhì*	v.	restrict, limit, confine
44	建造		*jiànzào*	v.	construct, build
45	面向		*miànxiàng*	v.	face, be geared to the needs of, cater to
46	争取	爭	*zhēngqǔ*	v.	strive for
47	功能		*gōngnéng*	n.	function
48	配套		*pèitào*	v.	form a complete set
49	设施	設	*shèshī*	n.	installation, facility
50	齐全	齊	*qíquán*	adj.	complete, well-stocked

课文

Skim the reading; then select the option below that best captures its main idea.

a 中国的住房建设

b 中国人的住房情况

c 中国人住房情况的改变

Read the text again carefully and answer the following questions.

1 对中国老百姓来说，早期的公房制度有什么好处和坏处？

_____

_____

2 政府为什么要把公房制改为私房制？

_____

_____

3 改革后，政府怎样帮助居民买房？

_____

_____

4 随着经济的快速发展和私房制的推行，中国市场上出现了什么新行业？

_____

_____

5 在住房制度改革以后，老百姓面临的新问题是什么？政府如何解决？

_____

_____

住房

最近几十年来，中国人的住房情况有了很大的改变。这个改变与政府住房政策及国家经济发展有直接关系。

从1950年到90年代初，中国住房采用的是公房制度。在公房制度下，老百姓的住房都由政府兴建，归国家所有，每个月的房租也由政府补助。一般来说，每家每月只需付几元到十几元房租，但是住宅面积很小。比如，在1980年，北京市居民平均每人住房面积才3点多平方米。公房制度在经济上帮助了老百姓，但是却使政府的负担越来越重。政府在房地产上的收入较少，很难维修旧房和兴建新房，所以广大居民的住房条件很差。同时，住房分配上的不公正，也成为一个严重的社会问题。

为了解决这些问题，政府决定从1988年开始改革住房制度，并决定要在1995到2000这五年内，把公房制度改成私房制度。1998年，中国政府正式停止了公房制，把公房卖给居民。为了鼓励个人及家庭购买私房，政府采取了一些措施：对于中低收入的居民，一是提供购房补助，帮助居民买房；二是调整贷款制度，让他们可以借钱买房；三是兴建更多面积小价格低的"经济适用住房"，让他们买得起房。不过，根据法律规定，中国的土地还是国家所有的，买房者只有70年的土地使用权。至于低收入居民，如果实在买不起住房，可以继续租房。1998年7月1日，在中国实行多年的公房制宣告结束。中国人终于可以自由买房、卖房和租房了，中国的住房也最终从国有化变为商品化和市场化了。

随着中国经济的迅速发展，人民收入越来越高。一些有钱人愿意购买更宽敞舒适的住宅，于是房地产开发公司应运而生。新建住宅使居民住房

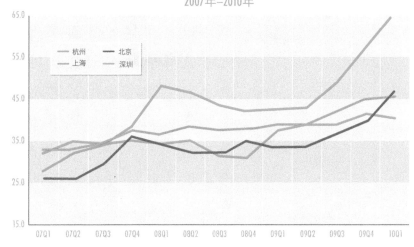

中国四个城市的房价租售比 (price-to-rent ratio)
2007年-2010年

杭州　北京
上海　深圳

数据来源：Wu, Jing & Gyourko, Joseph & Deng, Yongheng. 2012. "Evaluating conditions in major Chinese housing markets," Regional Science and Urban Economics, Elsevier, vol. 42(3), pages 531-543.

房价上涨的速度远远超过了普通百姓收入的增长速度，造成了'有房人不断买房，无房人买不起房'的情况。

面积不断扩大，条件不断改善。2014年，北京人均住房使用面积达到了31.5平方米。与1980年人均住宅面积只有3点多平方米的情况相比，北京人的居住条件不知道改善了多少倍。

当然，中国的房地产热也带来了房价的飞涨。特别是新式公寓楼和豪华别墅的纷纷出现，使房价成了"天价"。据中国国家统计局统计，从2003年到2013年，十年间全国房价平均上涨143%。而北京、上海等大城市竟超过了400%！房价上涨的速度远远超过了普通百姓收入的增长速度，造成了"有房人不断买房，无房人买不起房"的情况。为了限制房价上涨太快，政府每年都会制定房价调控政策，并鼓励开发商多建造面向普通百姓的住房，争取2020年基本做到"户均一套房、人均一间房、功能配套、设施齐全"。◆

住房

　　最近幾十年來，中國人的住房情況有了很大的改變。這個改變與政府住房政策及國家經濟發展有直接關係。

　　從1950年到90年代初，中國住房採用的是公房制度。在公房制度下，老百姓的住房都由政府興建，歸國家所有，每個月的房租也由政府補助。一般來說，每家每月只需付幾元到十幾元房租，但是住宅面積很小。比如，在1980年，北京市居民平均每人住房面積才3點多平方米。公房制度在經濟上幫助了老百姓，但是卻使政府的負擔越來越重。政府在房地產上的收入較少，很難維修舊房和興建新房，所以廣大居民的住房條件很差。同時，住房分配上的不公正，也成為一個嚴重的社會問題。

　　為了解決這些問題，政府決定從1988年開始改革住房制度，並決定要在1995到2000年這五年內，把公房制度改成私房制度。1998年，中國政府正式停止了公房制，把公房賣給居民。為了鼓勵個人及家庭購買私房，政府採取了一些措施：對於中低收入的居民，一是提供購房補助，幫助居民買房；二是調整貸款制度，讓他們可以借錢買房；三是興建

Reading Into a New China · 1

更多面積小價格低的"經濟適用住房"，讓他們買得起房。不過，根據法律規定，中國的土地還是國家所有的，買房者只有70年的土地使用權。至於低收入居民，如果實在買不起住房，可以繼續租房。1998年7月1日，在中國實行多年的公房制宣告結束。中國人終於可以自由買房、賣房和租房了，中國的住房也最終從國有化變為商品化和市場化了。

隨著中國經濟的迅速發展，人民收入越來越高。一些有錢人願意購買更寬敞舒適的住宅，於是房地產開發公司應運而生。新建住宅使居民住房面積不斷擴大，條件不斷改善。2014年，北京人均住房使用面積達到了31.5平方米。與1980年人均住宅面積只有3點多平方米的情況相比，北京人的居住條件不知道改善了多少倍。

當然，中國的房地產熱也帶來了房價的飛漲。特別是新式公寓樓和豪華別墅的紛紛出現，使房價成了"天價"。據中國國家統計局統計，從2003年到2013年，十年間全國房價平均上漲143%。而北京、上海等大城市竟超過了400%！房價上漲的速度遠遠超過了普通百姓收入的增長速度，造成了"有房人不斷買房，無房人買不起房"的情況。為了限制房價上漲太快，政府每年都會制定房價調控政策，並鼓勵開發商多建造面向普通百姓的住房，爭取2020年基本做到"戶均一套房、人均一間房、功能配套、設施齊全"。◆

阅读技巧

A 段落的主题 The Main Idea of a Paragraph

Very often, the main idea of a paragraph appears in the form of one general sentence, called the topic sentence. A topic sentence can occur anywhere in a paragraph (beginning, middle, or end), but is usually the first or second sentence. Below are five topic sentences from this lesson. Number them according to their corresponding paragraphs.

_____ 住房商品化也带来了问题。

_____ 住房制度改革改善了中国人的居住条件。

_____ 中国住房制度改革的经过。

_____ 中国以前的公房制度及其引起的问题。

_____ 最近几十年来，中国人的住房情况有了很大的改变。

B 篇章关联词：原因和结果
Discourse Connectives: Cause and Effect

While a cause always comes first in the real world, an author may give either the cause or the effect first. The skill of recognizing and using these signal words can help you become an effective reader and writer.

The following are among the most commonly used words to signal cause-and-effect relationships:

因为……所以……

由于……就……

……，因此／因而……

……使／使得……

……，结果……

之所以……是因为……

……，原因是……

……，于是……

The following words, though not connectives, can also signify a cause-and-effect relationship: A 跟 B 有关系 and A 带来／造成／导致 B.

C 阅读技巧练习 Reading Skill Practice

The following passages are from the text. Circle the connectives or words that signal cause and effect, and mark which part of the sentence is the cause and which is the effect.

1 这个改变与政府住房政策及国家经济发展有直接关系。

2 政府在房地产上的收入较少，很难维修旧房和兴建新房，所以广大居民的住房条件很差。

3 为了解决这些问题，政府决定从1988年开始改革住房制度。

4 为了帮助人民购买住宅，政府采取了一些措施。

5 随着中国经济的迅速发展，人民收入越来越高。

6 一些有钱人愿意购买更宽敞舒适的住宅，于是房地产开发公司应运而生。

7 当然，中国的房地产热也带来了房价的飞涨。

8 特别是新式公寓楼和豪华别墅的纷纷出现，使房价成了"天价"。

9 房价上涨的速度远远超过了普通百姓收入的增长速度，造成了"有房人不断买房，无房人买不起房"的情况。

Complete the following sentences, using appropriate connectives of cause and effect.

1 房价上涨 _____ 低收入的人们买不起房子。

2 _____ 房价上涨，_____ 低收入的人们买不起房子。

3 _____ 国家经济迅速发展，中国人的住房情况有了很大的改变。

4 国家经济迅速发展，_____ 中国人的住房情况有了很大的改变。

5 _____ 政府在房地产上的收入较少，_____ 很难维修旧房和兴建新房。

6 政府在房地产上的收入较少，_____ 很难维修旧房和兴建新房。

7 房地产开发公司 _____ 越来越多，_____ 越来越多有钱人想买更好的住房。

8 房地产开发公司越来越多，_____ 越来越多有钱人想买更舒适的住房。

词汇与句型

A A 跟 B 有关（系）
A has something to do with B

1 这个改变与政府住房政策及国家经济发展有直接关系。

This change is directly related to the government housing policy and the country's economic development.

2 很多老师指出，学生的学习成绩跟学习态度有明显的关系。

Many teachers have pointed out that a student's academic achievement is evidently related to his or her attitude towards learning.

3 他没上大学跟他家的经济状况没有关系。

That he didn't attend university had nothing to do with the financial condition of his family.

B 由 by

由 is used here to introduce an agent that assumes an official capacity to carry out a designated action. 由 is translated as "by" in English, but is only used in written language. The verbs used with 由 usually represent formal actions, such as:

决定	*juédìng*	to decide
陪同	*péitóng*	to accompany
主持	*zhǔchí*	to preside over (a meeting)
办理	*bànlǐ*	to handle, to conduct
分配	*fēnpèi*	to distribute, to allocate, to assign
领导	*lǐngdǎo*	to lead

1 在公房制度下，老百姓的住房都由政府兴建，归国家所有。

Under the public housing system, people's housing was constructed by the government and owned by the state.

2 今年的春季交易会将由北京电视台报道。

This year's Spring Trade Fair will be reported on by the Beijing Media Network.

3 公司新雇用了三名设计人员，他们的工作由经理分配。

The company recently hired three designers. Their tasks will be assigned by the manager.

4 我们找到了两个解决问题的方法，使用哪个得由校长决定。

We have found two ways to solve the problem. Which one should be used will depend on the principal's decision.

5 下个月的学生大会由张立主持。

Next month's student meeting will be presided over by Zhang Li.

C A 归 B 所有 : A belongs to B, A is owned by B

归……所有 is a rather formal usage. In informal contexts, 所有 can be omitted.

1 在公房制度下，老百姓的住房都归国家所有。

> Under the public housing system, people's housing was owned by the state.

2 中国所有的土地都归国家所有。

> All land in China is owned by the state.

3 宿舍设备归学校所有，但每个学生都可以使用。

> Facilities in the dorm belong to the school, but every student can use them.

4 他走了以后，这屋里的一切就归他弟弟（所有）了。

> After he left, everything in the house came into the possession of his brother.

D ……（来）说 ...speaking

1 一般来说，每家每月只需付很少的房租，但是住宅面积很小。

> Generally speaking, every household only needed to pay very little rent, but the living space was very small.

2 一般来说，公房房租都比较便宜。

> Generally speaking, rent for public housing is relatively cheap.

3 总的来说，这个制度是很成功的。

> As a whole, the system is quite successful.

4 老实说，我对贷款买房子这种方式还不太适应。

> Honestly speaking, I am still not very accustomed to getting a loan to buy a house.

5 客观地说，住房制度改革也带来了一些问题。

> Objectively speaking, the reform of the housing system also brought about some problems.

E 改成 vs. 变成 change into...

Both 改成 and 变成 are resultative verb compounds, in which 成 is the resultative ending, meaning "turn into" or "become." Although both 改成 and 变成 can be translated as "change into" in English, they are intrinsically different in Chinese. 改 (change, transform, alter) indicates that a change takes place due to an outside force. 变 (change, become different), by contrast, indicates a change that follows a natural development. In light of this explanation, we can see why 改成 and 变成 are used in two different patterns:

Subj. 把 A 改成 B

Subj. (从 A) 变成 B

1 政府决定在1995到2000年这五年内，把公房制度改成私房制度。

> The government decided to convert the public housing system to a private one within the five years from 1995 to 2000.

2 由于长期缺少雨水，那片土地逐渐变成了沙漠 (desert)。

> Due to a long period of drought, the land has gradually become a desert.

3 几年不见，她已经从小姑娘变成一位漂亮的少女了。

> I haven't seen her for some years. Now she has changed from a little girl to a pretty young lady.

4 因为学生太多，学校把一间大会议室改成了两间小教室。

> Because there are too many students, the school has converted the large conference room into two small classrooms.

5 你能不能帮我把这条长裤改成短裤？

> Could you please help me alter this pair of pants into shorts?

给 (to give) can be combined with different verbs to show different forms of transaction, such as 卖, 借, and 租.

1 政府决定把公房<u>卖给</u>居民。

The government decided to sell the state-owned houses to the residents.

2 如果你周末要去机场，我可以把车<u>借给</u>你。

If you need to go to the airport this weekend, I can lend you my car.

3 要是你把这所房子<u>租给</u>别人，每个月可以拿到不少租金。

If you rent out this big house, you will get a lot of rent every month.

4 经理把荣誉证书<u>颁发给</u>提前完成工作的职员。

The manager awarded the certificates of honor to the employees who had finished their work ahead of time.

G 于是 vs. 所以

于是 (so, then, hence, subsequently) is a conjunction/connective used to link two clauses to express a sequential relationship, indicating that the latter immediately follows the former and is usually an action that happened in the past. 所以 (so, therefore) is also a conjunction/connective linking two clauses of a logical cause-effect relationship.

Since many sequential occurrences also have a cause-effect relationship, 于是 and 所以 share some overlapping meaning and can be interchangeable in these situations. However, there are situations when only one of them is appropriate. The following table illustrates the overlapping and different properties of 于是 and 所以:

		所以	于是
SEMANTIC RELATIONSHIP	Cause-Effect Only	✓	
	Cause-Effect + Sequence	✓	✓
	Sequence Only		✓
TIME	Past	✓	✓
	Future	✓	
VERB TYPE	Action	✓	✓
	State	✓	

Examples of overlapping usages:

1 一些有钱人愿意购买更好的住宅，<u>于是／所以</u>房地产开发公司应运而生。

Some rich people wanted to buy better residences, therefore real estate developers emerged.

2 他的书找不着了，<u>于是／所以</u>他去买了一本新的。

He couldn't find his book, so he bought a new one.

3 小王听说他考上了大学，<u>于是／所以</u>立刻打电话过去祝贺他。

Xiao Wang heard that he was admitted into a university, so she called immediately to congratulate him.

4 那家餐馆生意很不错，<u>于是／所以</u>老板又开了一家分店。

The restaurant's business was prospering, so the owner opened a branch.

Examples of different usages:

5　我的书丢了，<u>所以</u>我考试没考好。⊗于是

I lost my book, so I didn't do well on the exam.

6　政府现在正在限制房价上涨，<u>所以</u>将来
　　老百姓也买得起房了。⊗于是

The government is trying to impose restrictions on housing prices so ordinary people can afford to buy houses in the future.

7　政府在房地产上的收入较少，<u>所以</u>很难
　　兴建新房。⊗于是

The government received very little money from the public housing, so it was very hard to build new houses.

8　他本来不太满意，听我这么一说，<u>于是</u>
　　接受了这个现实。⊗所以

At first he wasn't satisfied. After my talk, he then accepted this reality.

Summary:

于是 cannot be used if only a cause-effect relationship is involved (Sentence 5), if the action of the second clause is not in the past (Sentence 6), and if the verb in the second clause is not an action verb (Sentence 7).

所以 cannot be used if only a sequential relationship is involved (Sentence 8).

A 使役动词"使"和"让"
Causative verbs 使 and 让

In this lesson, we encounter 使 (cause, make, enable) and 让 (let, permit), which act as causative verbs to form constructions like those below:

A1 Pattern: A 使／让 B + adj. (or v.)

This pattern expresses the idea that "A (the cause or condition) makes B change to a specific state or take an action (i.e., result or effect)."

1 新式公寓楼和豪华别墅的纷纷出现，使房价成了"天价"。

The mushrooming of fancy apartment buildings and luxurious villas caused real estate prices to skyrocket (to become extremely high).

2 公房制度在经济上帮助了百姓，但却使政府的负担越来越重。

The public housing system helped ordinary people financially, but made the government's burden heavier and heavier.

3 二是调整贷款制度，让他们可以借钱买房。

The second (measure) is to adjust the mortgage system so as to enable them to buy housing with loans.

4 只有兴建"经济适用住房"，才能让他们买得起房。

Only when we construct "economical lodging" can they afford housing.

A2 "使"和"让"用法比较 Different usages of 使 and 让

Although both 使 and 让 can be translated as "make" in English, and are sometimes interchangeable, they differ in their usage due to their meanings. 使 tends to be used only in formal (written) situations, while 让 is used in a more colloquial style. In sentences with 使, the result tends to be a state (adjective), while in sentences with 让, the result can be either a state or an action.

1 对不起，让您久等了。

Sorry for making you wait so long. (in conversation, use 让, not 使)

2 音乐使／让我心情愉快。

The music makes me happy.

3 老板让他们不停地干活。

The boss makes them work without stopping.
(使 cannot be used)

A3 使役动词小结 A brief summary of causative verbs

Besides 使 and 让, we have also learned other verbs, ranging from "beg" to "force," that can also produce causative sentences.

1 他妹妹求他们不要再吵了。

His sister begged them not to quarrel any more.

2 明天小王要请我吃饭。

Xiao Wang is inviting me to dinner tomorrow.

3 今天妈妈没叫我去帮她做饭。

Mother didn't ask/tell/call me to help her in the kitchen today.

4 医生要病人按时吃药。

The doctor asked/told the patient to take his medicine on time.

5 老师要求学生早上八点以前到校。

The teacher requires the students to arrive on campus before 8 a.m.

6 大家都**劝** (quàn) 他不要买那么贵的
房子。

Everyone tried to persuade him not to buy such an
expensive house.

7 他爸爸妈妈不准他抽烟。

His parents don't allow him to smoke.

8 小孩不想吃饭，不要**逼**(bī)他。

The kid doesn't want to eat. Don't force him.

A4 Negation of causative sentences

Either the first verb or the second verb in a causative sentence
can be negated, depending on the intended meaning. For
examples of negating the first verb, see 3, 7, and 8 under A3.
For examples of negating the second verb, see 1 and 6.

B 在……上

pertaining to, in terms of, in the aspect of

The prepositional phrase 在……上 or 在……下 can be
used figuratively. It can appear either before or after the subject.
Semantically, this phrase is used to place the matter stated by the
sentence in a particular perspective. It can be translated as "in...,"
"pertaining to ...," "in terms of ...," or "...-ly."

1 中国和美国**在**文化**上**有许多不同的地方。

In terms of culture, there are many differences between China
and America.

2 **在**解决低收入居民的住房问题**上**，我们
应该向新加坡学习。

We should learn from Singapore in terms of solving the
housing problem for low-income residents.

3 我看到这个孩子**在**学习**上**有明显的进步。

I saw a noticeable improvement in this child's studies.

4 从1950年到1998年的公房制度**在**经济**上**
帮助了当时的老百姓。

The public housing policy from 1950 to 1998 had financially
helped ordinary people at that time.

C 在……下 under..., with...

1 **在**公房制度**下**，老百姓的住房都由政府
兴建，归国家所有。

Under the public housing system, people's residences were
built by the government and owned by the state.

2 **在**朋友的帮助**下**，他终于买到了满意的
房子。

With his friend's help, he finally bought a satisfactory house.

3 **在**政府鼓励**下**，老百姓开始向银行贷款
买房。

With the encouragement of the government, ordinary people
started to apply for housing loans from banks.

4 我们**在**专家的指导**下**改革了公司的管理
制度。

Under the experts' guidance, we reformed our company's
management system.

A 语音

Write the following underlined Chinese characters in *pinyin*. Pay special attention to their different pronunciations in different contexts:

高<u>兴</u>	（　）	<u>兴</u>建	（　）
<u>一</u>套房	（　）	<u>一</u>间房	（　）
<u>重</u>复	（　）	加<u>重</u>	（　）
条件<u>差</u>	（　）	<u>差</u>别	（　）
<u>应</u>该	（　）	<u>应</u>运而生	（　）
增<u>长</u>	（　）	<u>长</u>期	（　）

B 词汇与句型

B1 词语搭配 Match the following words by considering their appropriate collocations. (There may be multiple possible collocations, but each word can be used only once.)

Group One (Verb + Object)	Group Two (Noun + Noun)
1 采用 ＿＿条件	1 住宅 ＿＿开发公司
2 补助 ＿＿旧房	2 国家 ＿＿居民
3 维修 ＿＿负担	3 住房 ＿＿条件
4 解决 ＿＿制度	4 低收入 ＿＿制度
5 改善 ＿＿房租	5 居住 ＿＿经济发展
6 减轻 ＿＿问题	6 房地产 ＿＿面积

B2 选词填空 Choose the most appropriate words from the list to fill in the blanks of the sentences.

a	规定	h	至于
b	难上加难	i	应运而生
c	改革	j	公正
d	提前	k	由
e	负担	l	价格
f	造成	m	由于
g	维修	n	制度

1 最近的飞机票很难买，你要去旅行的话，最好＿＿＿＿＿＿几天买票。

2 我们学校＿＿＿＿＿＿，学生不准在宿舍喝酒。

3 除了养育自己的孩子，赵聪夫妇还要照顾四位老人，＿＿＿＿＿＿很重。

4 ＿＿＿＿＿＿经费问题，学校只能把原来的教学楼＿＿＿＿＿＿一下，不能盖新楼了。

5 去上海的普通火车票都很难买，要买有空调的特快车票就更是＿＿＿＿＿＿了。

6 我们公司原有的管理＿＿＿＿＿＿已经很难解决新的问题，实在需要＿＿＿＿＿＿。

7 政府兴建了很多经济适用房，＿＿＿＿＿＿很便宜，但是面积不大。

8 今年夏天我们想去中国旅行。＿＿＿＿＿＿去哪些地方，我们还没决定。

9 以前中国大学生的工作都＿＿＿＿＿＿政府分配，＿＿＿＿＿＿很多不＿＿＿＿＿＿的情况。

10 越来越多的老年人寻求保持活力的方法，于是老年人电子游戏也＿＿＿＿＿＿。

B3 用"于是"和"所以"填空 Fill in the blanks with 于是 and/or 所以.

1 孩子着了凉，_____生病了。

2 孩子生病了，_____我们赶快带她去医院。

3 孩子生病了，_____我们很着急。

4 孩子生病是因为着了凉，_____我们今后要小心。

5 孩子生病是因为着了凉，_____我们把房间里的温度调高了。

6 政府没有收入维修旧房和兴建新房，_____广大居民的住房条件很差。

7 广大居民的住房条件很差，_____政府决定改革住房制度。

8 一些有钱人想买更宽敞舒适的住宅，_____房地产开发公司应运而生。

B4 用括号内的词语完成句子 Complete the following sentences by using the expressions indicated in the parentheses.

1 城市里的空气质量不好，_____。（跟……有关）

2 春节期间，重庆火车站人山人海，_____。（改成）

3 中国的经济快速发展，_____。（使）

4 _____，当地居民种了很多树。（为了）

5 我们昨天开会决定_____。（由）

6 我现在没车了，_____。（把……V给……）

7 大家都说买房比租房好，_____。（于是）

8 小张是我最好的朋友，他常常_____帮助我。（在……上）

9 人们的健康状况通常_____。（跟……有关）

C 语法

C1 用"使、让"完成句子 Complete the following sentences with 使 or 让.

1 学习态度的改变_____他的学习成绩迅速提高。

2 今天晚上的聚会_____他忘记了那些不愉快的事情。

3 爸爸_____我每天晚上做两个小时的功课。

4 春节回家的旅客太多，_____火车上拥挤不堪。

5 政策的改变_____我们的经济发展得更快了。

6 饮酒过多_____他说了一些不该说的话。

7 对不起，我_____您失望了。

C2 选用合适的动词完成下列句子 Complete the following causative sentences with appropriate verbs from the list (some sentences may have more than one choice).

a 使   d 逼   g 要

b 让   e 叫   h 准

c 请   f 劝

1 他们分手的消息＿＿＿我们都感到意外。

2 这样做才能＿＿＿客人满意。

3 我女朋友不＿＿＿我抽烟。

4 坏人＿＿＿他说出银行卡的<u>密码</u> (mìmǎ) (PIN)。

5 老师＿＿＿我们写一篇关于中国人住房情况的作文。

6 她＿＿＿妹妹去洗手。

7 这个孩子真＿＿＿我生气！

8 我们都＿＿＿他不要跟那个说假话的人结婚。

9 要是你帮我做这件事，我明天＿＿＿你看电影。

10 他父母不＿＿＿孩子看太多电视。

C3 英译汉

1 She told me <u>not to</u> open the door.

_____

_____

2 She <u>doesn't allow</u> me to open the door.

_____

_____

3 He didn't <u>ask</u> you to go swimming with him.

4 He told you <u>not to</u> go swimming in that river.

_____

_____

5 He sold his house and car last week. I guess <u>it must have something to do</u> with his plan to move to New York.

_____

_____

6 Our next meeting on "population quality" <u>will be presided over</u> by our graduate student representative, Zhang Lin.

_____

_____

7 Generally speaking, Chinese people go home to celebrate the Chinese New Year with their families every year.

_____

_____

8 That village <u>has in recent years changed</u> into a small town.

_____

_____

9 In order to catch the 6 p.m. bus to Shanghai, Little Wang left the office two <u>hours earlier</u>.

_____

_____

10 He <u>has rented out</u> the first floor of his house to a small <u>restaurant</u> in order to make some money to pay back the bank loan.

_____

_____

11 If needed, we can easily <u>convert these meeting rooms into</u> a concert hall.

_____

_____

12 The real estate developers' summer convention had concluded, <u>therefore</u> all the reporters left.

_____

_____

13 The real estate developers' summer convention has concluded, <u>so</u> the convention center is empty now.

_____

_____

D 综合

D1 短文填空 Choose the most appropriate words from the list below to fill in the blanks and complete the article.

a 适用	g 分配	m 厨房
b 比	h 由	n 于是
c 所以	i 刚	o 努力
d 首先	j 为了	p 制度
e 公房	k 挤	q 付
f 经济	l 厕所	r 才

　　田大成和妻子_____结婚时，两个人在同一家工厂工作，住在工厂_____的一间职工宿舍房里，没有自己的_____和厕所。虽然不太方便，但是两个人赚钱两个人用，住的是_____，每月房租只要_____十几元，____他们觉得还不错。三年后，他们生了一个女儿，于是生活开始有了改变。_____是每个月的钱都不够用了。然后开始觉得三个人_____在一间房子里不舒服。就在这时，中国_____开始迅速发展，田大成和妻子商量了很久，最后决定_____孩子，两个人都离开工厂，去做个体生意。他们离开工厂后搬到田大成父母家住。每天两个人很早就出去工作，晚上很晚____回家，女儿____田大成的父母照顾。这样____地工作了几年，攒了不少钱。1998 年政府停止了公房_____，老百姓可以购买自己的房子了，_____田大成和妻子就用攒下来的钱，买了一套由政府兴建的_____房。现在他们有一套三室一厅的房子，也有自己的厨房和____，生活条件____以前好多了。

D2 根据这篇文章的意思，下面的说法对不对？(T/F)

1 _____田大成和妻子是为了工厂分配宿舍房才结的婚。

2 _____宿舍里只有公用厨房和厕所。

3 _____女儿的出生使他们的生活有了改变。

4 _____他们觉得三个人住在一间房子里很不错。

5 _____中国经济的发展改变了他们的工作。

6 _____田大成和妻子攒了不少钱，所以买了一套很豪华的房子。

7 _____要是政府没有改变住房政策，老百姓就不可能买自己的房子。

短文（一）
买房与中国人的消费观

　　有一个这样的故事：一个美国老太太和一个中国老太太在天堂 (heaven) 见面了。美国老太太说："我辛苦了一辈子，昨天终于还清了住房贷款"；中国老太太说："我辛苦了一辈子，昨天才存够钱买下了一套房子"。这个故事确实很有意思。

　　对很多北美家庭来说，贷款是一种很普通的购物方式，从买房到买车，从买家具到买电脑，人们已经习惯了先消费再付钱。但是传统的中国人认为，能省钱的地方就要省钱，最好想办法存点钱，尽量不要借钱。据统计，95%的中国家庭都有银行存款。

　　近年来在中国出现的贷款买房，改变了中国人的传统消费 (xiāofèi) (consumption) 观，因为大部分家庭无法一次付清全部房价，想买房的话，就必须向银行贷款。现在越来越多中国人明白了不但要存钱，还得学会用钱。他们不仅在购房或购车时贷款，就是在买家具、电脑、家用电器 (electrical appliance) 时也开始接受了"分期付款，先买后还"这种新消费方式。

E1 回答下面问题

1 在传统上，北美家庭和中国家庭对贷款的态度有什么不同？

_____

_____

2 中国人的传统消费观是怎样的？

_____

_____

3 中国人的新消费观是怎样的？

_____

_____

E2 根据短文内容，选择最佳答案回答问题

1 美国老太太和中国老太太的对话说明：

　a 美国老太太比中国老太太有钱。

　b 中国老太太比美国老太太工作努力。

　c 她们对人生的看法不同。

　d 她们对消费的看法不同。

2 关于分期付款，下面哪项说法不是原文的意思：

　a 贷款影响了中国人的消费观。

　b 大多数美国人能接受贷款的消费方式。

　c 中国人能接受分期付款买电脑，但不接受分期付款买房。

　d 以前中国人不习惯贷款买房，因为传统观念认为借钱不是一件好事。

3 传统的中国人对金钱的看法：

　a 能多赚就多赚些钱。

　b 生活上尽量少花钱，多存些钱。

　c 只有实在没办法时才向别人借钱。

　d 以上三个都正确。

4 根据短文，中国人的新消费观：

   a 使老百姓能够一次付清房价

   b 与中国经济迅速发展没有什么直接
     关系

   c 让所有的人都去银行贷款

   d 比较接近北美的消费观

5 随着新消费观的出现，中国人有哪些
  变化：

   a 越来越多的人向银行借钱买房。

   b 越来越少的人把所有的钱都存起来。

   c 越来越多的商品可以用分期付款的
     方式购买。

   d 以上三个都正确。

短文（二）
买房与中国人的家庭观

　　住房条件的改善，让中国人有了更
宽敞舒适的生活空间，不用再像六七十
年代那样，全家老小挤在一间小屋里。
现在，越来越多的年轻夫妇有了自己的
房子，然而新的难题也开始出现：谁来
照顾年老的父母？与父母一起住吧，两
代人常会在生活习惯和消费观上互相不
理解，关系不好处理。与父母分开住
呢，又不方便照顾他们的生活。于是，
不少人在买房时会仔细考虑这个问题，
并找到一些灵活的解决方法。比如，买
两套靠得较近的小房子，而不是买一
套大房子。这样，一套自己住，一套给
父母住；既有自己的生活空间，又方便
照顾父母，可说是一举两得 (one act achieves
two goals)。

E3 回答下面问题

1 现在中国人的家庭结构与六七十年代
  有什么不同？

  _____

  _____

2 现在年轻夫妇在买房时遇到的新问题
  是什么？

  _____

  _____

3 他们如何解决这个新问题？

  _____

  _____

E4 根据短文内容，选择最佳答案回答问题

1 现在中国人的住宅跟以前比有哪些
  变化？

   a 更贵

   b 更宽敞

   c 每人有自己的房间

   d 更适合老人居住

2 关于年轻夫妇买房时的考虑，下面
  哪项不符合原文？

   a 和父母同住，生活习惯不同会影响
     两代的关系。

   b 和父母同住，花的钱太多。

   c 和父母同住，方便照顾他们。

   d 和父母同住，缺少自己的空间。

3 年轻夫妇如何解决他们的新难题？

   a 买一套大房子，让父母有单独的房间

   b 买两套大房子，一套自己住，一套
     父母住

   c 买两套离得很近的小房子，自己
     一套，父母一套

   d 全家老小挤在一间小屋里

4 以下哪项最好地说明了这篇短文的主题？

a 随着时代的发展，年轻人与父母之间的生活习惯和消费观越来越不同。

b 现在的年轻夫妇不像六七十年代时那样尊敬父母。

c 年轻夫妇在买房时首先考虑的是如何让父母住得舒适。

d 随着中国人居住条件的改变，家庭结构也有了变化。

F 口语

F1 Discussion Topics

1 你认为公房制和私房制各有什么好处和坏处？

2 政府应该用什么方法解决低收入居民的住房问题？

3 对无家可归的人，社会和政府应该怎样帮助？

4 房价太高是什么原因？

5 买房和租房各有什么好处和坏处？

6 你对贷款消费的看法怎样？

F2 Presentation Topic: 不同的住房制度

Pick a country that you are interested in (or impressed by), and research the housing policy of that country. Consider the following questions. Prepare a short presentation in Chinese for the class.

1 这个国家的住房制度怎样？

2 这种住房制度好在哪里？

3 这种住房制度有什么问题？

4 你希望自己的国家采用这样的住房制度吗？

F3 Debate Topics

Research both sides of the following topics. The class will be divided into two sides. Each side will take turns presenting arguments.

1 住公寓比住独立屋好 vs. 住独立屋比住公寓好

2 公房制比私房制好 vs. 私房制比公房制好

F4 Extended Group Research Project

In a small group, choose one of the following topics to research. Prepare a presentation in Chinese with a visual component. Each member of the group should take turns presenting. Include a list of new vocabulary words for your classmates.

a 中国住房的改善
The Improvement of Housing Conditions in China

b 中国的房产泡沫
The Real Estate Bubble in China

c 鬼城现象 Deserted New Neighborhoods

d 中国住房政策的新变化
New Changes in China's Housing Policy

G 写作

作文题：任选一题（400-500字）

a 住房商品化的利弊 (libi)
The Pros and Cons of Commercialized Housing

b 怎样解决大城市的住房问题
How to Solve the Housing Problem in Big Cities

Write an essay of 400–500 characters on one of the topics above, using the grammar and vocabulary from this lesson.

The structure of your essay should be arranged in three parts, in the following order:

1 住房问题

2 问题产生原因及带来的影响

3 解决办法

教育

- 这张照片上的学生在做什么?
- 你对中国的教育制度有些什么了解?
- 教育的目的是什么? 一个人应该接受多少年的正式(学校)教育?
- 除了学校以外,还有什么地方可以让人接受教育?
- 你知道哪些跟"教育"有关的词汇?

阅读前讨论

The Chinese education system has undergone significant reforms in recent years. This lesson's expository reading describes the progress and development of the reforms, including their effects on teacher training and retention. The predominant structures used in the reading are categorization, comparison, and causation.

4

第四课

生词

自学生词

Match each new word with its English translation by deducing the word's meaning from its characters.
(The first one is done for you.)

学(學)成　　工商　　热门(熱門)　　　　初中　　　　青少年　　分成

校园(園)　　双(雙)向　　千军万马(軍萬馬)　　独(獨)木桥(橋)　　用人

1　青少年　youth, teenager

2　＿＿＿＿＿　thousands of soldiers and horses (a big army)

3　＿＿＿＿＿　popular, hot

4　＿＿＿＿＿　employ people

5　＿＿＿＿＿　divide (into)

6　＿＿＿＿＿　single-plank bridge

7　＿＿＿＿＿　campus, schoolyard

8　＿＿＿＿＿　junior high school

9　＿＿＿＿＿　two-way, bidirectional

10　＿＿＿＿＿　complete study

11　＿＿＿＿＿　industry and commerce

主要生词

	简体	繁体	拼音	词性	英文
1	受		shòu	v.	get, receive, suffer
2	损害	損	sǔnhài	v./n.	harm, injure; damage
3	恢复	復	huīfù	v.	recover, restore, reinstate
4	义务	義務	yìwù	n.	duty, obligation
5	程度		chéngdù	n.	extent, level, standard, degree
6	大专	專	dàzhuān	n.	junior college, technical college
7	本科		běnkē	n.	undergraduate
8	研究生		yánjiūshēng	n.	graduate student
9	师资	師資	shīzī	n.	teaching staff
10	入学	學	rùxué	v.o.	enter a school, be enrolled in, matriculate
11	高考		gāokǎo	n.	college entrance examination

	简体	繁体	拼音	词性	英文
12	竞争	競爭	jìngzhēng	v./n.	compete; competition
13	激烈		jīliè	adj.	intense, acute, fierce
14	家长	長	jiāzhǎng	n.	parents, head of a family
15	划	劃	huà	v.	draw or mark a line
16	句号	號	jùhào	n.	period, full stop
17	前途		qiántú	n.	future
18	硕士	碩	shuòshì	n.	master, master's degree
19	博士		bóshì	n.	Ph.D., doctoral degree
20	学位	學	xuéwèi	n.	academic degree
21	免费	費	miǎnfèi	v.o.	free of charge
22	人才		réncái	n.	person with ability
23	学历	學歷	xuélì	n.	educational background
24	逐渐	漸	zhújiàn	adv.	gradually
25	兴起	興	xīngqǐ	v.	rise, spring up
26	管理		guǎnlǐ	v./n.	manage, administer; management, administration
27	金融		jīnróng	n.	finance, banking
28	留学	學	liúxué	v.	study abroad
29	寄托	託	jìtuō	v.	place (hope, feeling, etc.) on
30	族		zú	n.	ethnicity, race, a group of people with common features
31	待遇		dàiyù	n.	salary, benefit, treatment
32	地位		dìwèi	n.	position, status
33	被迫		bèipò	v.	be forced, be compelled
34	转行	轉	zhuǎnháng	v.	change profession
35	主修		zhǔxiū	v.	major, specialize
36	师范	師範	shīfàn	n.	teachers' college, normal school
37	队伍	隊	duìwu	n.	team, profession, troops, army
38	颁布	頒	bānbù	v.	issue, publish
39	一系列		yíxìliè	attr.	a series of
40	逐		zhú	prep.	one by one

第一读：掌握课文大意

Skim the reading; then select the option below that best captures its main idea.

a 中国教育制度的发展

b 中国教师待遇的改革

c 中国教育改革后，教育制度和教师待遇的近况

第二读：细节和理解

Read the text again carefully and answer the following questions.

1 基础教育和高等教育各有多少年？都包括什么？

_____

_____

2 重点中学和非重点中学有什么不同？

_____

_____

3 高考为什么这么重要？

_____

_____

4 近年来大学校园里兴起什么热潮？为什么？

_____

_____

5 近年来最热门的研究生专业包括什么？

_____

_____

6 什么人被称为"寄托一族"？

_____

_____

7 什么情况使政府开始改革教师待遇？

_____

_____

8 为什么会出现"小留学生热"？

_____

_____

中国教育在1966年到1976年文化大革命期间，受到很大的损害。文革以后，经过几十年的改革，教育事业才得到恢复和发展。

现在在中国，每个孩子都要接受九年的义务教育，包括小学六年和初中三年。中国的教育，根据程度可以分成基础教育和高等教育。基础教育为小学六年和中学六年（其中包括初中三年，高中三年），高等教育为大专、本科和研究生。中国所有的学校，又可以根据质量分成两种：重点学校和普通学校。与普通学校相比，重点学校的学习条件和师资力量更好，但是很难考上。

中学生毕业后，想继续读大学，就要参加全国统一的大学入学考试，也就是高考。人们常常把竞争激烈的高考比作是"千军万马过独木桥"。由于高考在每年六月举行，很多学生和家长把

这个月称为"黑色六月"。两天的高考，不仅给学生们十二年的基础教育划上句号，也在很大程度上决定了他们未来的前途。

> 人们常常把竞争激烈的高考比作是'千军万马过独木桥'。

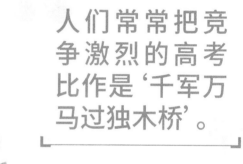

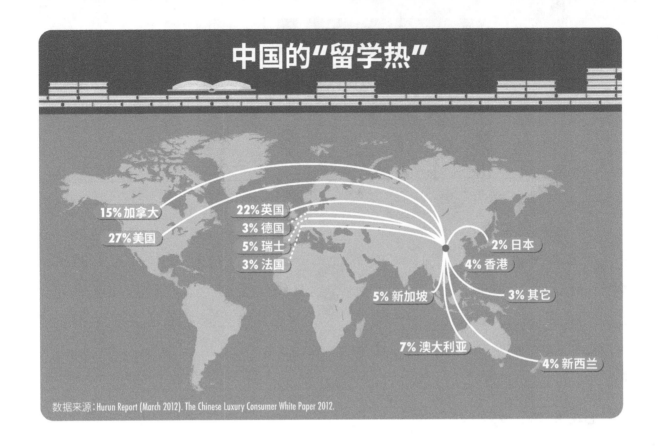

中国的"留学热"

15% 加拿大
27% 美国
22% 英国
3% 德国
5% 瑞士
3% 法国
2% 日本
4% 香港
5% 新加坡
3% 其它
7% 澳大利亚
4% 新西兰

数据来源：Hurun Report (March 2012). The Chinese Luxury Consumer White Paper 2012.

现在中国共有1000多所大学，提供本科、硕士和博士学位。以前上大学是免费的，毕业后的工作也由国家分配。从1989年起，大学开始收学费。现在，大学毕业生不再由国家分配工作，他们可以通过人才市场自己找工作，实现用人单位和大学生双向选择。

改革开放以来，由于用人单位对学历的要求逐渐提高，大学校园里又兴起了考研热和留学热。据统计，2014年全国考研人数达到172万人，最热门的专业包括工商管理（MBA）、法律、电脑、金融等。大学校园里，还有一批学生正在努力学习英文，准备出国留学去读研究生，他们被称为"寄托一族"（GRE 和 TOEFL）。

近年来，由于国内教育竞争激烈，压力太大，越来越多的本科生，中学生甚至小学生也开始出国留学。2013年，去美国读高中的中国学生达到32000人，比2005年增长了50倍！人们把这种现象称为"小留学生热"。

以前，中国教师的待遇非常差，工资低、住房旧、社会地位也不高，许多教师被迫转行，大学主修师范专业的学生也越来越少。教师队伍的不稳定严重地影响了教育质量。近年来，政府颁布了一系列政策来改善教师待遇。现在中小学教师工资不断提高。住房条件也大大改善，使很多已经离开学校的教师又回到学校。主修师范专业的学生逐年增加，连有些出国留学的人也选择学成回国教书。◆

教育

中國教育在1966年到1976年文化大革命期間，受到很大的損害。文革以後，經過幾十年的改革，教育事業才得到恢復和發展。

現在在中國，每個孩子都要接受九年的義務教育，包括小學六年和初中三年。中國的教育，根據程度可以分成基礎教育和高等教育。基礎教育為小學六年和中學六年（其中包括初中三年，高中三年），高等教育為大專、本科和研究生。中國所有的學校，又可以根據質量分成兩種：重點學校和普通學校。與普通學校相比，重點學校的學習條件和師資力量更好，但是很難考上。

中學生畢業后，想繼續讀大學，就要參加全國統一的大學入學考試，也就是高考。人們常常把競爭激烈的高考比作是"千軍萬馬過獨木橋"。由於高考在每年六月舉行，很多學生和家長把這個月稱為"黑色六月"。兩天的高考，不僅給學生們十二年的基礎教育劃上句號，也在很大程度上決定了他們未來的前途。

現在中國共有1000多所大學，提供本科、碩士和博士學位。以前上大學是免費的，畢業后的工作也由國家分配。從1989年起，大學開始收學費。現在，大學畢業生不再由國家分配工作，他們可以通過人才市場自己找工作，實現用人單位和大學生雙向選擇。

改革開放以來，由於用人單位對學歷的要求逐漸提高，大學校園裡又興起了考研熱和留學熱。據統計，2014年全國考研人數達到172萬人，最熱門的專業包括工商管理（MBA）、法律、電腦、金融等。大學校園裡，還有一批學生正在努力學習英文，准備出國留學去讀研究生，他們被稱為"寄托一族"（GRE 和 TOEFL）。

近年來，由於國內教育競爭激烈，壓力太大，越來越多的本科生，中學生甚至小學生也開始出國留學。2013年，去美國讀高中的中國學生達到32000人，比2005年增長了50倍！人們把這種現象稱為"小留學生熱"。

以前，中國教師的待遇非常差，工資低、住房舊、社會地位也不高，許多教師被迫轉行，大學主修師范專業的學生也越來越少。教師隊伍的不穩定嚴重地影響了教育質量。近年來，政府頒布了一系列政策來改善教師待遇。現在中小學教師工資不斷提高。住房條件也大大改善，使很多已經離開學校的教師又回到學校。主修師范專業的學生逐年增加，連有些出國留學的人也選擇學成回國教書。◆

说明文的结构 Understanding Organizational
Patterns in Expository Writing

The three predominant structures that the author uses to
organize this essay are: categorization (the use of 包括),
comparison (the use of 比), and causation (the use of 使).

Fill in the blanks below with information from the essay to see
how these organizational structures are used.

Categorization:

中国的义务教育包括

1 _____

2 _____

Comparison:

重点学校与普通学校相比

1 在学习条件方面_____

2 在师资力量方面_____

3 在学生成绩方面_____

Causation:

教师以前工资低、住房条件差，使

1 教师_____

2 念师范学校的学生_____

政府对教师工资和住房条件的提高，使

1 已经转业的教师_____

2 念师范学校的学生_____

3 出国留学的学生_____

词汇与句型

A ……，其中
within which, among them, of them

The 其 in 其中 is usually a plural pronoun. Depending on the context, it can be translated as "they/them," "these/those," etc. Thus, when 其中 is used, it requires an antecedent in plural form within or directly preceding the sentence.

1 果园里一共有5000棵果树，其中苹果树占80%。

There are five thousand fruit trees in the orchard in total, 80% of which are apple trees.

2 这些书，我已经看过其中的三本。

I have read three of these books.

3 公司新雇用了五个人，其中三个是日本人。

Our company has recently hired five people, of whom three are Japanese.

4 中学教育为六年，其中初中三年，高中三年。

High school education is six years, which consists of three years of junior high school and three years of senior high school.

B V1 来／去 V2

In this structure, 来／去 appears between two verb phrases. The first verb phrase expresses the means of the action, and the second verb phrase expresses the end or purpose. The order of these two phrases should not be reversed. 来 is used to express a closer relationship to the speaker, while 去 indicates a more remote relationship to the speaker.

1 学校开了个晚会来欢迎新同学。

The school threw an evening party to welcome the new students.

2 我们应该想个办法来解决这个问题。

We should think of a way to solve this problem.

3 政府通过一系列的政策来改善教师待遇。

The government has passed a series of policies to improve teachers' salaries and benefits.

4 春节时每个人都想回家去看望父母。

Everyone wants to go home to see their parents during the Spring Festival.

C ……热 hot, popular, trendy (action or event)

热 means "hot." As in English, 热 can also refer to "a popular trend." It can be used after a noun or verb phrase to suggest an upsurge of a certain trend, e.g., 考研热, 留学热, 英语热, and 汉语热.

1 在英语热背后，是中国老百姓对国际化的向往。

Behind the enthusiasm for learning English is the Chinese people's yearning for globalization.

2 这几年股票 (stock) 热降温了。

The stock craze has subsided in the past several years.

D ……族

族 used to only refer to a clan (家族), race (种族), or ethnicity (民族). In recent years, it has acquired a popular new usage referring to a group of people who share common features, behavior, or interests.

1 还有一批学生正在努力学习英文，准备出国留学去考研究生，他们被称为"寄托一族"（GRE 和 TOEFL）。

Some other students are working hard at their English to prepare for applying to graduate school abroad. They are called the "GRE and TOEFL test-taking tribe."

2 节日的地铁车厢里，<u>上班族</u>少了，旅游客多了。

During the holiday season, there were fewer office workers and more tourists riding the subway.

3 由于找工作竞争越来越激烈，不少大学生加入了<u>考研族</u>。

Due to the growing intensity of competition in the job market, many university students joined the graduate school application test-taking tribe.

4 他那个上初中的女儿是个疯狂的<u>追星族</u>。（星 short for 明星）

His daughter in junior high school is a crazy groupie (star chaser).

E 逐+N（逐年、逐步、逐一）

逐, a preposition, is often used with a monosyllabic noun to mean "one by one / N by N."

1 教师地位的改善使很多已经离开学校的教师又回到学校，主修师范专业的学生也<u>逐年</u>增加。

The improvement of teachers' social status brought many teachers back to school, and the number of students majoring in teaching is increasing year by year.

2 中国正在<u>逐步</u>改善农村的教育条件。

Step by step, China is improving the educational conditions in the countryside.

3 她向经理<u>逐一</u>介绍了外宾。

She introduced the foreign visitors to the manager one by one.

Students doing 早操 (zǎocāo) (morning exercises) at school

A 复习动词补语
Review of resultative-verb-compounds (RVCs)

You have already learned the structure of RVCs in first-year Chinese, but because the resultative endings are so unique in Chinese, they are difficult to render naturally into English. They need constant review before comprehension becomes automatic. This lesson has many RVCs. The resultative endings are -到 (arrive at or attain a goal, obtain), -成 (become, succeed, finish), -起 (rise, get up), and -上 (up), respectively.

- 受到 receive; suffer
- 得到 get, obtain, receive
- 分成 divide into
- 学成 complete study
- 考上 pass (the exam) to be admitted (by a school)
- 兴起 rise, spring up
- 划上 draw (up)

1 他的意见**受到**很多学者的注意。

His idea has received attention from many scholars.

2 校长的提议没有**得到**大多数老师的支持。

The principal's proposal wasn't supported by the majority of the teachers.

3 我们十个人可以**分成**两组，分别去北京和上海做市场调查。

The ten of us can divide into two groups to do market research in Beijing and Shanghai, respectively.

4 他在广州大学读了四年本科，**学成**后到日本继续读研究生。

Having finished four years of undergraduate study at Guangzhou University, he went to Japan for graduate study.

5 北京大学是最好的大学之一，只有那些高考分数极高的学生才**考得上**。

Beijing University is one of the top universities in China. Only those with extremely high scores on the College Entrance Exam can gain admission.

6 近年来，汉语热在很多国家迅速**兴起**。

In recent years, interest in learning Chinese has sprung up rapidly in many countries.

7 很多学生把重点大学与光明的前途之间**划上**等号。

Many students equate a key university with a promising future.

B Review of the usage of 为

为 is a frequently used word, but can be confusing. There are two different pronunciations of this character (*wéi* or *wèi*) with different meanings and functions. Let's review and summarize the most common usages of 为 that we have encountered so far:

B1 为 *(wéi)*

When 为 takes a second tone, it is a verb, which is usually used in a more formal style or in idiomatic expressions. The functions are:

A formal way of saying "to be (是)." For example:

1 基础教育**为**小学六年和中学六年。

Basic education is six years of elementary school and six years of middle school.

2 中国25岁以上人口平均受教育年限**为**7.5年。

For the population over twenty-five years of age, the average length of education is 7.5 years.

A formal version of "to do (做／作)." For example:

3 你放心，我一定尽力而<u>为</u>。

I assure you that I will do my best.

4 年轻人应该敢做敢<u>为</u>。

Young people should act with courage and determination.

A formal version of "as (作)." The meaning is derived from "to be." For example:

5 他被视<u>为</u>20世纪最伟大的中国作家之一。

He is regarded as one of the greatest Chinese writers of the twentieth century.

6 上海被称<u>为</u>中国的商业中心。

Shanghai is called (recognized as) the business center of China.

B2 为 *(wèi)*

When 为 is pronounced with the fourth tone, it is a preposition. Its functions are:

To introduce the target of a service or the beneficiary of an action. It can be translated as "for, about, on behalf of." For example:

1 我的病已经完全好了，你不必<u>为</u>我着急了。

I have completely recovered. You don't need to worry about me anymore.

2 政府在1993年到2000年间<u>为</u>教师盖了许多经济适用房。

Between 1993 and 2000, the government built many affordable houses for teachers.

To introduce the motive or purpose of the main action of the sentence. In this case, 为 can take a verb phrase as its object. This prepositional phrase can be positioned before or after the subject, but must precede the main verb. For example, Sentences 3 and 4 are both correct, but Sentence 5 is grammatically unacceptable.

3 那家商店<u>为</u>吸引顾客从日本进口了很多新型电视机。

That store, to attract more customers, has imported many new models of television sets from Japan.

4 <u>为</u>吸引顾客，那家商店从日本进口了很多新型电视机。

To attract more customers, that store has imported many new models of television sets from Japan.

5 ⊗ 那家商店从日本进口了很多新型电视机<u>为</u>吸引顾客。

That store has imported many new models of television sets from Japan to attract more customers. (This phrasing works in English but not in Chinese.)

B3 为 vs. 为了

为 and 为了 can both indicate the purpose of an action and are sometimes interchangeable, although 为 is more formal than 为了. Other times, they are used differently.

为了 is often placed before the subject to emphasize a purpose, while 为 phrases usually appear before the main verb.

1 <u>为</u>（了）解决教师转行问题，政府实行了一系列改革教师待遇的政策。

In order to solve the problem of teachers switching to other professions, the government instituted a series of policies to raise teachers' salaries and benefits.

2 他哥哥<u>为</u>出国留学正在努力学习英文。

His brother is diligently studying English in order to study abroad.

为 phrases can express the cause of an action or behavior, but 为了 cannot.

3 大家都<u>为</u>他考上重点大学高兴得不得了。

Everybody is thrilled about his successful enrollment at a key university.

⊗ 大家都<u>为了</u>他考上重点大学高兴得不得了。

C 标点符号的比喻用法
Metaphorical use of punctuation

Some punctuation marks and mathematical signs have clear and definite meanings, and thus can be used metaphorically: 句号 (period) denotes an end or conclusion, 等号 (equals sign) can mean equality or identification, and 问号 (question mark) is often used to express doubt or inquiry.

1 昨天的毕业典礼为他们的大学时代划上了句号。

Yesterday's graduation ceremony ended their college years.

2 很多学生把高考和压力划上等号。

Many students equate the university entrance examination with pressure.

3 那次事故以后，老板对他的工作能力打了一个大问号。

After that incident, the boss became doubtful of his capabilities.

D 双关语 Double entendre or pun

双关语 is a figure of speech in which a phrase can be understood in more than one way. These phrases deliberately exploit confusion between similar-sounding words for humorous or rhetorical effect. For example, many Chinese New Year traditions make good use of puns, e.g., 年年有余(鱼) and 福到(倒)了. The following are some more modern uses of puns:

1 出国留学是寄托一族的最大梦想。

To study abroad is the biggest dream of the GRE (寄) and TOEFL (托) examinees.

(The word-by-word translation of 寄托一族 is "reliance clan/tribe.")

2 他工资不低，可是每个月不到发工资那天就没钱了，真是个月光族。

Even though his salary is pretty decent, he is always out of money every month before payday. He's really one of those people whose wallet is always empty by the end of the month.

(The word-by-word translation of 月光族 is "moonlight clan." But 月 can also mean "month" while 光 can mean "finished or used up.")

3 你的生活比我强多了，你是月光族，可我已经是负翁了。

You live a much better life than I do. Your wallet is empty by the end of the month, but I have already become a man with a lot of debt.

("Man In debt" [负翁] is pronounced the same as "rich man" [富翁] in Chinese.)

练习

A 语音

A1 Write the following underlined Chinese characters in *pinyin*. Pay special attention to their different pronunciations in different contexts.

<u>教</u>育（　　） 　　<u>教</u>书（　　）

<u>划</u>上（　　） 　　<u>划</u>船（　　）

高<u>兴</u>（　　） 　　<u>兴</u>起（　　）

<u>行</u>为（　　） 　　转<u>行</u>（　　）

<u>重</u>新（　　） 　　<u>重</u>视（　　）

A2 给下列句子中的"为"字注音

1 从人口密度来看，中国<u>为</u>134人/平方公里。（　　）

2 住房分配上的不公正，也成<u>为</u>一个严重的社会问题。（　　）

3 <u>为</u>了解决这些问题，政府决定从1988年开始改革住房制度。（　　）

4 <u>为</u>了帮助人民购买住宅，政府采取了一些措施。（　　）

5 基础教育<u>为</u>小学六年和中学六年。（　　）

6 高等教育<u>为</u>大专、本科和研究生。（　　）

7 很多学生和家长把这个月称<u>为</u>"黑色六月"。（　　）

B 词汇与句型

B1 词语搭配

Group One
(Verb + Object)

1	解决	＿＿两种
2	颁布	＿＿待遇
3	提高	＿＿政策
4	分成	＿＿重点大学
5	通过	＿＿考试
6	考进	＿＿损害
7	受到	＿＿问题

Group Two
(Noun + Noun)

1	教育	＿＿市场
2	师范	＿＿待遇
3	学习	＿＿管理
4	教师	＿＿质量
5	人才	＿＿地位
6	社会	＿＿条件
7	工商	＿＿专业

B2 选择填空 Choose the most appropriate words to fill in the blanks. (Note: Not every word will be used.)

a	前途	h	激烈
b	划上	i	分成
c	待遇	j	义务
d	热门	k	兴起
e	被迫	l	一系列
f	硕士	m	考生
g	青少年	n	转行

1 我哥哥今年本科毕业，准备继续读 _____ 课程。

2 新来的老师在教学上遇到_____ 问题，但都一个一个解决了。

3 近年来，年轻人中间_____ 了 一股"韩剧热" (Korean TV drama craze)。

4 在练习口语的时候，老师把同学们 _____ 5个组，每组4个人。

5 现在连考重点中学的竞争都非常 _____，更别说考重点大学了。

6 别把我跟他_____ 等号，我们俩 很不一样。

7 那位足球运动员伤了脚，_____ 退出比赛。

8 很多人都想到那个公司工作，因为 他们的工资高、_____ 好。

9 现在电脑行业在中国还很_____， 你不如毕业以后去中国找工作吧！

10 王华决定不教书了，明年_____ 到大企业去。

11 小明马上就毕业了，可还没找到工作， 不禁有些为_____ 担忧。

B3 Match the words on the left with their meaning on the right.

1 有车族 _____ people who earn their living by labor/working for others

2 有房族 _____ people who travel/migrate to Beijing for job opportunities

3 月票族 _____ people who marry in haste

4 打工族 _____ people who own their own housing

5 急婚族 _____ people who don't want to marry

6 北漂族 _____ elderly people

7 不婚族 _____ people who have cars

8 银发族 _____ people who take public transportation regularly

B4 选词填空

a	逐条	d	逐日
b	逐个	e	逐字逐句
c	逐月	f	逐家逐户

1 使用新电器之前，一定要把说明 _____ 看清楚。

2 老师怕我们不懂，把课文_____ 地给我们讲解清楚。

3 为了安全，所有乘客进入飞机场以前 都得_____ 检查。

4 这位新市长上班第一天就去_____ 调查居民对住房的意见。

5 他的病情_____ 好转，大家都 很高兴。

6 物价不断上涨，工资却_____ 下降。老百姓日子不太好过。

C 语法

C1 Use the words covered in this lesson (in parentheses) to restate the following sentences.

1 那次失败结束了他的事业。（划上）

_____

_____

2 中国的1000多所大学里有100所重点大学。（其中）

_____

_____

3 虽然连着几天大风大雨，但是我家的房子没有什么问题。（受损害）

_____

_____

4 她是个好心人，常常帮助老人做家务事。（为）

_____

_____

5 正式教育一般由三个部分组成：小学、中学和大学。（分成）

_____

_____

6 老张同时做三份工作，因为他要存钱买房子。（为了）

_____

_____

7 为了解答同学们的问题，张老师在考试前增加了一次复习课。（来）

_____

C2 Using the words in parentheses, translate the following sentences into Chinese.

1 There are twenty people applying for the job of television reporter, among whom only three have previous work experience. （其中）

_____

_____

2 The government has built many affordable housing units for low-income citizens. （为）

_____

_____

3 I plan to use all of my bank savings to buy a small house. （去）

_____

_____

4 Why didn't the head of the village (村长) use the government aid to help those peasants? （去）

_____

_____

5 His plan to ask the company to raise employees' salaries was favorably received by everyone. （受到…的欢迎）

_____

_____

6 Project Hope (希望工程) has raised (筹集) a lot of money from both domestic and overseas resources to help children from poor and remote areas to go back to school. （来）

_____

_____

7 In order to prepare for the nationwide examination (全国统一考试), many students spend every minute on their studies. （为了）

_____

_____

D1 选词填空 Choose the most appropriate words from the list below to fill in the blanks. (Not every word will be used.)

a 发展	i 贵
b 条件	j 随着
c 为	k 制度
d 比	l 为了
e 期间	m 另外
f 关系	n 分成
g 而且	o 教育
h 才	p 迅速

中国的私立学校

从1949到1993年_____，中国没有任何私立学校，直到1993年，私立学校_____开始逐步发展起来。近年来，_____中国人的经济收入不断提高，私立学校也越来越多，遍及北京、上海、广州、天津等大城市。

私立学校基本上可以_____两种。一种是贵族式学校，是专门_____有钱人家的子女办的。这种私立学校的特点包括：学生都住校，教学上特别重视英文和电脑，多聘用有经验的教师和外籍教师，教师待遇也_____公立学校好。当然这种学校的学费非常_____，一般家庭的孩子根本上不起。

_____一种私立学校是专门为外来民工 (migrant workers) 的孩子办的。近年来，中国大城市经济的_____发展，吸引了大量来自农村的民工，同时也造成这些民工子女的_____问题。_____让这些"流动儿童"可以上学，面向民工子女的私立学校应运而生。这类学校的学费很低，但是学习_____一般都不太好。当然教学质量也不高。

D2 按照上面这篇文章的意思，下面的说法对不对？(T/F)

1 _____中国直到1993年才开始有私立学校。

2 _____中国的私立学校都比公立学校好。

3 _____北京、上海、广州、天津等大城市的私立学校都是贵族学校。

4 _____贵族学校的办学条件非常好。

5 _____为外来民工孩子办的私立学校并不贵。

6 _____民工孩子上的私立学校条件比较差。

7 _____"流动儿童"就是外来民工的孩子。

8 _____民工孩子的学习成绩可能都不太好。

E 阅读

短文（一）
大学的改变

近年来，随着社会的改变，大学也发生了变化，这些变化主要在四个方面：

一、收费方面。以前，学生上大学不必交费，所有的学费都是国家提供。但现在国家认为：第一、高等教育不是义务教育，不应该由国家提供学费。第二、国家在教育方面的经费 (budget) 不够，为学生提供学费以后，就没有钱去改善教学设备 (facilities, equipment) 和环境。因此，从1989年起，大学开始向学生收学费。

二、分配工作方面。以前大学生毕业后工作由国家统一分配，但现在毕业生得自己找工作。各地都有人才市场，用人单位可以挑选大学生，大学生也可以挑选用人单位。

三、课外时间方面。以前大学生课内课外都只是念书。可现在不少大学生利用课外时间工作。这样既能赚一点钱，又得到了一定的工作经验，有人甚至在毕业前就已经有了自己的公司。

四、大学内部的改变。为了适应社会的需要，许多大学开办了新的专业和课程。大学的考试制度、课程要求、毕业条件等，都有了很多改变。学校内部的管理(management)也在发生变化。

E1 按照这篇文章的意思，下面的说法对不对？(T/F)

1 _____ 大学的变化跟社会没有什么关系。

2 _____ 义务教育一般由国家提供学费。

3 _____ 国家现在向大学生收费，是为了把更多的钱用在购买教学设备上。

4 _____ 向大学生收费对中国教育的发展没有好处。

5 _____ 1989年之前，大学生念书不必交学费。

6 _____ 以前大学生毕业时，不用自己找工作。

7 _____ 用人单位就是大学生毕业的学校。

8 _____ 以前大学生课外工作的情况不普遍。

9 _____ 有工作经验的大学生更容易找到工作。

10 _____ 开办新课程、改变考试制度等都是大学内部的变化。

短文（二）
希望工程

在中国的贫困 (pínkùn) (poor) 地区，还有很多孩子因为家里穷而上不起学。中国青少年发展基金会 (foundation) 从 1989 年起开始了一项"希望工程" (gōngchéng) (project)，帮助失学 (be deprived of education) 儿童重新回到校园。1991年4月，一位记者在"希望工程"资助 (zīzhù) (aid financially) 的一群孩子中间发现了一双明亮的大眼睛，于是拍下了《我要读书》这张照片。这张照片后来成为"希望工程"的象征照片。

照片上那个拿着铅笔向前看的小女孩，就是苏明娟 (juān) (beautiful)。她眼中那种对知识的渴求 (kěqiú) (eagerly yearn for)，打动 (touch) 了很多人的心，推动了全社会来帮助贫困地区的失学儿童。苏明娟也在"希望工程"的帮助下，读完了小学和中学，又考进了大学。大学毕业后，她在一家银行找到工作，成为"希望工程"为社会培养 (péiyǎng) (train) 的第一批人才。

E2 按照上面这篇文章的意思，下面的说法对不对？(T/F)

1 ＿＿＿＿希望工程是政府为资助贫困儿童而发起的运动。

2 ＿＿＿＿希望工程从1991年开始。

3 ＿＿＿＿希望工程的主要帮助对象是贫困地区的孩子。

4 ＿＿＿＿希望工程除了帮助孩子们上学以外，也补助他们的生活费。

5 ＿＿＿＿《我要读书》这张照片上的人物很有名。

6 ＿＿＿＿照片上最打动人的是小姑娘手握铅笔的样子。

7 ＿＿＿＿苏明娟本人也接受了希望工程的资助，高中毕业后找到工作。

8 ＿＿＿＿希望工程对整个中国社会都产生影响。

9 ＿＿＿＿希望工程资助的贫困孩子在大学毕业后由国家分配工作。

10 ＿＿＿＿希望工程既推动社会关心失学儿童，又为社会培养了人才。

F 口语

F1 看图回答问题 Search for the famous picture of 苏明娟 online and discuss it with your classmates.

1 你从苏明娟的眼睛里看到了什么？

2 你身边也有这样的孩子吗？他们的问题是什么造成的？

3 希望工程能为他们做些什么？

F2 跟一位同学交谈你们自己考大学的经历。请做笔记，然后向全班同学复述你同学考大学的故事。

Tell a partner about your experience applying to colleges or universities. Then take notes as your partner tells you about his or her experience. Retell what you learned about your partner's experience to the class.

F3 谈谈你们国家的教育情况，有什么跟中国相同和不同的地方，还存在哪些问题。

Discuss the state of education in your country. How is it similar to and/or different from the state of education in China, and what other issues exist?

F4 小组讨论 Group Discussion

如果你是大学校长，想要改革你们学校的入学标准，你觉得下面列出的标准中哪个最重要？为什么？（请按照1-7给它们排名。）

If you were a university president seeking to reform the admissions process at your university, which of the following standards would you regard as most important? Rank them in order of importance from 1 to 7 (1 being the most important) and give reasons for your choices.

____ 推荐信 Reference letters

____ 大学出题的入学考试 University-designed admissions tests

____ 学生论文 Student-written essays

____ 学生来校面试表现 Student's interview with admissions officers

____ 中学成绩 High school grades

____ 全国统一考试 National standardized admissions tests

____ 其他？ Any others?

G 写作

G1 上网查一个中国大学对国际学生的入学要求，用一段话总结出来。

Visit a Chinese university's website and find out its admissions requirements for international students. Summarize your findings in one paragraph.

G2 作文题：教育的重要性（300-400字）

Write a short essay of 300–400 characters, using the new words and grammatical patterns that you have learned from the textbook so far. Follow these guidelines:

1 Begin your essay with an introductory paragraph, briefly stating the importance of education.

2 Develop your ideas with supporting statements using listing, cause and effect, and comparison. Provide examples to support your statements.

3 At the end of the essay, offer a general conclusion.

Use at least ten of the following vocabulary words from this lesson:

热门	待遇	根据	寄托
选择	留学	义务	为
师资	包括	程度	……热
竞争	划上	理想	一系列
前途	分成	逐渐	考上
毕业	激烈	人才	
学位	学成	地位	

Use at least five of the following sentence patterns from this lesson:

为了……

……来／去……

……使……

……，其中

以前……

近年来／现在……

与……相比……

阅读前讨论

- 这些学生在做什么？他们看起来怎么样？
- 你星期天一般做什么？
- 学生的星期天应该怎样度过？
- 你知道哪些跟"中学生"有关的词汇？

In order to be admitted into a senior high school, especially a "key" school, a Chinese student must pass the very competitive high school entrance examination. To prepare for the test, many students attend after-school classes, weekend review classes, or tutorial sessions in addition to their regular courses.

The essay in this lesson, written in a diary style, is about the life of a student in her last year of junior high school and her physical and psychological struggles.

5

第五课

生词

自学生词

Match each new word with its English translation by deducing the word's meaning from its characters.
(The first one is done for you.)

闹钟(鬧鐘)　　香甜　　睡梦(夢)　　紧(緊)接着(著)　　升学(學)　　路途

遥远(遙遠)　　书(書)架　　窗台(臺)　　低头(頭)　　宝(寶)石

1 窗台_____ windowsill

2 _____ alarm clock

3 _____ immediately, right after

4 _____ deep sleep, slumber

5 _____ distant, remote, far away

6 _____ hang or lower one's head

7 _____ precious stone, gem

8 _____ enter a higher school

9 _____ bookshelf

10 _____ fragrant and sweet, sound (sleep)

11 _____ road, journey

成语和惯用语

成语／惯用语	单字解释	意思
1　由此而来 *yóu cǐ ér lái* 云南的昆明四季如春，"春城"的名字就是由此而来。	由 from 此 this 而 a conjunction/connective to connect the prepositional phrase 由此 and the verb 来 来(來) come	(It) comes/originated from this (cause or source)
2　头昏脑胀 *tóu hūn nǎo zhàng* 一天的补习让我头昏脑胀。	头(頭) head 昏 faint, swoon 脑(腦) brain 胀(脹) swell	Dizzy, feel one's head swimming
3　精疲力尽 *jīng pí lì jìn* 精疲力尽的我躺在床上。	精 energy, spirit 疲 tired, exhausted 力 physical strength 尽(盡) use up	Exhausted, worn out
4　不知不觉 *bù zhī bù jué* 不知不觉中，我睡着了。	知 know 觉(覺) sense, feel	Unconsciously, unknowingly

	简体	繁体	拼音	词性	英文
1	圣经	聖經	*Shèngjīng*	p.n.	the Bible
2	上帝		*Shàngdì*	p.n.	God
3	创造	創	*chuàngzào*	v.	create
4	推行		*tuīxíng*	v.	carry out, implement
5	清晨		*qīngchén*	n.	early morning
6	叮呤呤		*dīnglínglíng*	ono.	ringing sound
7	阵	陣	*zhèn*	m.	a short period, a spell
8	一口气	氣	*yìkǒuqì*	adv.	in one breath, without a break
9	哈欠		*hāqian*	n.	yawn
10	摇	搖	*yáo*	v.	shake, wave, rock
11	优秀	優	*yōuxiù*	adj.	outstanding, excellent
12	拼		*pīn*	v.	go all out in work
13	丝	絲	*sī*	m.	thread
14	无奈	無	*wúnài*	adj.	helpless
15	唉		*ài*	intj.	sigh
16	压	壓	*yā*	v.	press, push down
17	喘		*chuǎn*	v.	breathe rapidly, gasp for air
18	科目		*kēmù*	n.	school subject or course
19	发火	發	*fāhuǒ*	v.o.	get angry, lose one's temper
20	期待		*qīdài*	v.	anticipate, expect
21	目光		*mùguāng*	n.	look, sight, vision
22	律师	師	*lǜshī*	n.	lawyer
23	工程师	師	*gōngchéngshī*	n.	engineer
24	堆		*duī*	v./n.	pile up; pile, heap
25	柜子	櫃	*guìzi*	n.	cupboard, cabinet
26	锁	鎖	*suǒ*	n.	lock
27	不由得		*bùyóude*	adv.	can't help
28	压抑	壓	*yāyì*	v.	constrain, inhibit, depress
29	颗	顆	*kē*	m.(n.)	small particles
30	眨		*zhǎ*	v.	(of eyes) blink, wink

课文

第一读：掌握课文大意

Skim the reading; then select the option below that best captures its main idea.

a 初三毕业生星期天的上课内容

b 初三毕业生的学习压力 (pressure)

c 父母亲和老师们怎么样帮助初三毕业生

第二读：细节和理解

Read the text again carefully and answer the following questions.

1 这篇日记的作者为什么觉得自己比上帝还忙？

_____

2 星期天上课时学生们有什么问题？为什么？

_____

_____

3 王老师认为学生们星期天上课的两个理由是什么？

_____

4 老师脸上为什么有"一丝无奈的苦笑"？

_____

5 母亲觉得星期天上课的目的是什么？

_____

6 作者对母亲买《中考试题》有什么感觉？

_____

7 作者下午得上什么课？中午休息了多长的时间？

_____

_____

8 作者的晚上是怎么过的？

_____

_____

9 上初三以后，作者的生活有了什么变化？

_____

10 作者羡慕 (xiànmù) (envy) 星星的什么？

_____

11 跟你的中学生生活相比，这位学生的星期天怎么样？

_____

_____

一个初三毕业生的星期天

《圣经》上说，上帝用六天创造世界后，第七天就休息了。据说，后来人们每周休息一天，就由此而来。现在，全国都推行"双休日"制度了，每周可以休息两天。可是我们这些初三毕业生，一周七天从早学到晚，比上帝都忙，连星期日都不能休息。

> 我们这些挤在'升学关'里的孩子，好像在爬一座几千米的高山，永远看不到头……

清晨

"叮呤呤……"一阵闹钟声把我从香甜的睡梦中吵醒。紧接着，妈妈敲门说："芳芳，芳芳！快起床，上课要迟到了！""星期天还得上课！"我很不高兴地从床上爬起来。

十分钟的穿衣、洗脸后，我准备出门了。"牛奶！"妈妈从厨房跑过来说："芳芳，芳芳！快喝，这一上午就靠它了。"我一口气把那一大杯牛奶喝了下去。哎！一个紧张的星期天就这样开始了。

上午

"咱们先讲到这儿，下面做练习。"王老师长长地吐了口气，旁边的几个同学已经开始打哈欠，我的眼睛也快要闭上了。

"陈力！"我被王老师的叫声吓了一跳，"上课怎么能睡觉呢？！"陈力站起来，不好意思地说："昨晚做功课做晚了……"王老师摇了摇头，说："坐下吧。我知道大家都不容易，可为了咱们学校的升学率，也为了你们自己，大家就拼这一年吧！等明年考上重点高中……"在她的脸上，我好像看到了一丝无奈的苦笑。唉，我们这些挤在"升学关"里的孩子，被各种各样的"率"压得喘不过气来，好像在爬一座几千米的高山，路途遥远，永远看不到头……

上午的四个小时总算过去了。中午总该有点儿休息时间了吧！

中午

刚进家门，妈妈就高兴地跑过来："芳芳，芳芳！快看，妈妈给你买了套最新的《中考试题》，听说这套试题非常好，买的人非常多，妈妈跑了好几家书店才买到呢。"我走进自己的房间，看到桌子上摆着一大堆不同科目的《中考试题》。书架上、窗台上、柜子里、床铺下，到处都堆满了书。还买！我真想发火，可是看到妈妈兴奋的笑脸和期待的目光，我又能说什么呢？妈妈说："芳芳，你一定要有优秀的成绩，才能考上重点高中，然后再考上重点大学。只要上了重点大学，就能当医生、律师、电脑工程师、CEO……"我什么也没说，很快地低头吃了几口饭，就带着半饱的肚子跑向英语辅导班。

晚上

一天的补习让我头昏脑胀。吃过晚饭，坐在书桌前，客厅传来电视里球赛的声音，我真想去看看，可是桌子上还有一大堆作业等着我去做。自从上了初三，我就不能看电视了。心爱的 iPad 和小说，也让妈妈锁起来了。想到这些，我不由得感到一种深深的压抑。

夜深了，精疲力尽的我躺在床上，窗外的星星像一颗颗宝石，眨着眼睛向我说话。它们多么快乐、自由啊！不知不觉中，我睡着了。明天，又是新的一周。◆

芳芳 <fangfang625@cheng-tsui.com>　　✍ 写邮件　📧 通讯录　　　　退出

05		7:00	早饭
2016年6月05日　星期日		7:30	复习班
丙申猴年　五月初一		12:00	午饭
		12:30	《中考试题》
◀　2016年6月　▶		2:00	补习班
日 一 二 三 四 五 六		6:00	晚饭
1　2　3　4		7:00	作业
5　6　7　8　9　10　11			
12　13　14　15　16　17　18			
19　20　21　22　23　24　25			
26　27　28　29　30			

一個初三
畢業生的星期天

《聖經》上說，上帝用六天創造世界後，第七天就休息了。據說，後來人們每周休息一天，就由此而來。現在，全國都推行"雙休日"制度了，每周可以休息兩天。可是我們這些初三畢業生，一周七天從早學到晚，比上帝都忙，連星期日都不能休息。

清晨

"叮呤呤……"一陣鬧鐘聲把我從香甜的睡夢中吵醒。緊接著，媽媽敲門說："芳芳，芳芳！快起床，上課要遲到了！""星期天還得上課！"我很不高興地從床上爬起來。

十分鐘的穿衣、洗臉後，我准備出門了。"牛奶！"媽媽從廚房跑過來說："芳芳，芳芳！快喝，這一上午就靠它了。"我一口氣把那一大杯牛奶喝了下去。哎！一個緊張的星期天就這樣開始了。

上午

"咱們先講到這兒，下面做練習。"王老師長長地吐了口氣，旁邊的幾個同學已經開始打哈欠，我的眼睛也快要閉上了。

"陳力！"我被王老師的叫聲嚇了一跳，"上課怎麼能睡覺呢？！"陳力站起來，不好意思地說："昨晚做功課做晚了……"王老師搖了搖頭，說："坐下吧。我知道大家都不容易，可為了咱們學校的升學率，也為了你們自己，大家就拼這一年吧！等明年考上

第五課 · 一个初三毕业生的星期天 · 课文 95

重點高中……"在她的臉上，我好像看到了一絲無奈的苦笑。唉，我們這些擠在"升學關"裡的孩子，被各種各樣的"率"壓得喘不過氣來，好像在爬一座幾千米的高山，路途遙遠，永遠看不到頭……

上午的四個小時總算過去了。中午總該有點兒休息時間了吧！

中午

剛進家門，媽媽就高興地跑過來："芳芳，芳芳！快看，媽媽給你買了套最新的《中考試題》，聽說這套試題非常好，買的人非常多，媽媽跑了好幾家書店才買到呢。"我走進自己的房間，看到桌子上擺著一大堆不同科目的《中考試題》。書架上、窗台上、櫃子裡、床鋪下，到處都堆滿了書。還買！我真想發火，可是看到媽媽興奮的笑臉和期待的目光，我又能說什麼呢？媽媽說："芳芳，你一定要有優秀的成績，才能考上重點高中，然後再考上重點大學。只要上了重點大學，就能當醫生、律師、電腦工程師、CEO……"我什麼也沒說，很快地低頭吃了幾口飯，就帶著半飽的肚子跑向英語輔導班。

晚上

一天的補習讓我頭昏腦脹。吃過晚飯，坐在書桌前，客廳傳來電視裡球賽的聲音，我真想去看看，可是桌子上還有一大堆作業等著我去做。自從上了初三，我就不能看電視了。心愛的 iPad 和小說，也讓媽媽鎖起來了。想到這些，我不由得感到一種深深的壓抑。

夜深了，精疲力盡的我躺在床上，窗外的星星像一顆顆寶石，眨著眼睛向我說話。它們多麼快樂、自由啊！不知不覺中，我睡著了。明天，又是新的一周。◆

A 叙述文的结构 The Structure of Narratives

The structure of a narrative includes time, location, characters, and sequential events related through a causal or thematic chain. Both psychological and physical causality might be incorporated in the actions to show the mood and state of mind of the characters. More often than not, the author will use the story to make a statement of opinion or an assessment of the experience.

Please answer the following questions:

1 "我"是谁?

_____

_____

2 故事发生在哪些地方?

_____

_____

3 故事里除了"我"以外，还有谁? 他们
  跟"我"关系怎么样?

_____

_____

4 故事把星期天分成哪几个部分? 为什么
  这么分?

_____

_____

5 你认为作者写这个故事的目的是什么?

_____

_____

词汇与句型

A 据说 + clause : "it is said that ..."

据说 is the short form of "根据有人所说," meaning "according to what someone said...." Syntactically, 据说 is usually followed by a clause that includes the information to be conveyed. The speaker is not the source of the information.

1 据说那个小学毕业的学生考上重点中学的特别多。

It is said that many students who graduated from that elementary school get admitted to (pass the entrance examination for) key high schools.

2 据说那个地方的空气质量越来越差。

It is said that the air quality in that place is getting worse.

3 据说中国的中学生每天要上8个小时的课。

I heard that high school students in China have to take eight hours of classes every day.

4 据说中国父母对孩子的期望特别高。

People say that Chinese parents have exceptionally high expectations of their children.

B 由此而来 coming from this (source or reason)

Modern formal written language often uses expressions that evolved from classical Chinese, such as 由此而来. 由 is a preposition, meaning "from"; 而 is a connective that connects the prepositional phrase 由此 and the verb 来, and requires no English word in translation. 此 is a demonstrative pronoun, corresponding to "this." Here, 此 refers back to the entire clause preceding it.

1 中国由于人口过多而从70年代开始实行计划生育政策，可是由此而来的其他问题又形成了新的挑战。

Due to its excessive population, China has been implementing a family planning policy since the 70s. However, other issues arising from this policy are creating new challenges.

2 云南的昆明四季如春，"春城"的名字就是由此而来。

Kunming City in Yunnan has a very mild climate. The four seasons all feel like spring. That's the reason why it's called the "Spring City."

3 陈力经常做功课做到半夜两、三点，由此可知，他为什么上课总是没有精神。

Chen Li often does homework until two or three o'clock in the morning. From this (fact) we know why he always looks very tired in class.

C 总算 finally, at last, in the end

总算 is an adverb that precedes the main verb. A clause with the expression 总算 emphasizes that hopes or expectations are fulfilled after a long time, with many difficulties.

1 连着下了三天大雪，今天总算停下来了。

It has snowed heavily for three days, but it finally stopped today.

2 改善教师待遇的政策，经过多年的努力以后，现在总算得到效果，教师的工资提高了，住房条件也比以前好得多了。

After many years of hard work, the policy to improve teachers' working conditions has (now) finally produced some effect. Teachers' pay has increased, and their housing conditions are also much better than before.

3 小王结婚已经五年了，可是一直住在父母家里。五年来，他努力工作，存了一笔钱，最近又向银行贷了款，现在总算可以买一套小公寓了。

Xiao Wang got married five years ago, but has been living with his parents. He worked hard during those five years and saved some money. Recently, he was also able to obtain a loan from the bank. At long last, he can now buy a small apartment.

D 一口气 + V
do something in one breath or without break

1 我昨天晚上<u>一口气</u>做完了三套化学试题。

I finished three sets of chemistry tests in one go last night.

2 他渴极了，<u>一口气</u>喝完了一大瓶水。

He was very thirsty. He drank a large bottle of water in one gulp.

3 她<u>一口气</u>读完了那本小说。

She finished reading that novel in one sitting.

E 不由得 can't help, cannot but

1 回家的路上，想到爸爸妈妈一定会问我的考试成绩，心情<u>不由得</u>沉重起来。

On the way home, thinking that my parents would definitely ask me about my test scores, I couldn't help but feel my heart sink heavily.

2 她看到这个可怜的孩子，<u>不由得</u>流下泪来。

When she saw the poor child, she couldn't hold back her tears.

3 这个女孩长得特别漂亮，路上的人都<u>不由得</u>要多看她两眼。

That girl is so pretty that passersby can't help but take a few glances at her.

A 话题链与"零代词"
Topic chains and "zero-pronouns"

In Lesson 1, you learned the special Chinese syntactic structure of the "topic-comment" sentence. A topic, once set up, can extend across successive clauses to form a "topic chain," which is introduced in this lesson. This unique structure is an important organizing feature of Chinese language discourse.

A topic chain is a chain of clauses sharing an identical topic, which is usually the noun phrase (NP) in the first clause. Subsequent mentions of the same NP within the chain (usually represented by a co-referential pronoun in English) are left unstated. The unspecified pronoun is referred to as a "zero-pronoun" (ø), which functions as a cohesive device tying all the clauses together to form a topic-chain structure. Semantically, a topic chain structure is like a network of information, with the topic as its nucleus and the clauses providing different information surrounding the topic, bound together by the zero-pronouns. The following sentence is an example taken from this lesson.

1 芳芳，你一定要成绩优秀，才能考上重点高中，然后（ø）再考上重点大学。（ø）只要上了重点大学，（ø）就能当医生、律师、电脑工程师、CEO……

Fangfang, you must get into a key high school with excellent scores, then you will be able to go to a top university. As long as you go to a top university, you can become a doctor, a lawyer, a computer engineer, or a CEO....

Sentence 1 includes four clauses, providing four pieces of different information about the topic, 你, which only appears in the first clause. Subsequent mention of the topic has been omitted (hence the zero-pronouns).

Here are more examples taken from this lesson. Pay special attention to the zero pronouns in each topic chain and the differences between the Chinese sentences and their English translations:

2 我什么也没说，（ø）很快地低头吃了几口饭，（ø）就带着半饱的肚子跑向英语辅导班。

I didn't say anything. I quickly lowered my head and ate a little food, then I ran to the English tutorial with a half-full stomach.

3 吃过晚饭，我坐在书桌前，（ø）听到客厅传来电视里球赛的声音。（ø）真想去看看，可是桌子上还有一大堆作业等着我。

After dinner, I sat at my desk. I heard the sound of the sports game on TV coming from the living room. I really wanted to go and watch it, but there was still a huge pile of homework waiting for me on the desk.

4 我们这些挤在"升学关"里的孩子们，被各种各样的"率"压得喘不过气来，（ø）好像在爬一座几千米的高山，（ø）永远看不到（ø）头。

Kids like us who are jostling our way through the "high school entrance barrier" are weighed down and made breathless by the pressure from all kinds of "rankings." It's like we're trying to climb up a big mountain thousands of meters high, but we can never see the top of the mountain.

Sentences 2 and 3 have one topic, but Sentence 4 is an example of a complex topic chain. It has a secondary topic, 高山, such that the last clause has two zero pronouns, the first one referring to the first topic, 我们, and the second referring to 高山.

Identifying the co-referential topics depends highly on contextual clues and logical reasoning, not grammar. As an analogy, a topic-chain structure in Chinese is like a run-on sentence in English (and would be considered ungrammatical in English). But it's acceptable, or even preferable, in Chinese; this structure is commonly used, especially in formal, written language.

A common problem for learners (especially English-speaking learners) is the tendency to repeat co-referential pronouns in every clause, due to their habit of overtly coding these co-referential pronouns in English. But in Chinese, this is considered redundant and cumbersome because the repetitive use of these pronouns is quite unnecessary, and what's worse, it breaks the smooth flow of discourse.

B Review of existential sentences

An existential sentence indicates the existence of someone or something in a particular location (or time). This is a type of "topic-comment sentence" in Chinese. With a "place/time word" at the initial position of the sentence as the topic, the rest of the clause serves as the comment on the topic. Below, we review the three types of existential sentences that we have learned:

B1 Place (Time) + 有 + NP

The most commonly used verb in existential sentences is 有.

1 桌子上还有一大堆作业。

2 明天有两门考试，三节课。

B2 Place + V 满了 + NP (for V 满, review Grammar in Lesson 1)

1 树上开满了花。

B3 Place + V 着 + NP

Existence is also conveyed by V 着. These verbs usually denote placement or posture that may cause an entity to exist in a certain manner as a result. The topic of this kind of existence sentence is always a place. These sentences are more descriptive than sentences with just 有.

1 桌子上堆着各种科目的中考试题和没做完的作业。

There are all kinds of high school entrance tests and unfinished assignments piled up on the table.

2 背上压着各种各样的"率"。

All kinds of "ratings/rankings" weigh heavily on our backs.

3 大门上挂着一个木牌，上面写着公司的名字。

There is a wooden signboard hanging on the main gate, with the company's name written on it.

4 床旁边放着一个闹钟和第二天要穿的衣服。

An alarm clock and clothing for the next day were placed beside the bed.

5 床上躺着一个病人。床边坐着他的母亲。

In the bed lay a patient. At his bedside sat his mother. (There was a patient lying in the bed. His mother was sitting at his bedside.)

C 量词 Measure words

There are a few new measure words in this lesson. Their usage is illustrated by the following examples:

1 丝 (silk, thread; used for something very thin, slim or light)

一丝白发	a white hair
一丝希望	a gleam of hope
一丝悲哀	a tinge of sadness
一丝风	a breath of wind

2 颗 (for something small and round)

一颗星星	a star
一颗善良的心	a kind heart
一颗种子	a seed

3 阵 (a short period of time, a spell)

一阵微风	a puff of breeze
一阵笑声	a burst of laughter
一阵雨	a shower of rain
哭了一阵	cried for a while

4 口 (mouth, mouthful)

喘了口气	took a breath
咬了一口	took a bite
喝了口酒	took a sip of wine

5 堆 (heap, mound, pile)

有一大堆工作要做
have a heap of work to do

有一大堆盘子要洗
have a stack of dishes to wash

有一大堆英文书要读
have a pile of English books to read

D 怎么能……呢？ A rhetorical question
（反问）

A rhetorical question is a figure of speech in the form of a question to which no answer is expected. It is a device used by the speaker to assert or deny something. For example, in English, "Who cares?" actually means "I don't care." By implying that the answer is obvious, a rhetorical question can achieve an emphasis stronger than a direct statement.

1 这个问题这么严重，<u>怎么能</u>不让大家知道<u>呢</u>？

  This is such a serious problem. How could we not let everyone know?

  (We should let everyone know about this problem.)

2 看到妈妈兴奋的神情和期待的目光，我<u>怎么能</u>对她发火<u>呢</u>？

  Seeing my mother so excited and expectant, how could I be angry at her?

Examples with other question words are:

3 <u>谁</u>不想得第一名<u>呢</u>？可是第一名只有一个啊。

  Who doesn't want to be Number One? But there is only one Number One.

4 我这样做是为了你好，你<u>难道</u>不知道<u>吗</u>？

  I am doing this for your benefit. Don't you know?

5 您这样做是为了我好，我<u>哪</u>能不知道<u>呢</u>？

  You are doing this for my own good. How could I not know?

6 孩子昨天晚上睡得那么晚，<u>为什么不让</u>他多睡一会儿<u>呢</u>？

  The kid went to bed so late last night. Why not let him sleep a little longer?

练习

A 语音

Write the following underlined Chinese characters in *pinyin*. Pay special attention to their different pronunciations in different contexts.

<u>得</u>上课（　　）　　　　压<u>得</u>很重（　　）

高<u>兴</u>（　　）　　　　<u>兴</u>奋（　　）

<u>重</u>新（　　）　　　　<u>重</u>点（　　）

<u>吐</u>气（　　）　　　　呕<u>吐</u>（　　）

B 词汇与句型

B1 词语搭配 Match the following words by considering their appropriate collocations.

Group One (Verb + Object)	Group Two (Adj. + Noun)
1 创造 ＿＿制度	1 无奈的 ＿＿路程
2 推行 ＿＿哈欠	2 遥远的 ＿＿升学率
3 打 ＿＿世界	3 香甜的 ＿＿时刻
4 考上 ＿＿压抑感	4 优秀的 ＿＿苦笑
5 产生 ＿＿大学	5 紧张的 ＿＿睡梦

B2 选词填空

a 推行　　　　h 香甜
b 喘　　　　　i 拼
c 一口气　　　j 不知不觉
d 一丝　　　　k 总算
e 不由得　　　l 叮呤呤
f 压抑　　　　m 期待
g 由此而来　　n 筋疲力尽

1 我刚进家门，电话就＿＿＿＿响了起来。

2 考上重点高中确实让人兴奋，但＿＿＿＿的学业竞争给我很大压力。

3 他对那部新电影没有＿＿＿＿兴趣，还是你陪我去看吧。

4 昨晚下了一场暴雨，凉快了很多，我睡得很＿＿＿＿。

5 他＿＿＿＿吹灭了生日蛋糕上的十根蜡烛。

6 我们连着加了三天班，同事们都已经累得＿＿＿＿了。

7 阴沉的天气让人觉得很＿＿＿＿。

8 中国从70年代开始＿＿＿＿计划生育政策。

9 她们以＿＿＿＿的心情等着歌星出场。

10 看到女儿可爱的样子，她＿＿＿＿微笑起来。

11 我们在火车上被挤得＿＿＿＿不过气来。

12 他的梦想＿＿＿＿实现了，今年出版了第一本诗集。

13 我们聊得很开心，＿＿＿＿好几个小时过去了。

14 为了高考，他整整＿＿＿＿了一年，现在终于被清华大学录取了。

B3 下面的句子里，用哪个成语最合适？

a 不知不觉 　　c 精疲力尽
b 头昏脑胀 　　d 由此而来

1 昨天准备考试，看了6个小时的书，看得我_____。

2 一口气爬上这么高的山，我真是_____了。

3 "鱼"跟"余"(surplus) 听起来一样。过年吃饭一定要有鱼（年年有余）的传统就是_____。

4 他专心做功课，_____已经是半夜了。

5 让学生们从早学到晚，难道学校的优秀升学率就_____吗？

6 她_____地说："我已经跑遍了全城，还是没买到，不能再走了！"

C 语法

C1 汉译英 Translate the following passage (a topic chain) into English, paying special attention to the different use of co-referential pronouns in Chinese and English.

我哥给我买的那辆二手车，又笨又重，颜色很难看，而且特别费油，我真不喜欢，可是又不好意思告诉他，只好留着，以后再说吧。

_____

_____

_____

C2 The following groups of sentences are considered "cumbersome" in Chinese. Rewrite them into natural Chinese, using topic chain structures.

1 我一听，我就明白了。

_____

2 小文在大学学的是经济学。他特别希望能在银行工作。但是他毕业三年了，他还没有找到银行的工作。

_____

_____

3 田老师从银行贷到一笔款，他用那笔款买了一所房子。他这几天正在忙着搬家。

_____

_____

4 政府决定从1988年开始改革住房制度。政府把公房卖给居民。他们还鼓励个人及家庭购买私房。

_____

_____

5 以前，中国教师的待遇非常差。他们的工资低，他们的住房旧，他们的社会地位也不高。这种情况使许多教师被迫转行。

_____

C3 根据英文意思，用合适的量词完成下列短语 Complete the following phrases with appropriate measure words according to the English translation given.

一（　　）掌声　　　　a round of applause

一（　　）美丽的宝石　a beautiful gemstone

一（　　）笑容　　　　a glimmer of a smile

一（　　）参考书　　　a set of reference books

一（　　）高楼　　　　a high building

叹了一（　　）气　　　uttered a sigh

有一大（　　）问题要问　have a flurry of questions to ask

C4 Replace 有 in the following sentences with appropriate V 着 phrases chosen from the list below. Note the difference the changes make.

a 长着　　　　　f 藏着
b 坐着　　　　　g 站着
c 游着　　　　　h 放着
d 亮着　　　　　i 开着
e 拿着　　　　　j 压着

1 水里有很多漂亮的金鱼。

　水里_____很多漂亮的金鱼。

2 教室前面有一棵大树。

　教室前面_____一棵大树。

3 远处的屋子里有灯光。

　远处的屋子里_____灯光。

4 床底下的那个鞋盒里有她最秘密的信件。

　床底下的那个鞋盒里_____她最秘密的信件。

5 门外地上有一封信，信上有一块石头。

　门外地上_____一封信，信上_____一块石头。

6 大门口有两个高大的士兵 (shìbīng) (soldier)。

　大门口_____两个高大的士兵。

7 花园里有五颜六色的玫瑰花。

　花园里_____五颜六色的玫瑰花。

8 车厢里有很多来中国旅游的外国人。

　车厢里_____很多来中国旅游的外国人。

C5 Change the following statements into rhetorical questions to add more emphasis, using the cues provided in the parentheses.

1 大家都想考上重点中学。（谁）

_____

2 我不能忘记那些可爱的学生。（怎么）

_____

3 这儿是医院，你不能抽烟。（怎么）

_____

4 别人能做到的事，我也做得到。（难道）

_____

5 他送的礼物那么好，我非常喜欢。（哪儿）

_____

6 这么简单的文章，你应该看得懂。（为什么）

_____

7 好好的东西你却扔掉了，真是太浪费了。（不是……吗？）

_____

C6 完成句子

1 据说中国的中学生＿＿＿＿＿＿＿＿＿。

2 这确实是你的错，你怎么能
＿＿＿＿＿＿呢？

3 他每次英语考试都是全班第一，"英语天才"的称号＿＿＿＿＿＿＿＿＿。

4 老师和家长都希望我们考上重点高中，可是由此而来的＿＿＿＿＿＿＿＿＿。

5 父母一直期待我放假时回家，我怎么能＿＿＿＿＿＿呢？

6 今天早上，我一口气＿＿＿＿＿＿＿。

7 经过三年的努力，他总算＿＿＿＿＿＿。

8 公共汽车里挤满了＿＿＿＿＿＿＿。

9 只要再拼一年，我就＿＿＿＿＿＿。

10 高考总算结束了，我不由得
＿＿＿＿＿＿＿＿＿＿＿＿＿＿。

C7 英译汉 Translate the following sentences into Chinese, paying special attention to the underlined words.

1 The small restaurant is packed with foreign tourists.

＿＿＿＿＿＿＿＿＿＿＿＿＿＿＿＿＿

2 It is said that he can speak quite a few foreign languages.

＿＿＿＿＿＿＿＿＿＿＿＿＿＿＿＿＿

3 All the articles published in our newspaper express the opinions of their authors. We don't take any responsibility for issues brought about by them.

＿＿＿＿＿＿＿＿＿＿＿＿＿＿＿＿＿

＿＿＿＿＿＿＿＿＿＿＿＿＿＿＿＿＿

＿＿＿＿＿＿＿＿＿＿＿＿＿＿＿＿＿

4 There is a large painting hanging on the wall of her bedroom. (Place + V 着 + NP)

＿＿＿＿＿＿＿＿＿＿＿＿＿＿＿＿＿

5 My parents don't even allow me to go out for a walk. How can I accompany you to see the late-night movie? I have to stay home to prepare for my tests tomorrow.

＿＿＿＿＿＿＿＿＿＿＿＿＿＿＿＿＿

＿＿＿＿＿＿＿＿＿＿＿＿＿＿＿＿＿

6 The little boy was taken aback by the big dog that suddenly ran out of the house.

＿＿＿＿＿＿＿＿＿＿＿＿＿＿＿＿＿

＿＿＿＿＿＿＿＿＿＿＿＿＿＿＿＿＿

7 As long as you work hard, you will have an opportunity to be promoted by the boss.

＿＿＿＿＿＿＿＿＿＿＿＿＿＿＿＿＿

＿＿＿＿＿＿＿＿＿＿＿＿＿＿＿＿＿

D 阅读

D1 Scanning for specific information

For this exercise, keep the pre-reading questions in mind as you read. Seek answers only for those questions, and ignore unnecessary information. Try not to worry about words you don't know. You can answer the post-reading questions through more careful reading.

1 作者学的是什么专业？

＿＿＿＿＿＿＿＿＿＿＿＿＿＿＿＿＿

2 学校规定几门主课不及格的学生就不能毕业？

＿＿＿＿＿＿＿＿＿＿＿＿＿＿＿＿＿

3 职业高中毕业生工资要求高不高？

＿＿＿＿＿＿＿＿＿＿＿＿＿＿＿＿＿

4 职业高中毕业生找工作容易不容易？

＿＿＿＿＿＿＿＿＿＿＿＿＿＿＿＿＿

短文（一）
职业高中

我是一个职业高中生 (vocational high school student)，可是跟那些找不到工作的大学毕业生相比，我觉得自己是个幸运儿 (xìngyùn'ér) (lucky guy)。你知道现在大学生的困难吗？为了上大学，他们花了很多时间和金钱，拿到学位后，却找不到合适的工作。我们虽然没有大学学位，却有很多实用 (shíyòng) (practical) 的技能，不担心找不到工作。而且以后还可以一边工作一边参加自学考试。我学的是会计 (kuàijì) (accounting) 专业。现在社会上有不少企业需要会计，我们还没毕业就有企业来学校要我们去他们单位工作。

社会上有些人对职业高中有错误的想法，他们认为职业高中没有普通高中好，职业高中比较容易，学的课程比较少，也没有普通高中那么严格。其实，我们要学的课程相当多，不但要学会计学、经济学、企业 (qǐyè) (business) 管理等专业课，还要学普通高中的基础课程。我们每天除了上课以外，就是做功课，很少有时间做别的事情。另外，学校还规定，两门主课不及格 (jígé) (pass a test) 的学生，就不能毕业。这有时会压得我们喘不过气来，但是一想到那么多找不到工作的人，我们又觉得太幸运了。我们职业高中生学的东西都很实用，学了就可以立刻用上，我们班不少同学都在利用假期给小公司工作。而且我们经过培训 (péixùn) (training)，技术熟练 (jìshù shúliàn)

(skilled in techniques)、适应力 (shìyìnglì) (adaptability) 强，对工资的要求不高，加上适合社会和企业的需求，所以毕业后找工作比大学生还容易。

D2 根据短文内容，选择最佳答案回答问题

1 作者为什么说自己是"幸运儿"？
- a 因为职业高中生的课程比较少。
- b 因为职业高中生有时候比大学生容易找工作。
- c 因为职业高中生不用学普通高中的基础课程。
- d 因为职业高中生可以参加自学考试。

2 职业高中生找工作有哪些优势 (advantages)？
- a 他们的技术熟练。
- b 他们对工资的要求不太高。
- c 他们学的知识很实用。
- d 以上都是。

3 根据作者观点，以下对职业高中的看法中哪项不正确？
- a 职业高中学生学的知识很实用。
- b 职业高中课程不比普通高中课程容易。
- c 职业高中要求不严。
- d 职业高中生一般不担心找不到工作。

4 以下哪项最好地说明了这篇短文的主题？
- a 职业高中比普通高中好。
- b 职业高中比大学好。
- c 读职业高中的好处。
- d 社会上有些人对职业高中错误的看法。

1 孩子上幼儿园 (kindergarten) 以前，美国的父母关不关心他们的学习？

_____

2 美国孩子跟日本孩子相比，谁更早开始学习阅读识字？

_____

3 日本幼儿园一天的活动中有多少时间是教阅读和数学？

_____

4 亚洲父母认为对孩子的早期教育重要不重要？

_____

短文（二）
儿童教育

据某报纸报道，美国儿童开始接受教育的年龄比日本的儿童早。美国的妈妈们非常注意孩子上幼儿园 (kindergarten) 以前的学习。他们常常带孩子出去开眼界，给他们买书，还要读书给他们听。而亚裔 (Asian descent) 的父母则更关心孩子的身体健康，一定要让孩子吃得好，睡得好。美国的孩子上小学以后，父母就认为对孩子的教育是学校的事了，他们不必教孩子做功课。可是亚裔的父母却正好相反 (on the contrary)，他们在这个时候才认真注意孩子的学习成绩 (schoolwork)，并对孩子的功课进行辅导。

在美国，一半以上的孩子在两岁以前就开始学习阅读了，而在亚洲 (Asian) 国家这种现象不到30%。在孩子上幼儿园以前，美国有85%的母亲会教孩子读书认字。在日本这样做的母亲只有40%。美国幼儿园一天的活动中有30%是教阅读和数学，而这些课程在日本幼儿园一天的活动中还不到1%。日本的学龄前儿童中有40%的时间是用来学习怎样听老师的话，跟老师一样清楚地说话。这些活动在美国幼儿园一天的课程中仅占14%。美国幼儿园的这种教育方式反映 (reflect) 了美国人的一种看法，那就是如果大人不在孩子小时候培养 (foster, develop) 他们的兴趣，将来他们长大就不可能有所作为。而亚洲父母则认为对孩子进行不进行早期教育没关系，关键是要努力。因为一个人无论在什么时候，只要努力就一定能够成功。不过，近年来，由于社会竞争压力越来越大，亚洲父母也越来越重视幼儿的早期教育了。

D4 根据短文内容，选择最佳答案回答问题

1 这篇文章说的是儿童的：

  a 小学教育   c 早期教育

  b 中学教育   d 大学教育

2 孩子上幼儿园以前，亚裔父母特别关心的是：

  a 孩子的身体健康

  b 孩子的学习成绩

  c 孩子的读书和写字

  d 孩子听话和说话的能力

3 亚裔父母什么时候开始重视孩子的学习成绩？

  a 两岁以前

  b 上幼儿园以前

  c 上幼儿园的时候

  d 读小学的时候

4 比较日美两国的幼儿园，日本的幼儿园更重视儿童的：

  a 阅读书籍的能力

  b 读书认字的能力

  c 阅读和数学方面的能力

  d 听话和说话的能力

5 美国的孩子两岁以前开始学习阅读的占：

  a 50%以上   c 85%

  b 30%   d 不到30%

6 美国的父母为什么在孩子上小学以后，不对孩子的功课进行辅导？

  a 因为他们认为这时教育小孩应该是学校的事情了。

  b 因为他们以前已经对孩子的功课进行了辅导。

  c 因为他们认为培养孩子的兴趣比得到好成绩更重要。

  d 因为他们这时候最关心的是孩子的身体健康。

7 美国幼儿园的教育方式反映了美国人这样一种看法：

  a 小孩努力不努力不要紧，只要他们有兴趣。

  b 儿童小时候的兴趣培养会影响他们以后的生活。

  c 教孩子怎么读书比教他怎么听话更重要。

  d 一个人不论什么时候努力都能成功。

8 这篇文章主要说的是：

  a 东西方幼儿园教育方式的不同

  b 儿童教育在不同的时候有不同的特点

  c 东西方社会在儿童早期教育方面，看法和做法都不一样

  d 一个人无论在什么时候，只要努力就一定会成功

E 口语

E1 采访 Oral Interview

Interview a classmate about his or her high school experience. If possible, interview someone from a different background or culture. You may use the example questions below and add other questions of your own.

1 你们那儿有没有重点中学和普通中学？你上的是什么中学？

2 你最喜欢中学生活中的什么？最不喜欢的呢？

3 你的学习压力很大吗？请举例说明。

4 你的父母对你的学习很关心吗？请举例说明。

5 你们的老师对你们很严格吗？请举例说明。

6 你们周末都做些什么?

7 你们申请大学时需不需要考试?是什么样的考试?

8 大学录取学生主要是看什么条件?

E2 报告 Oral Presentation

Give an oral presentation about your classmate's high school experience based on the interview.

E3 讨论 Discussion Topics

1 我们为什么上大学?

2 压力是否有利于学习?

3 教育最重要的目的是什么?

4 中小学生可以有手机吗?

5 学龄儿童必须上学吗?

E4 辩论 Debate Topics

Research both sides of the following topics. The class will be divided into two sides. Each side will take turns presenting arguments.

1 学龄儿童必须上学 vs. 不能强迫学龄儿童上学

2 高考对学生压力太大，应该废除 vs. 高考是唯一公平的考试，应该保留

E5 衍生小组项目 Extended Group Research Project

In a small group, choose one of the following topics to research. Prepare a presentation in Chinese with a visual component. Each member of the group should take turns presenting. Include a list of new vocabulary words for your classmates.

a 城市农民工子女的教育问题
The Education of Migrant Workers' Children

b 中国的考试制度
The Examination System of China

c 虎妈教育方式
The "Tiger Mother" Education Style

F 写作

作文题：中学时最难忘的一件事(350-450字)

Write a short story of 350-450 characters about the most unforgettable event in your high school experience. Use the words and grammatical points that you have learned from the textbook so far. Your story should describe the event's time, location, participants, and sequence. Also include your feelings and opinions about the event. To make your writing more cohesive, try to use topic chain structures and connectives such as:

Temporal sequence 先，然后，后来，接着

Contrast 虽然，可是，不过

Condition 只有……才……，只要……就……

全新变化 大学生就业

- 你有过找工作的经历吗？如果找过，请谈一谈找工作的经过和结果。

- 大学生学什么专业比较好找工作？

- 你选择专业的时候，会不会考虑这个专业对你将来找工作的影响？为什么？

- 找工作的时候，什么对你最重要？

- 上面这张照片是一场大学生招聘会现场。你对这种场面的印象如何？

College-educated people in China used to be highly privileged and secure in the job market. However, as part of the continuous reform of the education system, the government abolished its policy of controlling and assigning jobs for all university graduates in 2000. People's perceptions, attitudes, and behavior related to employing university graduates have also undergone a tremendous change. In order to support its main idea and pique the interest of readers, the article in this lesson cites three news stories about the experiences of university students searching for jobs.

6

第六课

生词

自学生词

Match each new word with its English translation by deducing the word's meaning from its characters.
(The first one is done for you.)

首选(選)　　　　铁饭(鐵飯)碗　　　　招生　　　　求职(職)　　　　择业(擇業)

回收　　　　　　再生　　　　　　　新浪网(網)　　　心理　　　　　自主

1	择业 select a career	6	_____ apply for a job
2	_____ psychology, mentality; mental	7	_____ first choice
3	_____ iron rice bowl, secure job	8	_____ Sina News website
4	_____ collect to be recycled	9	_____ regrow, reproduce, recycle
5	_____ recruit students	10	_____ of one's own will

成语和惯用语

成语／惯用语	单字解释	意思
天之骄子 *tiān zhī jiāo zǐ* 1 不要以为你爸爸是经理你就是天之骄子。人人都得自己努力创业才有前途。	天 Heaven, God 之 possessive particle, literary equivalent of 的 骄(驕) proud, arrogant 子 son	God's favored one, an unusually privileged person

主要生词

	简体	繁体	拼音	词性	英文
1	如下		*rúxià*	v.	as follows
2	机关	機關	*jīguān*	n.	office
3	无所谓	無謂	*wúsuǒwèi*	i.e.	(do) not care, be indifferent
4	创业	創業	*chuàngyè*	v.o.	start an undertaking
5	感慨		*gǎnkǎi*	v./n.	sigh with emotion
6	描述		*miáoshù*	v.	describe
7	差异	異	*chāyì*	n.	differentiation, difference

	简体	繁体	拼音	词性	英文
8	几乎	幾	*jīhū*	adv.	almost, nearly
9	肯定		*kěndìng*	adv.	definitely, undoubtedly
10	终身	終	*zhōngshēn*	n.	lifetime
11	胆量	膽	*dǎnliàng*	n.	courage, guts, nerve
12	流行		*liúxíng*	adj.	popular, fashionable
13	就业	業	*jiùyè*	v.o.	obtain employment
14	简历	簡歷	*jiǎnlì*	n.	résumé
15	失败	敗	*shībài*	v./n.	fail, lose; failure, loss
16	充满	滿	*chōngmǎn*	v.	be full of
17	焦虑	慮	*jiāolù*	adj.	agitated, anxious
18	交流		*jiāoliú*	v.	exchange, communicate
19	招聘		*zhāopìn*	v.	advertise job offers, recruit employees
20	网站	網	*wǎngzhàn*	n.	website
21	涌	湧	*yǒng*	v./n.	(of water or clouds) gush, surge
22	日益		*rìyì*	adv.	more and more
23	建筑	築	*jiànzhù*	n.	architecture, building
24	辞	辭	*cí*	v.	resign, dismiss, decline
25	废品	廢	*fèipǐn*	n.	waste product, reject
26	破烂	爛	*pòlàn*	n.	junk, scrap
27	浪费	費	*làngfèi*	v.	waste
28	贡献	貢獻	*gòngxiàn*	v./n.	contribute; contribution
29	环保	環	*huánbǎo*	attr.	environmental protection
30	行业	業	*hángyè*	n.	trade, profession, industry
31	促进	進	*cùjìn*	v.	promote, advance, accelerate
32	塑料		*sùliào*	n.	plastic
33	财富	財	*cáifù*	n.	wealth
34	获得	獲	*huòdé*	v.	obtain, acquire
35	利润	潤	*lìrùn*	n.	profit, profit return
36	网络	網絡	*wǎngluò*	n.	(computer) network
37	老板	闆	*lǎobǎn*	n.	boss
38	失去		*shīqù*	v.	lose, miss
39	保障		*bǎozhàng*	v./n.	safeguard; protection, guarantee

第一读：掌握课文大意

Skim the reading; then select the option below that best captures its main idea.

a 几个大学生找工作的故事

b 激烈的就业竞争对大学生心理的影响

c 大学生就业情况在2000年以后的重要改变

第二读：细节和理解

Read the text again carefully and answer the following questions.

1 80年代大学毕业生认为最好的工作是什么？为什么？

_____

_____

2 为什么那时候大学毕业生不能自己选择工作？

_____

_____

3 是什么改变了大学生就业情况？

_____

_____

4 大学生刘刚的求职经历怎么样？

_____

_____

5 近年来大学生就业观念与择业标准有些什么改变？

_____

_____

6 "收破烂"与"废品回收公司"有什么不同？

_____

_____

7 按照黄义的看法，什么样的人才算是人才？

_____

_____

8 冯小兵对现在的就业情况有什么看法？

_____

_____

9 国家停止对大学生统一分配，对什么人是一种挑战？对什么人是一种自由？

_____

_____

大学生就业全新变化

2003年12月12日，新浪网完成了一项共有6070人参加的调查[1]，问题是"刚走出校园的你，在找工作时首选什么？"调查结果如下：

公司、企业 59.14%

政府部门、机关 26.21%

无所谓 8.57%

个人创业 6.08%

这份调查的结果，让20年前的一位大学毕业生感慨万千。他用下面的一段话描述了两代人的差异：

"那时候几乎没有人会首选'公司、企业'，而且公司、企业本来就没有几家。那时候的首选肯定是'政府部门和国家机关'，因为那是终身可靠的铁饭碗。那时候，不会也不敢有什么'无所谓'，也没有胆量'个人自主创业'，更不可能有人做这样的调查，因为那个时候的流行语不是'你选择什么'，而是'政府分配你做什么，你就做什么'。"

随着近年来的教育改革，高校扩大招生，大学生们的就业已经在各方面发生了改变。从2000年起，教育部停止了多年来"国家统一分配高校毕业生"的工作方式，从此，找工作要由毕业生自己负责。这种变化，对有的学生来说，是一种挑战，但对另一些学生来说，却是一种自由。

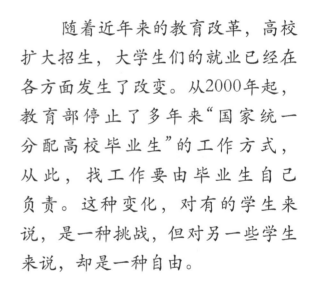

[1] Huang, Yong 黄勇, "Xinwen zongshu: ershi nian Zhongguo daxuesheng jiuye zoushi huimou" 新闻综述: 20年中国大学生就业走势回眸 [News Roundup: A Look Back at a 20-year Trend of College Student Employment], *Zhongguo qingnian bao* 中国青年报, Dec. 19, 2003, at *Xinlang xinwen zhongxin* 新浪新闻中心, available at <http://news.sina.com.cn/c/2003-12-19/04111376314s.shtml>.

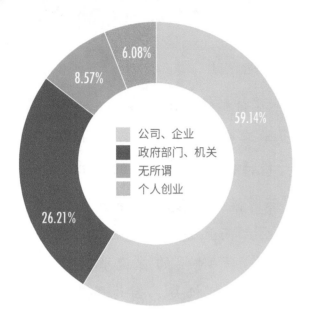

6.08%

8.57%

59.14%

26.21%

公司、企业
政府部门、机关
无所谓
个人创业

河南省黄河科技学院本科生刘刚，一年内先后寄出近200份简历，得到了42次面试机会，他参加了其中的23次，平均每两周一次，而每次面试都失败了。竞争激烈的就业形势使不少大学生心中充满了焦虑与不安。人才交流会上，排队求职的大学生人山人海；招聘网站上，千万封求职 e-mail 涌入各个企业的信箱；甚至连招聘人的手机上，每天都能收到100多人的求职短信……可以说，找工作的大学生们把所有能用的办法都用上了。

面对日益激烈的就业竞争，越来越多的大学生已经在心理上改变了传统的就业观念与择业标准。他们不再认为自己是"天之骄子"，而称自己为"有知识的劳动者"了。

山西大学毕业生黄义，在学校里学的是建筑工程专业，今年年初，他辞掉在企业的工作，开办了一个网上废品回收公司。有人认为他读了那么多书，却去"收破烂"，真是浪费人才。但黄义觉得，读书多的人不一定是人才；能适应社会，并能对社会发展做出贡献的人，才算人才。他认为废品回收是一种环保行业。他的工作是利用在大学里学到的知识，更好地促进废品的再利用。比如回收的塑料有几十种，如果没有一定的专业知识，就只能简单地把它做为一般的废品处理；但是如果把它细分，就可以在再生资源利用上创造更多的财富，并获得更多的利润。

那个时候的流行语不是'你选择什么'，而是'政府分配你做什么，你就做什么'。

清华大学学生冯小兵毕业后和两个同学一起开了一家网络公司，当起了"老板"。虽然这个老板当得很辛苦，但他们觉得是"自己给自己打工，做自己喜欢的事"。现在的大学毕业生虽然失去了国家计划分配的保障，但却获得了选择的自由。◆

大學生就業全新變化

2006年12月12日，新浪網完成了一項共有6070人參加的調查，問題是"剛走出校園的你，在找工作時首選什麼？"調查結果如下：

公司、企業　　　　59.14%

政府部門、機關　　26.21%

無所謂　　　　　　8.57%

個人創業　　　　　6.08%

這份調查的結果，讓20年前的一位大學畢業生感慨萬千。他用下面的一段話描述了兩代人的差異：

"那時候幾乎沒有人會首選'公司、企業'，而且公司、企業本來就沒有幾家。那時候的首選肯定是'政府部門和國家機關'，因為那是終身可靠的鐵飯碗。那時候，不會也不敢有什麼'無所謂'，也沒有膽量'個人自主創業'，更不可能有人做這樣的調查，因為那個時候的流行語不是'你選擇什麼'，而是'政府分配你做什麼，你就做什麼'。"

隨著近年來的教育改革，高校擴大招生，大學生們的就業已經在各方面發生了改變。從2000年起，教育部停止了多年來"國家統一分配高校畢業生"的工作方式，從此，找工作要由畢業生自己負責。這種變化，對有的學生來說，是一種挑戰，但對另一些學生來說，卻是一種自由。

河南省黃河科技學院本科生劉剛，一年內先後寄出近200份簡歷，得到了42次面試機會，他參加了其中的23次，平均每兩周一次，而每次面試都失敗了。競爭激烈的就業形勢使不少大學生心中充滿了焦慮與不安。人才交流會上，排隊求職的大學生人山人海；招聘網站上，千萬封求職 e-mail 涌入各個企業的信箱；甚至連招聘人的手機上，每天都能收到100多人的求職短信⋯⋯可以說，找工作的大學生們把所有能用的辦法都用上了。

面對日益激烈的就業競爭，越來越多的大學生已經在心理上改變了傳統的就業觀念與擇業標准。他們不再認為自己是"天之驕子"，而稱自己為"有知識的勞動者"了。

山西大學畢業生黃義，在學校裡學的是建筑工程專業，今年年初，他辭掉在企業的工作，開辦了一個網上廢品回收公司。有人認為他讀了那麼多書，卻去"收破爛"，真是浪費人才。但黃義覺得，讀書多的人不一定是人才；能適應社會，並能對社會發展做出貢獻的人，才算人才。他認為廢品回收是一種環保行業。他的工作是利用在大學裡學到的知識，更好地促進廢品的再利用。比如回收的塑料有幾十種，如果沒有一定的專業知識，就只能簡單地把它做為一般的廢品處理；但是如果把它細分，就可以在再生資源利用上創造更多的財富，並獲得更多的利潤。

清華大學學生馮小兵畢業後和兩個同學一起開了一家網絡公司，當起了"老闆"。雖然這個老闆當得很辛苦，但他們覺得是"自己給自己打工，做自己喜歡的事"。現在的大學畢業生雖然失去了國家計劃分配的保障，但卻獲得了選擇的自由。◆

阅读技巧

A 推论 Making Inferences

Making inferences requires understanding the author's ideas through clue words and phrases that imply information without stating it, since ideas and information in the text are not always given directly. Inferences can also be made from your own experience and previous knowledge. The following excerpt is taken from the reading in this lesson:

面对日益激烈的就业竞争，越来越多的大学生已经在心理上改变了传统的就业观念与择业标准。他们不再认为自己是"天之骄子"，而称自己为"有知识的劳动者"了。

Which inference can you make based on the information stated above?

a 现在的大学生都是"天之骄子"。

b 很多大学生以前都有比较传统的就业观念。

c 以前的大学生找工作比现在更难。

The answer is (b). We can infer that "越来越多的大学生已经在心理上<u>改变了</u>传统的就业观念" means they used to have a more "traditional concept of employment."

B 阅读技巧练习：推论 Reading Skill Practice: Making Inferences

Choose the best inference from the three possible choices for each sentence, and underline the clue(s) that helped you choose your answer.

1 有人认为他读了那么多书，却去"收破烂"，真是浪费人才。

　a 做收破烂的工作需要读很多书。

　b 收破烂的工作是被人看不起的工作。

　c 人才是收破烂的没有用的人。

2 清华大学冯小兵毕业后和两个同学一起开了一家网络公司，当起了"老板"。

　a 冯小兵的公司很小。

　b 冯小兵是一个很有能力的老板。

　c 冯小兵在同学开的网络公司里工作。

3 这种变化，对有的学生是一种挑战；但对另一些学生来说，却是一种自由。

　a 这种变化很受同学们欢迎。

　b 大家都觉得自由择业是一件好事。

　c 不同的学生对这个变化有不同的看法。

4 "那时的流行语不是'你选择什么'而是'政府分配你做什么，你就做什么'。"

　a 那时候大家都能选择流行的工作。

　b 那时候大家都得服从政府的分配。

　c 那时候大家想做什么工作就做什么工作。

词汇与句型

A 如下 as follows, as shown below

1 今年我校博士毕业生名单<u>如下</u>：……

The Ph.D. graduates of our university this year are as follows: ...

2 这次抽样调查的结果<u>如下</u>：……

The results of the sample survey are as follows: ...

3 我们为晚会准备工作做了<u>如下</u>安排：……

We have made the following arrangements in order to prepare for the party: ...

B 先后 successively, one after another

1 刘刚一年内<u>先后</u>寄出近100份简历。

Liu Gang sent out nearly one hundred résumés in succession in a single year.

2 两年内，政府为当地居民<u>先后</u>兴建了六栋公寓楼。

In two years, the government built six successive apartment buildings for the local residents.

3 爷爷病得很厉害，亲戚们<u>先后</u>从各地赶回家看望他。

Grandpa got seriously ill. Relatives rushed home one after another to visit him.

C 听从 obey, heed

1 中国的传统观念认为，在家里应该<u>听从</u>父母，在单位应该<u>听从</u>领导。

According to traditional Chinese thinking, you should obey your parents at home and obey your boss at work.

2 你是老板。我们<u>听从</u>你的安排。

You are the boss. We are at your disposal.

3 小李没<u>听从</u>医生的意见，结果他的病越来越<u>严重</u>了。

Xiao Li didn't follow his doctor's advice. As a result, his illness got worse and worse.

D 流行…… popular, widespread…

1 <u>流行</u>语 (popular saying, catchphrase, watchword)

世界杯期间，"你今天看球了吗？"一下子成了<u>流行</u>语。

During the World Cup season, "Did you watch the game today?" suddenly became a popular greeting.

2 <u>流行</u>病 (epidemic)

天花曾经是常见的<u>流行</u>病，现在基本上得到了控制。

Smallpox used to be a common epidemic, but it's basically under control now.

3 <u>流行</u>感冒／<u>流</u>感 (influenza)

我们办公室有几乎三分之一的人得了<u>流</u>感，不能上班。

Almost a third of the people in our office are down with the flu and cannot come to work.

4 <u>流行</u>音乐 (pop music)

与古典音乐相比，我更喜欢流行音乐。

I prefer pop music to classical music.

E (将) 近 almost, nearly
(usually used with a number)

(将)近 is similar to 差不多, but more formal in style.

1 火车站售票窗口前，近千人在排队
   买票，急着回家。

   Nearly a thousand people lined up at the ticket windows of the train station, anxious to go home.

2 我爷爷已年近九十，身体依然很健康。

   My grandpa is almost ninety, but still remains in good health.

3 她用了（将）近三个小时读那篇课文，
   可还是不懂。

   She spent almost three hours reading that lesson, but she still didn't understand it.

F 日益 more and more..., increasingly, growing day by day

1 在就业竞争日益激烈的形势下，为了
   增加就业机会，很多大学毕业生选择
   继续读研究生。

   Under circumstances of increasingly intense competition for employment, many university graduates chose to pursue postgraduate education to increase their chances of finding a job.

2 随着城市人口的增长，城市住房日益
   紧张。

   With the increase of the urban population, urban housing and accommodation have become more and more strained.

3 自去年年底以来，公司的财政状况日益
   好转。

   Since the end of last year, our company's financial situation has been taking a favorable turn.

G 无所谓 (do) not care, indifferent

1 无论我们讨论什么，她总是一副无所谓
   的样子。

   No matter what we discuss, she always seems indifferent.

2 去哪儿吃我都无所谓，我只想尽快吃饭。

   I don't care where we are going to eat. I just want to eat as soon as possible.

3 我无所谓走路去还是骑车去，你们来
   决定吧。

   It doesn't matter to me whether we walk there or bike there. It's up to you guys.

H 几乎 almost, nearly

1 功课太多，压得我几乎喘不过气来。

   The burden of coursework is so heavy that I am almost out of breath.

2 在现代城市里，传统的大家庭几乎
   不存在了。

   In modern cities, the traditional extended family has almost become extinct.

3 电影太没有意思了，我几乎睡着了。

   The movie was so boring that I almost fell asleep.

I 只有……才能……

only when... can someone...

只有 introduces a conditional phrase or clause indicating that it is the necessary and sufficient condition for the result introduced by 才能.

1 <u>只有</u>能适应社会并且能对社会发展做出贡献的人<u>才能</u>算是人才。

Only if you meet the needs of and make a contribution to societal development can you be considered a distinguished person.

2 <u>只有</u>不断努力、不怕失败，<u>才能</u>创立起自己的事业。

Only when you continue to strive, without fear of failure, can you establish your own career.

J 不是 A 而是 B: it is not A but B

This structure is used to comment on or explain something by contrasting A and B (negating A and confirming B). Syntactically, A and B can be noun phrases, verb phrases, or even clauses. Sometimes 并 is added to 不是 for more emphasis.

1 现在的大学生们明白了他们<u>并不是</u>"天之骄子"<u>而是</u>普通劳动者。

Today's university graduates realize that they are not actually "Heaven's favorites" but ordinary workers.

2 小王上课没有精神，<u>不是</u>因为身体不好，<u>而是</u>因为最近找工作的压力太大。

Xiao Wang has no energy in class. It is not because of poor health but rather the terrible pressure of job hunting.

3 老万买得起房子，<u>不是</u>因为他收入高，<u>而是</u>在银行贷到了一笔款。

The reason why Lao Wan can afford a new house is not because of his high income, but because he obtained a bank loan.

A 中文构词法简介 （一）
Introduction to Chinese word formation (I)

One of the unique (and fun) challenges of learning Chinese relates to the ways in which Chinese words are created. You have been practicing "Vocabulary-Building Skills," in which you make intelligent guesses about the meanings of new words based on your knowledge of each character, since Lesson 1. In Lessons 6 and 7, we will introduce you to the basic system of Chinese word formation.

A1 合成词 Compound words

In the early history of the Chinese language, each word consisted of only one character. Even now, almost every character has at least one complete and independent meaning, and therefore can be an independent word (e.g., 人, 写, 我, 四, 啊, and 涌).

But language evolves. In modern Chinese, most words are formed by combining two or more characters. These are called compound words. Compounding is a very productive mechanism for creating new words, since each character can be combined with dozens or even hundreds of other characters to form compounds. The number of combinations is almost unlimited. Today about 80% of Chinese words are compounds, of which two-character compounds are by far the most preferred word form, accounting for more than 70% of modern Chinese words. Below are some examples of Chinese compound words (mostly taken from Lesson 6):

Word	Individual Character Meaning	Compound Meaning
网站	net, web + stop, station, service center	website
求职	ask, seek + job, position	seek employment
售货员	sell + goods + person	salesclerk
无所谓	none + (particle) + say	doesn't care
二氧化碳	two + oxygen + transform + carbon	carbon dioxide
非政府主义	non + government + -ism	anarchism

A2 The meanings of compound words

In many cases, the meanings of compound words can be derived from the meanings of their constituent characters, although not always directly. For example, the character 业 means "trade," "profession," "job," "career," "cause," "business," "course of study," etc. In Lesson 6, there are seven compounds that contain the character 业. The following table demonstrates how we can understand and differentiate the meanings of these compounds by processing the meaning of their respective component characters:

Word	Individual Character Meaning	Compound Meaning
行业	trade + business	profession
就业	take up + job	obtain employment
择业	choose + job	career selection
创业	establish + business	establish business
企业	attempt + business	enterprise, business
专业	concentrate + study	major, specialty
毕业	finish + course of study	graduate

There are some compound words with meanings that may not be apparent from their constituent parts. For example, 马上 (horse + upon) means "at once," and the playful word 马马虎虎 (horse + horse + tiger + tiger) means "so-so, nothing special." However, these exceptions are relatively few in number.

A3 简缩词 Abbreviations

Abbreviation (缩写、简称) is another word formation process. Abbreviations are formed by taking one character from each word in the longer corresponding form, though not necessarily the first character in each word. Most abbreviations come from proper names of institutions, companies, and organizations, so there are far more abbreviated nouns than verbs. From the following examples, you may also notice that most of the abbreviations are realized in the popular two-character form:

Original	Abbreviation	Meaning
高等学校	高校	university, higher education
高校入学考试	高考	university entrance examination
环境保护	环保	environmental protection
超级市场	超市	supermarket
手提电话机	手机	cell phone
广东出口商品展销会	广交会	Guangzhou Export Commodities Fair

In summary, learning and using new words can be made much easier, more meaningful, and more effective if you know about the underlying cognitive mechanisms of word formation in addition to their contextual information. Many new words that you encounter may be made of characters you already know. Learning a new word often means arranging old characters (or words) into a new combination.

B Non-interrogative usage of question words

Question words in Chinese can be used as indefinite pronouns (corresponding to "anyone," "everything," "nowhere," etc.), especially when used with 都 or 也. For example:

1 我没什么问题。
   I don't have any questions/problems (in particular).

2 谁都喜欢她。
   Everybody likes her.

3 谁都不喜欢她。
   Nobody likes her.

4 今天晚上他哪儿也不想去。
   He doesn't want to go anywhere tonight.

When interrogative pronouns are used in pairs with 就 (or 也), they function as indefinite pronouns with the suffix "-ever." For example:

5 政府分配你做什么，你就做什么。
   You have to take whatever job the government assigns you.

6 我不知道怎么点法国菜。你点什么我也点什么。
   I don't know how to order French food. I'll order whatever you order.

7 老板什么时候来，我们就什么时候开始。
   We'll start whenever the boss comes.

8 哪儿天气好我们就去哪儿。
   We'll go wherever the weather is good.

C Metaphorical usage of words

C1 铁······ iron... (metaphorically: hard, strong, solid, tough)

1 铁饭碗 (iron rice bowl, secure job)

毕业后，王明去政府部门工作，拿到了那时人人羡慕的"铁饭碗"。

After graduation, Wang Ming worked as a government officer, which was an "iron rice bowl" job that everyone coveted at that time.

2 铁人 (iron man, strong man)

一整天没吃饭还能干活？你真是个铁人啊！

Still working without eating all day? You are truly an iron man!

3 铁证如山 (irrefutable evidence as strong as mountains)

铁证如山，你这一次逃不掉了。

This is irrefutable evidence. You can't get away with it this time.

C2 涌 (of water) gush, well, pour, surge (metaphorically: emerge or move in large numbers or quantity)

1 招聘网站上，千万封求职电子邮件涌入各个企业的信箱。

Through job sites, thousands of e-mail applications poured into the mailboxes of various companies.

2 每年五月，大量游客开始涌入温哥华。

Every May, tourists begin swarming into Vancouver.

3 看着奶奶留下的旧相册，多少回忆涌上我的心头。

Looking through the old photo album Grandma left, so many memories welled up in my mind.

D Prepositional phrases that may occur before the subject/topic

Prepositional phrases (preposition + N) usually occur after the subject/topic but before the main verb phrase, indicating a place, direction, source, method, etc., relevant to the action or event. However, there are a number of prepositional phrases that can freely go either before or after the subject/topic of a sentence. They qualify not the main verb phrase but the entire sentence, providing a situational frame within which the action/event happens. These propositional phases include 随着···，关于···，由于···，对于···, etc. This lesson features another one: 面对 "facing..., confronting..."

Pattern: S + (面对 + NP) + V + O or (面对 + NP) S + V + O

1 许多大学生，面对越来越激烈的就业竞争，已经在心理上改变了传统的就业观念与选择事业标准。

Many college students, faced with increasingly intense job competition, have changed their traditional mentality about employment and their criteria for choosing professions.

2 面对发展经济的挑战，中国政府决定终止实行了几十年的公房制度。

Facing the challenge of economic development, the Chinese government decided to abolish the public housing system, which had been in practice for several decades.

3 面对多次创业的失败，他决定不再自己开公司而去大企业申请工作。

Facing several setbacks in running his own business, he decided not to start any more new undertakings of his own, but to apply for jobs at big companies.

练习

A 语音

Write the following underlined Chinese characters in *pinyin*.
Pay special attention to their different pronunciations in different contexts.

出<u>差</u>（　　）　　<u>差</u>异（　　）

测<u>量</u>（　　）　　胆<u>量</u>（　　）

适<u>应</u>（　　）　　<u>应</u>该（　　）

<u>调</u>查（　　）　　<u>调</u>整（　　）

B 词汇与句型

B1 词语搭配 Match the following words by considering their appropriate collocations.

Group One
(Verb + Object)

1 投递　　＿＿＿贡献
2 开办　　＿＿＿机会
3 回收　　＿＿＿公司
4 获得　　＿＿＿财富
5 创造　　＿＿＿简历
6 做出　　＿＿＿废品

Group Two
(Noun + Noun)

1 政府　　＿＿＿结果
2 专业　　＿＿＿形势
3 自然　　＿＿＿部门
4 竞争　　＿＿＿行业
5 调查　　＿＿＿资源
6 网络　　＿＿＿知识

Group Three
(Adj. + Noun)

1 激烈　　＿＿＿分配
2 全新　　＿＿＿消息
3 流行　　＿＿＿观念
4 可靠　　＿＿＿竞争
5 统一　　＿＿＿音乐
6 传统　　＿＿＿节日

B2 选择填空 Choose the most appropriate words to fill in the blanks.

a 创业　　e 贡献　　i 几乎
b 差异　　f 招聘　　j 日益
c 感慨　　g 求职　　k 网站
d 简历　　h 失败　　l 肯定

1 他辞掉了银行的铁饭碗，选择
自己＿＿＿＿＿＿，真有胆量！

2 这是一个很不错的音乐＿＿＿＿＿＿，
我常常在这里下载最新的流行歌曲。

3 随着污染问题＿＿＿＿＿＿严重，政府
越来越意识到环境保护的重要性。

4 在海外生活了四十年后，老人终于
回到故乡，心中＿＿＿＿＿＿万千。

5 别担心，现在才十点半，
我们＿＿＿＿＿＿能赶上飞机。

6 美国文化与中国文化有很大的
＿＿＿＿＿＿，比如不同的消费观。

7 高三学生的生活很紧张，学习压力
很大，＿＿＿＿＿＿没有时间出去玩。

8 小林认为，只有先适应社会，才能
最终对社会有所＿＿＿＿＿＿。

9 我们公司在报纸上登了一则广告，要_____一位销售部经理。

10 妹妹参加了十几次面试，但都_____了，最后决定自己创业开公司。

11 我上个月就把申请表和_____寄给那家公司了，可是到现在还没消息。

12 她有丰富的工作经验，比其他_____者具有更多优势。

B3 完成句子

1 随着电脑和网络的流行，_____。

2 只有得到父母的同意，我才能_____。

3 各种各样的招聘网站使大学毕业生们_____。

4 面对_____，小雪决定回中国找工作。

5 有人认为_____，但李医生觉得_____。

6 对喜欢艺术片 (art films) 的人来说，这部电影_____；但对喜欢动作片 (action movies) 的人来说，它_____。

7 我来美国读书不是因为国内学习压力大，而是_____。

8 两代人之间有很多差异，在我父母上学的时候，他们不会_____，也没有_____，更不可能_____。

9 _____，只有有钱人才买得起。

C 语法

C1 选词填空 Fill in the blanks with the most appropriate compounds from the list provided.

首 (first ...) 首都、首要、首位、首选

1 刚走出校园的你，找工作时_____什么？

2 有人把事业放在首位，有人把家庭放在_____。你呢？

3 现在的_____任务是改善住房条件。

4 北京是中国的_____。

再 (re-...) 再婚、再生、再利用

1 近年来，陈教授主要研究水资源的净化与_____。

2 太阳能是一种可_____能源。

3 听说他离婚半年后就_____了，我们都很吃惊。

业 (...employment) 待业、就业、失业、创业

1 旅游业的开发为当地居民创造了许多_____机会。

2 在家_____了几年以后，她终于在一家宾馆找到了工作。

3 降低_____率应是政府经济政策中的首要大事。

4 大学生自主_____很难，社会各界应该支持他们。

C2 Match words in the left column with their abbreviations in the right column.

1 免费 _____ 初中三年级

2 文革 _____ 找工作

3 考研 _____ 中等学校入学考试

4 初三 _____ 文化大革命

5 双休 _____ 国家统计局

6 中考 _____ 报考研究生

7 求职 _____ 两天休息

8 国统局 _____ 免除费用

C3 Write out the abbreviated forms of the following.

1 公有住房 _____

2 私有住房 _____

3 每人平均 _____

4 选择职业 _____

5 参加考试的学生 _____

6 两个方向 _____

C4 英译汉 Translate the following sentences, using question words as indefinite pronouns.

1 As a news agency, we report <u>whatever</u> society pays close attention to.

_____

_____

2 Marriage is my own business. I will marry <u>whomever</u> I want to.

_____

_____

3 He is our boss. We have to do it in <u>whatever way</u> he directs us.

_____

_____

4 问： When are we leaving?

答： We'll leave <u>whenever</u> you are ready.

_____

_____

5 问： What would you like to eat for dinner?

答： I'll eat <u>whatever</u> you cook.

_____

_____

6 问： Where do you plan to go after graduation?

答： I'll go <u>wherever</u> I can find a job.

_____

_____

C5 英译汉

1 Hong Kong is <u>the first choice</u> in investment for many big companies. (noun)

_____

_____

2 <u>Only</u> those who are willing to accept challenges with courage <u>can</u> succeed.

_____

_____

3 The purpose of this survey is <u>not to count</u> how many students want to start their own businesses, <u>but to find</u> out the reasons for such a choice.

_____

_____

4 Nowadays, it is very difficult for university graduates to find a good job that they really like. I will be happy <u>as long as</u> I can find an ordinary job.

_____

_____

5 <u>Facing</u> ever-increasing market demand, this corporation has decided to invest more.

_____

_____

6 As far as university graduates <u>are concerned</u>, job fairs and job sites offer a large number of opportunities.

D 综合

D1 短文填空

a 而是	d 并不是	g 职业
b 就业	e 难上加难	h 人才
c 招聘	f 激烈	i 大学

今年在福建的＿＿＿＿会上出现了一个有意思的现象：＿＿＿高中毕业生的薪水正在上涨，月薪4000元，甚至5000到6000元也有；就业率达到98%，而＿＿＿毕业生普遍月薪只有3000到4000元。很多大学生感到＿＿＿市场竞争太＿＿＿了，连一般的工作都有很多人申请，要找到一份理想的工作简直是＿＿＿。为什么会出现这种情况呢？有人认为，职业高中生一般都是技术工或者是熟练工，他们拿高薪的原因＿＿＿因为学历高，＿＿＿因为他们能马上为企业创造经济价值。而大学生呢，虽然有高学历却没有实践技能。一些高校在培养＿＿＿的过程中只重视理论教育，所以他们的毕业生一般都缺乏企业所需要的实际能力。

D2 按照这篇文章的意思，下面的说法对不对？(T/F)

1 ＿＿＿＿今年福建的职业高中毕业生很受欢迎。

2 ＿＿＿＿大学生的工资不如职业高中的毕业生。

3 ＿＿＿＿职业高中毕业生的学历很高。

4 ＿＿＿＿目前大学毕业生没有实际能力。

5 ＿＿＿＿职业高中毕业生的工资越来越高。

6 ＿＿＿＿作者不理解为什么会出现这种情况。

7 ＿＿＿＿高校就是高等学校。

8 ＿＿＿＿高校的教育应该改革。

短文（一）
就业——我自己的选择

我是一个幸运儿。毕业时，同时有三个单位对我感兴趣，让我去面试。一家是中国建设银行；一家是广州本田 (Honda) 汽车公司，也就是日本本田汽车公司在中国的合资 (joint venture) 企业；还有一家是一个叫"易趣"的网站。我高兴地把面试的好消息告诉了家人。

我爷爷在银行工作过40多年，当然希望我去建设银行。他翻出了多年不用的电话本，找领导、找大学同学、找老同事帮忙。结果大家都告诉他，现在银行用人光靠关系不行，还要看能力。后来，我没有通过建行最后一次面试。听到这个消息，爷爷难受了好多天。

我父母希望我去本田，因为它是那年"中国企业500强"中的第8名。但我对汽车工业实在没什么兴趣。我看中的是网络业，因为我觉得这是一个充满生命力 (vitality) 的新行业，虽然易趣提供的工资连本田的三分之一都不到。

不久，本田公司的录用通知来了，爸爸妈妈兴奋极了。从来舍不得 (shěbude) (begrudge) 买衣服的爸爸，拿出一个月的工资，要妈妈为我买来一套高级西装。他们说："去大企业总得有一套像样 (presentable) 的衣服。"

刚试完西装，电话响了。一接电话，原来是"易趣"面试我的那位总经理。他说："我们决定录用你，明天可以来上班吗？"

放下电话，我做出了最后的决定。我平静地对父母说，我不去本田，要去那家小网站。爸爸看着我，半天说不出话来，然后从我手中夺 (duó) (seize) 过那套西装，扔在地上。妈妈一个人躲在房里哭了半天，我知道她一半是为我哭，一半是为她自己哭，因为她已经把儿子要去本田上班的消息告诉她认识的每一个人了。可现在她儿子不去"中国企业500强"了！不过我并不后悔 (hòuhuǐ) (regret)，虽然父母把我养育成人 (bring up)，可是事业发展的方向，还得我自己选择。

E1 根据短文内容，选择最佳答案回答问题

1 作者没参加哪个单位的面试？
  a 日本本田汽车
  b 中国建设银行
  c 易趣网站
  d 广州本田汽车

2 作者为什么说自己是"幸运儿"？
  a 因为爷爷在银行工作过40年，可以帮他找关系。
  b 因为他面试的单位都录用他了。
  c 因为全家都支持他去易趣网站工作。
  d 因为同时有三个单位让他去面试。

3 父母为什么希望作者去本田？
  a 本田的工资高。
  b 本田是大企业。
  c 本田是"中国企业500强"的第8名。
  d 以上都是。

4 作者选择易趣网站的最主要原因是：

   a 易趣的工资是本田的三倍。

   b 他对新兴的网络业很感兴趣。

   c 易趣是大网站，有发展前途。

   d 他不喜欢父母为他做决定。

5 在找工作时，作者没有考虑以下哪个因素？

   a 个人事业发展的方向

   b 个人的兴趣

   c 企业的发展前途

   d 工资

6 以下哪项最好地说明了这篇短文的主题？

   a 一个人事业发展的方向，应该由自己选择。

   b 被易趣网站录用，是一件很幸运的事情。

   c 我是一个幸运儿，毕业时，同时有三家企业让我去面试。

   d 我进不了"中国企业500强"，让父母很难过。

短文（二）

老板，要招小工吗？

我大学毕业半年了，却找不到工作。虽然条件一次次降低，还是没人要我。今天我决定去人才市场试试，看能不能找个工资最低的小工的工作。虽然只想当个小工，但要去北京最大的人才市场找工作，总得穿得像个样儿吧！于是我穿上西装，打起领带，皮鞋擦得亮亮的，就上路了。

人才市场上，人山人海，到处都是找工作的人。我问了很多招工单位，都说不需要小工。直到天要黑了，人才市场要关门了，我还没找到工作。眼看就要没希望了，我也累得精疲力尽，只好在一把椅子上坐下了。这时，一个穿

西装的人快步朝我走过来，我连忙站起来，整理了一下头发，心想：只要他开口，无论什么条件，我都答应了。

他说："老板，您要招小工吗？"

E2 **按照这篇文章的意思，下面的说法对不对？(T/F)**

1 _____ 我刚开始找工作的时候要求比现在高。

2 _____ 小工并不是我最想要的工作。

3 _____ 因为我的要求太高，所以找了一天也没找到工作。

4 _____ 我对找得到找不到工作无所谓。

5 _____ 我以为跟我说话的人是老板。

6 _____ 跟我说话的人以为我是老板。

7 _____ 跟我说话的人也想招小工。

8 _____ 我们的条件已经降到最低了，可是还是找不到工作。

短文（三）

讲个笑话吧！

公司老板亲自面试，我小心地送上简历。老板没问别的，只是说："讲个笑话吧！"我想了半天，终于想出一个关于鹦鹉(yīngwǔ)(parrot)的笑话：

"一个人去店里买鹦鹉，店主对他说：'我们有三只鹦鹉，蓝的会讲四种语言，卖3000元；红的能讲六种语言，卖4000元；那只黄的不会讲话，卖5000元。'为什么？'顾客问道，'它可什么都不会啊！'是这样的，'店主解释道，'我们也不知道怎么回事，但其它两只鹦鹉都叫它老板。'"

讲完后我一看，老板脸色非常难看，心里知道，这次又完了！

E3 按照这篇文章的意思，下面的说法对不对？(T/F)

1 _____ 老板的面试就是要我讲个笑话。

2 _____ 在笑话里，当老板的鹦鹉什么都不会。

3 _____ 老板听了我的笑话后，非常难受。

4 _____ 我的面试顺利完成了，下周可以去上班了。

5 _____ 我没得到这个工作机会。

6 _____ 这是我第一次工作面试。

7 _____ "这次又完了"的意思是"现在我讲完了"。

F 口语

F1 下面是人们择业时一般要考虑的几个因素。对你来说哪个因素最重要？请用数字（1-8）把他们按重要性排列。最重要的用1，最不重要的用8。

Eight factors that people generally consider when choosing a career are listed below. Think about your own career choices and rank them from 1 to 8, with 1 being the most important factor and 8 being the least important.

_____ 薪水高

_____ 有意思

_____ 精神上没有压力

_____ 体力上不累

_____ 能发挥我的专长

_____ 离家很近

_____ 工作时间比较<u>灵活</u> (flexible)

_____ 有升职的机会

F2 如果你觉得还有重要的因素没有列出来，请加上，并请用数字也标注上重要性。

If you think any other important factors are missing from this list, please add them, and use additional numbers to mark their importance.

F3 跟同学讨论，比较你们的答案，看看你们的观点有什么不同。

Discuss your answers with a group of classmates and see what differences of opinion you have.

G 写作

作文题：任选一题（450-500字）

a 我最理想的工作

b 我第一次找工作的经历

Use the new vocabulary you have learned in this lesson to write an essay of 450–500 characters about your dream job or the experience of finding your first job. Use topic-chain sentences and connectives to link your sentences.

Useful connectives:

Contrast

而，却，不过，可是，不是……而是……

Condition

只有……才……，只要……就……

Sequential order

首先，再说，同时，于是，然后，一……就……

Further development

不但……而且

Reason or cause

因为……所以，由于

大学生与快餐中转站

- 看了课文题目，你能不能猜出来快餐中转站是做什么的？

- 如果大学毕业找不到理想的工作，你会怎么办？

- 你愿意做收入一般，但比较稳定的工作，还是有机会发展，但要冒险的工作？

- 你知道哪些跟"创业"有关的词汇？

This lesson tells the story of a female college graduate looking for a job and establishing her own business. Her experience reflects how the booming economy and highly competitive labor market have changed the concept of a career for the young and educated in China, who for hundreds of years had considered themselves a privileged class entitled to good jobs. Although the message of this lesson and Lesson 6 are similar, their styles differ. Whereas Lesson 6 centers on a feature news article, this lesson showcases a narrative. Pay special attention to how the narrative presents sequential events by means of temporal connectives.

7

第七课

生词

🔊 自学生词

Match each new word with its English translation by deducing the word's meaning from its characters.
(The first one is done for you.)

盒饭(飯)　　口味　　　　菜单(單)　　送餐　　　饭(飯)菜　　小吃　　　　面(麵)食

店名　　　订单(訂單)　　升级(級)　　餐饮(飲)　　价位(價位)　　脸红(臉紅)心跳

1　__升级__　go up (in grade, etc.)

2　_____　food made of wheat

3　_____　blush with shame or shyness

4　_____　price level

5　_____　rice and other dishes, meal

6　_____　delivery

7　_____　name of a store

8　_____　menu

9　_____　snacks

10　_____　food and drink

11　_____　box lunch

12　_____　order form

13　_____　taste

🔊 主要生词

	简体	繁体	拼音	词性	英文
1	碰壁		*pèngbì*	v.o.	be rebuffed
2	写字楼	寫　樓	*xiězìlóu*	n.	office building
3	白领	領	*báilǐng*	n.	white-collar (worker)
4	快餐		*kuàicān*	n.	fast food
5	答复	復	*dáfù*	v.	answer, reply
6	价值	價	*jiàzhí*	n.	value
7	特色		*tèsè*	n.	salient feature, characteristic
8	改进	進	*gǎijìn*	v.	improve
9	流泪	淚	*liúlèi*	v.o.	shed tears
10	客户	戶	*kèhù*	n.	client, customer
11	责备	責備	*zébèi*	v.	accuse, blame
12	放弃	棄	*fàngqì*	v.	abandon, give up

	简体	繁体	拼音	词性	英文
13	业务	業務	*yèwù*	n.	business
14	详细	詳細	*xiángxì*	adj.	detailed, elaborate
15	收集		*shōují*	v.	collect, gather
16	信息		*xìnxī*	n.	information
17	当地	當	*dāngdì*	n.	local
18	风味	風	*fēngwèi*	n.	special flavor
19	风格	風	*fēnggé*	n.	style, manner
20	中转	轉	*zhōngzhuǎn*	v.	transfer, change hands
21	赚取	賺	*zhuànqǔ*	v.	earn, make a profit
22	差价	價	*chājià*	n.	price difference
23	订购	訂購	*dìnggòu*	v.	order (goods)
24	事先		*shìxiān*	adv.	in advance, beforehand
25	优惠	優	*yōuhuì*	n.	favor, discount
26	价	價	*jià*	n.	price
27	聘请	請	*pìnqǐng*	v.	hire
28	过后	過後	*guòhòu*	adv.	afterwards, later
29	亲自	親	*qīnzì*	adv.	personally, in person
30	推销	銷	*tuīxiāo*	v.	promote (goods)
31	保证	證	*bǎozhèng*	v.	pledge, guarantee, assure
32	满足	滿	*mǎnzú*	v.	satisfy
33	及时	時	*jíshí*	adj.	timely, prompt
34	营养	營養	*yíngyǎng*	n.	nutrition
35	变换	變換	*biànhuàn*	v.	vary, alternate
36	起初		*qǐchū*	adv.	at first, in the beginning
37	怀疑	懷	*huáiyí*	v.	doubt, suspect, distrust
38	尝试	嘗試	*chángshì*	v.	attempt, try
39	果然		*guǒrán*	conj.	really, indeed, as expected
40	专门	專門	*zhuānmén*	adj.	special, specialized
41	创	創	*chuàng*	v.	begin, initiate, establish
42	知名		*zhīmíng*	adj.	well-known, famous
43	突破		*tūpò*	v.	break through

课文

第一读：掌握课文大意

Skim the reading; then select the option below that best captures its main idea.

a 大学生何英自主创业的经过
b 大学生在快餐店打工的故事
c 大学生与快餐店

第二读：细节和理解

Read the text again carefully and answer the following questions.

1 何英为什么去快餐店打工？

_____

_____

2 何英刚在快餐店上班时感觉怎么样，为什么？

_____

_____

3 是什么事情让何英有了自己创业的想法？

_____

_____

4 何英为创业作了一些什么准备？

_____

_____

5 何英为什么选春节时期开始她的业务？

_____

_____

6 春节过后，何英是怎样对付快餐业激烈竞争的？

_____

_____

7 怎么证明何英创业成功了？

_____

_____

8 何英创业成功的原因是什么？她的做法跟别人有什么不同？

_____

_____

大学生与快餐中转站

　　从大四开始，何英就开始找工作，没想到却到处碰壁。毕业几个月以后，她仍然在寻找工作机会。直到有一天，一家快餐店的老板看中了她的简历，给了她肯定的答复。

　　终于有工作了，可她刚上班时却很不好意思。难道读了四年大学，就是为了有一天在快餐店打工吗？作为大学毕业生，自己的价值在哪里呢？因此，每次店里进来一个人，她就脸红心跳，恐怕是熟人。几个星期之后，才慢慢适应过来。

　　不久，老板要何英给写字楼的白领们送餐。刚到第一家公司，就听见他们说："你们店做的饭菜太没特色，再不改进，我们就换别的店了。"送了餐出来，何英看到另一家快餐店的送餐女孩正在流泪，原来她也被客户责备了。那个女孩说："客户对饭菜不满意，就怪我们。可我每次把客户的意见告诉老板，他都不理，还说白领要求太高，以后不给他们送餐了。"

　　女孩的话使何英忽然想到，有的快餐店认为白领们要求高而放弃给他们送餐的业务，我为什么不把这笔业务接过来呢？从此，每次送餐时，何英都会详细记下客户的电话和用餐要求。春节前，何英已经收集好一批客户信息，并开始对快餐市场进行调查。她找到当地各种风味的快餐店，从东北菜到四川菜，从南方小吃到北方面食，然后记下他们的店名、电话、快餐风格和价位。几天之后，她想出一个"快餐中转站"的计划：按照写字楼白领们的要求，从各家快餐店订购不同风味快餐，然后提供送餐服务，从中赚取差价。

1. 记下客户的电话和用餐要求
2. 对快餐市场进行调查
3. 按照客户的要求订购不同风味的快餐
4. 提供送餐服务，从中赚取差价

她租了一间20平方米的小房间作办公室，请了两个送餐工，还作了三套送餐制服。接下来，何英开始给各个写字楼打电话联系业务。因为那时正是春节期间，很多快餐店放假，所以她很快就拿到了100多份订单，其中有些是她的老客户。因为事先做过调查，何英马上根据订单要求，找到了一家合适的快餐店，那家老板一听何英要50份快餐，立刻答应给她优惠价。然后，她又去另外一家饭店，订了50份特色菜。等两家饭菜都送到了，何英就和聘请的两名员工一起去送餐。那天，除去各种费用，何英赚了150元钱。第二天，她多订了50份，很快又送完了。

春节过后，快餐店的竞争一天比一天激烈，何英的订单没有以前那么多了。她就亲自上门推销，把自己的快餐菜单拿给客户看，还保证说："你们想吃什么菜，我都可以满足。送餐及时，保证营养，还能常常变换口味！"不少公司起初抱着怀疑的态度订餐，但尝试之后，觉得果然不错，就都不去其他餐馆了。一个月下来，何英外送盒饭3600多份，利润达到4000多元。

第二个月，何英又多聘了两名员工，这样自己就能专门去各家餐馆和公司联系订餐及送餐业务了。同时，她还不断想出各种方法改进服务。一方面，她寻找到更多各具风味、干净又便宜的小饭馆，让快餐店菜单日益丰富，白领们有更多选择；另一方面，她到各公司发放调查问卷，统计白领最爱吃的饭菜，然后自己设计新菜单，交给饭馆去做。她还建了一个网站，客人们可以在网站上选菜、订餐、评论服务、提意见或建议。

慢慢地，她的快餐服务创出了知名度。一年后，何英每月收入几万元；三年后，年利润突破100万元，她的"快餐中转站"也升级为餐饮公司。◆

大學生與快餐中轉站

從大四開始，何英就開始找工作，沒想到卻到處碰壁。畢業幾個月以後，她仍然在尋找工作機會。直到有一天，一家快餐店的老闆看中了她的簡歷，給了她肯定的答復。

終於有工作了，可她剛上班時卻很不好意思。難道讀了四年大學，就是為了有一天在快餐店打工嗎？作為大學畢業生，自己的價值在哪裡呢？因此，每次店裡進來一個人，她就臉紅心跳，恐怕是熟人。幾個星期之後，才慢慢適應過來。

不久，老闆要何英給寫字樓的白領們送餐。剛到第一家公司，就聽見他們說："你們店做的飯菜太沒特色，再不改進，我們就換別的店了。"送了餐出來，何英看到另一家快餐店的送餐女孩正在流淚，原來她也被客戶責備了。那個女孩說："客戶對飯菜不滿意，就怪我們。可我每次把客戶的意見告訴老闆，他都不理，還說白領要求太高，以後不給他們送餐了。"

女孩的話使何英忽然想到，有的快餐店認為白領們要求高而放棄給他們送餐的業務，我為什麼不把這筆業務接過來呢？從此，每次送餐時，何英都會詳細記下客戶的電話和用餐要求。春節前，何英已經收集好一批客戶信息，並開始對快餐市場進行調查。她找到當地各種風味的快餐店，從東北菜到四川菜，從南方小吃到北方麵食，然後記下他們的店名、電話、快餐風格和價位。幾天之後，她想出一個

"快餐中轉站"的計劃：按照寫字樓白領們的要求，從各家快餐店訂購不同風味快餐，然後提供送餐服務，從中賺取差價。

她租了一間20平方米的小房間作辦公室，請了兩個送餐工，還作了三套送餐制服。接下來，何英開始給各個寫字樓打電話聯系業務。因為那時正是春節期間，很多快餐店放假，所以她很快就拿到了100多份訂單，其中有些是她的老客戶。因為事先做過調查，何英馬上根據訂單要求，找到了一家合適的快餐店，那家老闆一聽何英要50份快餐，立刻答應給她優惠價。然後，她又去另外一家飯店，訂了50份特色菜。等兩家飯菜都送到了，何英就和聘請的兩名員工一起去送餐。那天，除去各種費用，何英賺了150元錢。第二天，她多訂了50份，很快又送完了。

春節過後，快餐店的競爭一天比一天激烈，何英的訂單沒有以前那麼多了。她就親自上門推銷，把自己的快餐菜單拿給客戶看，還保証說："你們想吃什麼菜，我都可以滿足。送餐及時，保証營養，還能常常變換口味！"不少公司起初抱著懷疑的態度訂餐，但嘗試之後，覺得果然不錯，就都不去其他餐館了。一個月下來，何英外送盒飯3600多份，利潤達到4000多元。

第二個月，何英又多聘了兩名員工，這樣自己就能專門去各家餐館和公司聯系訂餐及送餐業務了。同時，她還不斷想出各種方法改進服務。 一方面，她尋找到更多各具風味、乾淨又便宜的小飯館，讓快餐店菜單日益豐富，白領們有更多選擇；另一方面，她到各公司發放調查問卷，統計白領最愛吃的飯菜，然後自己設計新菜單，交給飯館去做。她還建了一個網站，客人們可以在網站上選菜、訂餐、評論服務、提意見或建議。

慢慢地，她的快餐服務創出了知名度。一年後，何英每月收入幾萬元；三年後，年利潤突破100萬元，她的"快餐中轉站"也升級為餐飲公司。◆

A 时序关联词 Temporal Connectives

This lesson features a narrative about a young entrepreneur establishing and developing her career. In a narrative, the content is usually arranged in chronological order, which can be indicated by time words (e.g., 1999年, 前天), prepositional and adverbial phrases (e.g., 从昨天起, 刚刚, 后来), or time clauses (e.g. ……的时候, ……以前). (Please see more details in Grammar Point B: Temporal Connectives.)

A timeline with the key dates and times from this narrative is shown below. Reread the text and record the events that happened at those times in the spaces provided. Then use the timeline to retell the story to a classmate.

从大四开始，_____

_____

直到有一天，_____

_____

不久，_____

_____

从此，_____

_____

春节期间，_____

_____

春节过后，_____

_____

一个月下来，_____

_____

第二个月，_____

_____

一年后，_____

_____

三年后，_____

_____

B 阅读技巧练习：推论 Reading Skill Practice: Making Inferences

Choose the best inference from the three possible choices for each sentence. Underline the clue(s) that helped you choose.

1 难道读了四年大学，就是为了有一天在快餐店打工吗？

  a 读大学就是为了有一天在快餐店打工。

  b 读了四年大学，却在快餐店打工，实在是浪费人才。

  c 在快餐店打工不必读四年大学，三年就够了。

2 每次店里进来一个人，她就脸红心跳，恐怕是熟人。

  a 她一看见熟人就兴奋，因为她终于有工作了。

  b 她一看见熟人就脸红，因为她是一个胆小的人。

  c 她一看见熟人就害怕，因为她的这个工作太差了。

3 她租了一间20平米的房作办公室，请了
   两个送餐工，还做了三套送餐制服。

   a 她租了办公室，请了送餐工，自己
      就不必去送餐了。

   b 她租了办公室，请了送餐工，自己
      还打算去送餐。

   c 她租了办公室，请了送餐工，可是
      多做了一套送餐制服。

4 春节过后，快餐店的竞争一天比一天
   激烈。

   a 这是因为人们吃得很多。

   b 这是因为快餐店都越做越好。

   c 这是因为放假的快餐店又开业了。

5 三年后，年利润突破100万元，她的
   "快餐中转站"也升级为餐饮公司。

   a 三年后，她的公司大大发展了。

   b 三年后，她的公司平均每年赚了
      30多万元。

   c 三年后，她转到了另一个餐饮公司。

词汇与句型

A 优惠 favor, discount (price)

1 所有商品，七折优惠。

All goods are 30% off.

In Chinese, a discount is advertised as the amount the customer pays (in this case, 70%). In North America, this is advertised as the amount taken off the price (in this case, 30%). These are actually just different ways of expressing the same idea.

2 中国的投资政策为外国投资者提供了特别的优惠。

China's investment policy provides preferential treatment to foreign investors.

3 我们饭店提供比其他饭店更优惠的价格。

Our hotel offers more favorable prices than others.

Useful derived phrases:

优惠价	special price
优惠券	coupon
优惠政策	preferential policy
优惠条件	favorable terms

B 知名度 popularity, fame

1 张教授在古典文学领域有很高的知名度。

Professor Zhang enjoys a high reputation in the field of classical literature.

2 这个电视广告大大提高了我们企业的知名度。

This TV advertisement greatly boosted our corporation's popularity.

3 经过多年努力，这位导演终于在电影界创下知名度。

After years of effort, this director finally established a reputation in the film industry.

Useful derived phrases:

知名学者	well-known scholar
知名人士（人物）	famous person (figure)
知名画家	well-known artist
知名作家	well-known writer
知名品牌	famous brand
满意度	(level of) satisfaction
自由度	(degree of) freedom

C 亲自 (亲眼／亲耳／亲手／亲口)
personally, in person

1 厨师生病了，今天没来工作，餐馆老板只好亲自下厨做饭。

The chef was sick and didn't come to work today. The restaurant owner had to cook in the kitchen himself.

2 小何没走，我昨天亲眼看见他在学校门口的快餐店打工。

Xiao He didn't leave. Yesterday I saw him working in the fast-food restaurant by the school gate with my own eyes.

3 相信我，我亲耳听到他要去银行上班的消息。

Trust me. I heard the news with my own ears that he is going to work at a bank.

4 这封信非常重要，你一定要亲手交给他。

This is a very important letter. You must deliver it to him in person.

5 这个消息是他亲口告诉我的。

He told me this news himself.

D 不理
pay no attention to, ignore, refuse to acknowledge

1 我跟他打招呼，可是他<u>不理</u>我。

I said hello to him, but he ignored me.

2 顾客已经向服务台提了几次意见，可是他们根本<u>不理</u>。

The customers have already made several complaints to the people at the front desk, who didn't pay any attention at all.

3 他<u>不理</u>我的劝告，坚持按自己的方法做。

He totally ignored my advice, and adhered to his own way (of doing things).

E 突破
breach, break through; breakthrough

1 三年下来，何英的快餐中转站营业利润<u>突破</u>了100万元。

After three years, He Ying's profit from the fast-food service station topped one million yuan.

2 这是电脑技术史上的一次重大<u>突破</u>。

This is a significant breakthrough in the history of computer technology.

3 他们最近在医学研究方面取得<u>突破</u>性进展。

They have made breakthrough progress in the field of medical research recently.

F 没想到
didn't expect that…, little does one think

1 我<u>没想到</u>何英毕业后找了一份送快餐的工作。

I didn't expect that He Ying would find a fast-food delivery job after graduation.

2 谁都<u>没想到</u>黄义辞掉了企业的工作，然后办了一个网上废品回收公司。

No one would have expected Huang Yi to resign from his corporate job and start an online waste recycling company.

3 <u>没想到</u>有这么多大学毕业生参加这次人才交流会。

Nobody expected so many college graduates would attend this career fair.

G 果然
(just) as expected

1 天气预报说今天下午有雨，<u>果然</u>，吃过午饭就下起雨来了。

The weather forecast said that it would rain this afternoon. As expected, it started to rain right after lunch.

2 教练对那名新队员很有信心，<u>果然</u>，他在今天的篮球比赛中表现出色。

The coach has a lot of confidence in the new player. Sure enough, he performed very well in today's basketball game.

3 他说过要给我买件生日礼物，今天<u>果然</u>给我买了一本书。

He promised to buy me a birthday present. He did indeed buy me a book today.

H 因此
so, therefore, for this reason

1 客户对饭菜不满意，<u>因此</u>取消了跟这家餐馆订餐的业务。

The customers were dissatisfied with the food, so they canceled their order from this restaurant.

2 有人喜欢广东菜，有人喜欢东北菜，<u>因此</u>我们从不同的餐馆订餐。

Some people like Cantonese food, but others like Northeastern food, so we ordered dishes from different restaurants.

3 他工作很勤奋，<u>因此</u>很快被老板提升了。

He works very diligently. That's why he has been promoted by the boss.

因此 and 所以 are both connectives linking clauses of cause-result relationships. They are usually interchangeable. For example, in the previous sentences (1-3) with 因此, 所以 can also be used. However, they differ in following ways:

因此 is more formal than 所以. It is rarely used in oral communication.

4 我昨天生病了，<u>所以</u>没去你们家帮忙。
对不起啊！ （⊗ 因此）

所以 is often used together with 因为 (e.g., 因为……，
所以……), while 因此 seldom goes with 因为.

5 因为他昨天生病了，<u>所以</u>我替他上了
一天班。 （⊗ 因此）

For emphatic effect, the clause introduced by 所以 (the result) can occur before the clause introduced by 因为, which is usually realized as "之所以……，是因为……." But 因此 cannot be used in this way.

6 她<u>之所以</u>不敢见客人，是因为怕碰见
熟人。 （⊗ 因此）

I 从此 (from + this [time]) since then; from now on

1 何英送的午餐很不错，<u>从此</u>同事们就不
去其他餐馆了。

The lunch boxes delivered by He Ying were very good. Since then, my colleagues stopped going to other restaurants.

2 这是爸爸给我的最后一笔生活费，
<u>从此</u>，我就要自己打工赚钱了。

This is the last installment of financial support from my father. From now on, I have to earn money through my own work.

3 生孩子以后，姐姐辞了工作，<u>从此</u>成为
"全职母亲"。

After her baby was born, my elder sister resigned from her job and has been a "full-time mother" ever since.

J 一天比一天 more and more; day by day
(cf. 一年比一年)

1 春天来了，天气<u>一天比一天</u>暖和。

Spring has come. It is getting warmer every day.

2 她来加拿大两个月了，<u>一天比一天</u>更
适应这里的生活方式。

She has been in Canada for two months. She is getting more and more used to the lifestyle here.

3 地球的气温<u>一年比一年</u>高，就是因为
人类不重视保护环境。

The Earth is getting warmer year by year as a result of humanity's neglect of the environment.

K 起初 at first, in the beginning

1 不少公司<u>起初</u>抱着怀疑的态度订餐，
但尝试之后，觉得果然不错，就都不
去其他餐馆了。

In the beginning, some companies' staff ordered the food with a skeptical attitude. But after trying it, they found the food was indeed excellent, and haven't ordered from any other restaurant since then.

2 <u>起初</u>，他认为自己找工作太难了，
但后来又觉得这实际上是一种自由。

At first, he considered it too difficult to have to find a job himself; but later on, he realized that looking for a job was actually a kind of freedom.

3 我们<u>起初</u>有十五名员工，后来公司业务
扩大，老板又聘请了五名。

We had fifteen employees in the beginning. Later, the company's business expanded, so the boss hired five more.

L 从中 (from which) vs.
其中 (of which; among which)

1 学校推荐了五位学生，我们要<u>从中</u>选一位参加全国演讲比赛。

The school recommended five students, out of whom we will select one for the national speech contest.

2 虽然第一场比赛失败了，但是我们<u>从中</u>学到很多宝贵经验。

Although we lost the first game, we did learn valuable lessons from it.

3 我们中文班一共有20位学生，<u>其中</u>12位男生，8位女生。

In our Chinese class there are twenty students, of whom twelve are male and eight are female.

4 这家餐馆有很多好吃的菜，<u>其中</u>我最喜欢的是芥兰牛肉。

This restaurant offers a lot of delicious dishes, among which beef with broccoli is my favorite.

A 中文构词法简介 (二)
Introduction to Chinese word formation (II)

A1 Major types of (bi-syllabic) compounding

As discussed in Lesson 6, compounding is the most productive mechanism to create new words. The number of combinations is almost unlimited, and the ways to make them are very flexible. The table below illustrates major types of (bisyllabic) compounding:

	Combination	Example 1	Example 2	Example 3	Result
1	N + N	盒饭 box + meal boxed meal	菜单 dish + list menu	价值 price + worth value	N
2	A + N	白领 white + collar white-collar	快餐 fast + meal fast food	简历 brief + history résumé	N
3	V + N	升级 raise + level upgrade, promote	开车 operate + vehicle drive	怀疑 have + suspicion suspect	V/N
4	N + V	日出 sun + out sunrise	地震 earth + quake earthquake	心跳 heart + jump heartbeat	N/V
5	N + A	脸红 face + red blush	年轻 year + light young	心狠 heart + cruel cruel	A
6	V + V	答复 answer + reply reply	变换 change + change change	放弃 release + abandon abandon, give up	V/N
7	V + A	提高 lift + high raise	推广 push + broad popularize	突破 dash + broken breakthrough	V/N
8	A + V	好看 good + look good-looking	新建 new + build newly built	难受 hard + endure uncomfortable	A
9	A + A	详细 detail + fine detailed	满足 full + ample satisfied	干净 dry + clean clean	A

Note: The part of speech categorization of the resulting compounds is only for general information. There are exceptions in every category.

Method	Type	Example Words				
Reduplication	N	姐姐	妹妹	太太	星星	
	V	看看	想想	休息休息	讨论讨论	
	Adj.	高高的	瘦瘦的	漂漂亮亮的		
Prefix (very few)	老	老虎	老乡	老外	老师	老板 老百姓
	第	第一	第二	第三		
	阿	阿姨	阿妹	阿哥	阿乡	
Suffix (very few)	子	刀子	胖子	桌子	椅子	
	头	石头	苦头	木头	日头	
	儿	花儿	马儿	官儿	鸟儿	玩儿
	化	西化	现代化	自动化		
Loan Words (外来词)	音译	沙发 sofa	咖啡 coffee	麦当劳 McDonald's		
	意译	白领 white-collar	计算机／电脑 computer			
	音意译	酒吧 bar	可口可乐 Coca-Cola	因特网 Internet		

Understanding how Chinese words are constructed and used is critical for a full understanding of how the Chinese language operates. Through studying and analyzing rules of Chinese word formation, Chinese learners can enlarge their vocabulary, enhance meaningful memorization, and ensure appropriate usage. For example, a compound formed by "V + N" has the syntactic relationship verb + object (e.g., 结婚, 见面, 谈话), so it cannot take another noun as its object. Knowledge like this can help learners avoid common mistakes such as ⊗"结婚我的朋友," ⊗"见面我的老师," and ⊗"谈话他."

B 时序关联词 Temporal connectives

Discourse connectives (or linking words) are used to link an author's ideas, sentences, and paragraphs, and denote the relationships between them (e.g., contrasting, conditional, causal, temporal, sequential, etc.). Syntactically, they are like conjunctions or adverbial phrases.

In a narrative, the temporal connectives are the main linking devices to arrange ideas and events in time or order. In some narratives, chronological order is strictly followed. Events are listed or discussed exactly in the order in which they occurred. However, there are also narratives that list events out of order for special purposes.

Commonly used temporal connectives are:

Time adverbs: 就、才、又、已经、曾经、马上、立刻、刚刚、正、后来、正在

Conjunctions: 首先、起先、起初、以前、以后、于是、然后、接着、跟着、从而

Prepositional phrases: 从……、自……、到……、随着……、当……

Temporal connectives function to sustain a continuous flow of content. Learning how to use them helps to facilitate construction and comprehension of a coherent text and make the relationships between sentences and paragraphs obvious.

C 反问句 Rhetorical questions

C1 难道……吗？ Could it be possible that...?
(showing strong surprise or disbelief)

1 他们公司的知名度非常高，<u>难道</u>你从来没听说过吗？

Their company is very famous. Are you sure you have never heard of it?

2 他们能够做到那样，我们<u>难道</u>就做不到吗？

If they could achieve so much, why can't we?

C2 为什么不……呢？ Why not...? (making suggestions, giving advice or reprimand)

1 既然那家饭馆饭菜可口、价格便宜，<u>为什么不</u>让他们每天来送餐呢？

Since that restaurant offers delicious food at good prices, why not let them deliver food to us every day?

2 如果那些西药没有效果，<u>为什么不</u>试一试中药呢？

If the Western medicine has no effect, why not try some Chinese medicine?

3 你知道明天有考试，<u>为什么不</u>把功课复习好再出去呢？

You know you have a test tomorrow; why didn't you finish reviewing your lessons before going out?

练习

A 语音

Write the following underlined Chinese characters in *pinyin*. Pay special attention to their different pronunciations in different contexts.

中<u>转</u>（　　）　　<u>转</u>动（　　）

看<u>中</u>（　　）　　<u>中</u>国（　　）

放<u>假</u>（　　）　　真<u>假</u>（　　）

<u>要</u>求（　　）　　重<u>要</u>（　　）

适<u>应</u>（　　）　　<u>应</u>该（　　）

她<u>的</u>（　　）　　<u>的</u>确（　　）

很<u>差</u>（　　）　　<u>差</u>别（　　）

开<u>会</u>（　　）　　<u>会</u>计（　　）

B 词汇与句型

B1 Match the following words on the left with the words appropriately associated with them on the right.

Group One
(Verb + Object)

1　进行　____机会

2　放弃　____调查

3　收集　____要求

4　创出　____员工

5　按照　____知名度

6　聘请　____信息

Group Two
(Adj. + Noun)

1　营养　____信息

2　特殊　____答复

3　优惠　____快餐

4　肯定　____客户

5　老　　____风味

6　详细　____价格

B2 选择填空 Choose the most appropriate words to fill in the blanks.

a　碰壁　　　　h　优惠

b　从此　　　　i　不理

c　起初　　　　j　突破

d　从中　　　　k　亲自

e　其中　　　　l　下来

f　知名度　　　m　亲眼

g　一天比一天　n　为什么不

1　他已经对你说过几次"对不起"了，你要再_____他，就太狠心了。

2　期末考试快到了，我们的学习压力_____大。

3　_____他一句中文都不会，可是现在他已经能用中文跟客户聊天了。

4　别人要你做什么你就做什么，_____自己用脑子想一想呢?

5　毕业以后他去了法国，_____我们就再也没见过面了。

6 经过几次＿＿＿＿＿＿＿之后，小叶不想再找工作了，她想自己开个网络花店。

7 如果你们公司一次订货超过100万，我们可以提供特别的＿＿＿＿＿＿＿价。

8 几年＿＿＿＿＿＿＿，他的＿＿＿＿＿＿＿越来越高，去年收入＿＿＿＿＿＿＿了两百万。

9 这件事情太奇怪了，我要不是＿＿＿＿＿＿看见，也绝不会相信的。

10 这么点儿小事就不必你＿＿＿＿＿＿＿来了。

11 我们学校共有7000个学生，＿＿＿＿＿＿＿15%是留学生。

12 王先生专为海外华人在北京买房，第一年就＿＿＿＿＿＿＿获利几十万。

B3 完成句子

1 ＿＿＿＿＿＿＿＿＿＿＿＿＿＿＿＿＿＿，

所以我很了解他。

2 ＿＿＿＿＿＿＿＿＿＿＿＿＿＿＿＿＿＿，

没想到自己创业也不容易。

3 ＿＿＿＿＿＿＿＿＿＿＿＿＿＿＿＿＿＿，

第二天他果然来了。

4 ＿＿＿＿＿＿＿＿＿＿＿＿＿＿＿＿＿＿，

为什么不早来问我呢？

5 ＿＿＿＿＿＿＿＿＿＿＿＿＿＿＿＿＿＿，

难道你就永远靠父母生活吗？

C 语法

C1 Match the Chinese loan words with their English originals, and write down the way they are translated: M (meaning translation), S (sound translation), or M+S (combination of meaning and sound). (The first one has been done for you.)

Chinese	Match	Translation	English
奥巴马	(e)	S	a (fashion) model
星巴克	( )		b e-mail
视窗	( )		c Olympic
奥林匹克	( )		d Windows
幽默	( )		e Obama
浪漫	( )		f Starbucks
华尔街	( )		g humor
啤酒	( )		h romantic
高尔夫球	( )		i X-ray
电邮	( )		j beer
软件	( )		k golf
模特儿	( )		l software
阿司匹林	( )		m aspirin
爱克斯光	( )		n Ikea
宜家	( )		o Wall Street

C2 The story in this lesson is easy to follow because the episodes are clearly marked by temporal connectives. Review the following excerpts from the lesson and mark the temporal connectives in the text. Then determine what functions these connectives play (time, frequency, sequence).

1 从大四开始，何英就开始找工作，没想到却到处碰壁。毕业以后，她仍然在寻找机会。直到有一天，一家快餐店老板看中了她的简历，给了她肯定答复。

2 不久，老板要何英给写字楼送餐。刚到第一家公司，就听见他们说……

3 从此，每次送餐时，何英都会详细记下客户的电话和用餐要求。春节前，何英已经收集好了一批客户信息，并开始对快餐市场进行调查。她找到当地各种风味的快餐店，从东北菜到四川菜，从南方小吃到北方面食，然后记下他们的店名、电话、快餐风格和价位。几天之后，她想出一个"快餐中转站"的计划。

C3 这是一组有关职业的名词。请将它们按最后一个字（差不多等于后缀）分类。并尽量加上你能找到的其他同类名词。

The following nouns all denote jobs. Group them by their ending characters (which function almost like suffixes and can create many different words). Add as many other jobs as you can find to each category.

会计师　服务员　教师
演员　　理发师　军人
技术员　运动员　摄影师
建筑师　厨师　　艺术家
画家　　制片人　清洁工
小工　　水管工　民工

飞行员　电工　　企业家
修理工　渔人　　律师
作家　　工程师　救生员
船员　　录音师　矿工
气象员　音乐家　机修工
官员　　店员　　建筑工
设计师　外交家　职员
医师　　加油工　工人
推销员　艺人　　科学家
数学家　诗人　　售货员

___师 (master)	___员 (member)	___家 (expert)	___工 (worker)	___人 (person)

C4 选词填空 Fill in each blank with an appropriate metaphorical phrase from the options listed below.

a 人山人海　　d 天之骄子

b 碰壁　　　　e 铁饭碗

c 发火

1 老林说他愿意把房子优惠卖给我，可是我的钱不够，去找银行贷款也是到处_____，只好放弃这个机会。

2 我理想的工作是那种有挑战性，有发展前途的工作。政府部门的_____对我没有什么吸引力。

3 我的老板脾气不好，特别容易_____。我们都很怕他。

4 每年新年除夕，纽约 (New York) 的时代广场上_____，特别热闹。

5 现在的大学生已经不再是_____了，因为能上大学的人一年比一年多了。

D 综合

D1 短文填空

a 终于　　　　h 选择

b 起初　　　　i 适合

c 知名度　　　j 竞争

d 因此　　　　k 听从

e 为什么不　　l 怀疑

f 工作　　　　m 专业

g 稳定

我朋友的择业观

　　我朋友是个美籍华人。他跟孩子讨论_____专业时，常会问下面几个问题：第一，你是否喜欢这一行？一个人的爱好与_____的区别是：爱好是自己花钱去做，而且特别想做。比方说看电影，打高尔夫球；而工作是别人付钱让我去做，比方说每天上班。如果工作与爱好是同一件事，_____一边高高兴兴地做事，一边开开心心地赚钱呢？

　　第二，你是不是_____做这一行？大家当然都喜欢做自己爱好的事情，但问题是，你有没有能力在这一行发展？同样是打高尔夫球，有人挣钱，有人花钱；_____，选择_____不仅要考虑自己的爱好，更要了解自己的客观条件。

　　第三，你是否可以靠这一行生存？有的行业，_____太激烈，成功的机会太少。比方说，很多学音乐，绘画，表演的人，辛苦了几十年，结果不但创不出_____，甚至连饭都可能吃不上。而学工程管理，医疗教育等专业的人，因为市场需求量大，比较容易找到_____的工作。

　　我朋友说，_____，孩子常常抱着_____的态度，以为家长要强求他们_____大人安排。但通过几次讨论之后，他们_____明白了家长的一片好意，当然，做最后选择的还是孩子。

D2 按照这篇文章的意思，下面的说法对不对？(T/F)

1 _____ 一个人的爱好和他的工作可以是一样的。

2 _____ 爱好和工作的区别是，一个花钱，一个挣钱。

3 _____ 按照我朋友的说法，找工作不能只看自己喜不喜欢。

4 _____ 我朋友不希望他的孩子找竞争性太强的工作。

5 _____ 学音乐，绘画的人得辛苦几十年才能成功。

6 _____ 我朋友不会同意他的孩子当老师。

7 _____ 我朋友觉得打高尔夫球的工作最好，又能挣钱，又能花钱。

8 _____ 我朋友的择业观比较实际 (practical)。

D3 英译汉

1 You interviewed twenty applicants today. Don't tell me that you haven't found a single one who can meet our requirements.

_____

_____

_____

2 There are numerous enterprises that offer a high salary and good benefits in China now. Therefore, many Chinese students studying overseas are going back to work after finishing their studies.

_____

_____

_____

3 At first he didn't believe that He Ying could become so well-known in the fast-food business. But after he watched the news story about her success, he decided to give up his job at the government office and start his own business too.

_____

_____

_____

4 Even though the salesman was rebuffed everywhere, he didn't give up. He finally achieved the sales target successfully.

_____

_____

5 The book that she ordered two months ago has not yet arrived. Could there be a problem?

_____

_____

6 As winter comes, it's getting colder day by day.

_____

7 During the period from 1998 to 2002, the Yuan Da (远大) Real Estate Development Company built many good-quality but moderate-cost houses for low-income families. From then on it has been a highly successful company.

_____

_____

8 The dishes in that restaurant are truly, as you said, really good.

_____

9 He learns a Chinese idiom every day. After one year, he has memorized more than three hundred idioms. (Don't use 以后)

_____

_____

短文
求职难，女生求职难上加难

广州某高校大四女生小玲，最近到一家IT企业面试后，收到招聘负责人的明确答复："你的条件很不错，但是单位领导要求只招男生。"小玲成绩优秀，还曾经花了近万元参加校外Java高级软件(ruǎnjiàn)(software)工程师培训班，并获得资格证书。在她班上，不少成绩不如她的男生早已找到满意的工作，而她却在就业上不断碰壁。

最近，西南大学组织了一次女大学生就业情况调查。调查结果显示，在就业过程中，女大学生面临的最大困难是性别歧视(qíshì)(discrimination)。约70%的女大学生认为，在求职时存在男女不平等现象，有的女博士只能与男硕士同等录用，而女硕士只能与男本科生同等录用。一些单位甚至向女生明确提出"两年内不能结婚生子"的条件，虽然这一要求并不会出现在聘用合同(hétong)(contract)上。

不过，用人单位也有他们的难处。不少企业表示，女生参加工作以后，过不了多久就要面临怀孕(huáiyùn)(pregnancy)、生育等一系列问题。在女员工生育期间，公司不仅要照常付她的工资，而且还得另外聘请一名工作人员来替她工作。而当女员工回来工作时，公司又得解决新聘员工的工作问题。他们说："聘用男性员工，要少很多麻烦。"

据了解，女员工的生育问题，以及她们不便出<u>差</u> (chūchāi) (go on a business trip)、不能陪老板出去喝酒等限制，都可能造成招聘中的重男轻女现象。当前就业中的性别歧视，不仅影响了女大学生学习、生活的积极性，也使越来越多的女学生接受"学得好不如<u>嫁</u> (jià) (marry) 得好"的观念。

E1 根据短文内容，选择最佳答案回答问题

1 小玲在就业上不断碰壁，是因为：

　a 她的成绩不好。

　b 她虽然参加了软件工程师培训班，却没能获得资格证书。

　c 她对工资的要求太高。

　d 她是女生。

2 根据西南大学的调查，在就业时，

　a 70% 的女大学生找不到工作。

　b 女大学生面临的最大困难是男女不平等现象。

　c 女硕士往往和男博士同等录用。

　d 有些单位向女生提出"三年内不能结婚生子"的条件。

3 以下哪项被认为是女员工的限制？

　a 怀孕生育

　b 不便出差

　c 不能陪老板出去喝酒

　d 以上都是

4 以下哪项不符合短文内容？

　a 就业中的男女不平等现象影响了女大学生的生活态度。

　b 就业中的男女不平等现象影响了女大学生的婚姻观念。

　c 就业中的男女不平等现象影响了女大学生的身体健康。

　d 就业中的男女不平等现象影响了女大学生的学习积极性。

5 以下哪项最好地说明了这篇短文的主题？

　a 学得好不如嫁得好。

　b 聘用男性员工，要少很多麻烦。

　c 在就业过程中，女大学生面临的最大困难是性别歧视。

　d 就业中的性别歧视影响了女大学生学习和生活的积极性。

F 口语

F1 请完成右边的职业排行表并与同学一起讨论

1 比较下列职业，谈谈它们各有什么优缺点（优点打√，缺点打×）

2 哪个职业是你最理想的？ 为什么？请按你的想法把它们排列起来。（最理想1—最不理想8，可以写在最下面的一行里）

3 跟同学比较一下你们的排行表，看有什么不一样。说说你们各自的理由。

F2 右边是中国2008年和2015年的十大最佳职业排行表。请跟同学讨论中国职场在这段时间内发生了什么变化，并解释导致这些变化的可能原因。

F3 请上网查询中国最近的十大最佳职业排行表。跟同学讨论中国职场在最近这段时间内又发生了什么变化，并解释导致这些变化的可能原因。

	会计师	警察	医生	大学教授	电脑专家	水管工	电影演员	餐馆服务员
收入高								
学历要求低								
工作环境好								
不辛苦								
不危险								
社会地位高								
有创造性								
稳定								
自由								
有挑战性								
职业排行								

中国2008年最佳职业

1　销售 Marketing
2　IT工程师 IT Engineer
3　建筑设计师 Architect
4　高级技师 Senior Technician
5　公务员 Government Official
6　职业经理人 Career Manager
7　人力资源经理 Human Resources Manager
8　市场研究分析师 Market Research Analyst
9　财务顾问 Financial Advisor
10　律师 Lawyer

中国2015年最佳职业

1　软件工程师 Software Engineer
2　设计师 Designer
3　机械工程师 Mechanical Engineer
4　销售总监 Marketing Director
5　教师 Teacher
6　采购经理 Purchasing Manager
7　理财／投资顾问 Financial/Investment Advisor
8　网络市场营销 Online Marketing
9　店长／楼面经理 Store Manager
10　财务经理 Financial Manager

写一个名人的（创业）故事（400-500字）

Write a narrative of a famous person's life, focusing especially on stories about the beginning of his or her career. Organize paragraphs in chronological order, including important dates, times, and events. Here are some people you may want to write about (you may also come up with someone on your own):

张艺谋 (Zhang Yimou), 马云 (Jack Ma), 姚明 (Yao Ming), 孙中山 (Sun Yat-sen), 奥巴马 (Barack Obama), 希拉莉·克林顿 (Hillary Clinton), 比尔·盖茨 (Bill Gates), 乔布斯 (Steve Jobs), 奥普拉·温弗瑞 (Oprah Winfrey), 昂山素季 (Aung San Suu Kyi)...

Helpful time expressions (from this lesson):

从 from
不久 before long
起初 at first, at the outset
期间 during
先……然后 first... then
过后 afterwards
前 before
（一年前，三天前）
(三年)下来
马上 immediately
直到 until, up to

之后（以后）after
刚 a very short time ago
正在 in the midst of
随着 along with
随后 soon afterwards
从此 from then on
后 after
（一年后, 三个月后）
事先 prior to
就 then
终于 finally

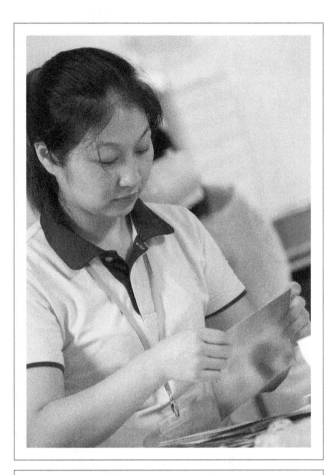

恋爱婚姻

- 你过情人节的时候，最想收到什么礼物？
- 情人节是属于谁的？老人和儿童也可以过情人节吗？
- 爱情的结果一定是婚姻吗？没有爱情的婚姻应该怎么办？
- 你知道哪些跟"爱情、婚姻"有关的词汇？

For thousands of years, the Chinese people lived according to strict moral and social codes. Under the constraints of traditional Confucian ethics, marriage was seen as a family affair, arranged by parents in accordance with social hierarchy, with the purpose of producing a male heir to carry on the family line. Love was never a factor for consideration. Changes began to take place at the turn of the twentieth century. But it is the Open Door Policy, which began in the late 1970s, and the thriving economy of the past few decades that have truly transformed the Chinese people's fundamental attitude and behavior toward love and marriage.

As in Lesson 2, the reading begins with a story that leads into a discussion of the subject of interest — in this case, China's changing values and norms regarding love and marriage.

8
第八课

生词

自学生词

Match each new word with its English translation by deducing the word's meaning from its characters.
(The first one is done for you.)

情人　　情人节(節)　　西洋　　巧克力　　心上人　　求爱(愛)　　表白

花店　　大多　　双(雙)方　　婚恋(戀)　　外力　　高于(於)　　再次

1 花店 ____ florist

2 ____ chocolate

3 ____ superior to, higher than

4 ____ marriage and courtship

5 ____ woo, court

6 ____ mostly

7 ____ outside or external force

8 ____ express or state clearly

9 ____ second time, once more

10 ____ the West, the Occident

11 ____ lover, sweetheart

12 ____ Valentine's Day

13 ____ both sides, two parties

14 ____ sweetheart, heart's desire

成语和惯用语

成语／惯用语	单字解释	意思
1 门当户对 *mén dāng hù duì* 他们的婚姻要由父母决定，讲究的是<u>门当户对</u>。	门(門) gate 当(當) equal 相当 户(戶) gate, family status 对(對) suit, match 对称	Be well-matched in social and economic status for marriage
2 传宗接代 *chuán zōng jiē dài* 婚姻的主要功能不再是为家族"<u>传宗接代</u>"。	传(傳) pass on 宗 ancestor, clan 接 connect 代 generation	Have a son to carry on the family name, continue the ancestral line
3 从一而终 *cóng yī ér zhōng* 中国老人也由以前的"<u>从一而终</u>"到现在愿意考虑再次结婚⋯⋯	从(從) follow 一 one (partner) 而 particle 终(終) end, die, death	Be faithful to one's husband (or be faithful to one's master)

	简体	繁体	拼音	词性	英文
1	束		shù	m.	bundle, bunch
2	玫瑰		méiguī	n.	rose
3	等候		děnghòu	v.	wait, await
4	浪漫		làngmàn	adj.	romantic
5	经典	經	jīngdiǎn	n./adj.	classics; classical
6	感动	動	gǎndòng	v.	move, touch (emotionally)
7	登陆	陸	dēnglù	v.o.	land, disembark
8	流传	傳	liúchuán	v.	circulate, spread
9	惊喜	驚	jīngxǐ	n.	pleasant surprise
10	讲究	講	jiǎngjiu	v.	pay attention to, strive for
11	情感		qínggǎn	n.	emotion, feeling
12	含蓄		hánxù	adj.	implicit, veiled, reserved
13	开放	開	kāifàng	adj.	open-minded
14	追求		zhuīqiú	v.	seek, pursue, court (a person)
15	主动	動	zhǔdòng	adj.	active, voluntary
16	封建		fēngjiàn	adj./n.	feudal; feudalism
17	娶		qǔ	v.	marry (a woman)
18	嫁		jià	v.	marry (a man)
19	穷人	窮	qióngrén	n.	poor people
20	离婚	離	líhūn	v.o.	divorce
21	即使		jíshǐ	conj.	even if, even though
22	牺牲	犧	xīshēng	v.	sacrifice
23	勇敢		yǒnggǎn	adj.	brave, courageous
24	家族		jiāzú	n.	clan, family
25	强调	強調	qiángdiào	v.	stress, emphasize
26	融洽		róngqià	adj.	harmonious
27	期望		qīwàng	v./n.	hope, expect; expectation
28	值		zhí	n.	value, worth
29	调和	調	tiáohé	v.	mediate, reconcile
30	矛盾		máodùn	n.	conflict, contradiction
31	凑合	湊	còuhe	v.	make do (with), passable, improvise
32	接近		jiējìn	v.	be close to, approximate

主要生词

第一读：掌握课文大意

Skim the reading; then select the option below that best captures its main idea.

a 现代中国年轻人喜欢过情人节

b 现代中国人恋爱、婚姻观念的变化

c 现代中国青年男女对恋爱和婚姻的看法

第二读：细节和理解

A Read the text again carefully and answer the following questions.

1 情人节"登陆"中国是什么意思？

_____

2 为什么中国年轻人这么快就接受了西方的情人节？

_____

_____

3 中国传统社会中，人们的恋爱婚姻受到哪些限制？

_____

_____

4 中国传统婚姻制度是什么时候开始改变的？最重要的改变是什么？

_____

_____

5 是什么情况大大地改变了中国人对恋爱和婚姻的观念？

_____

6 "门当户对、传宗接代、从一而终"是什么意思？

_____

_____

7 中国人现在对理想婚姻的看法跟以前有什么不一样？

_____

_____

B Choose the best inference from the three possible choices. Underline the clue(s) that helped you choose.

1 南京花店店主小林的话说明了什么？

a 以前中国女孩子在追求爱情方面不太主动。

b 不少中国女孩子喜欢买玫瑰花。

c 中国女孩子在追求爱情方面非常主动。

2 传统的中国家庭很"稳定"意思是：

a 夫妻感情很好。

b 离婚的家庭不多。

c 婚姻由父母决定。

3 "随着中国经济改革和对外开放带来的社会和思想进步，人们的婚恋观念也开放起来。"这句话说明：

a 婚恋观念的开放是人们思想进步的结果。

b 婚恋观念的开放带来了对外开放。

c 婚恋观念的开放带来了中国经济改革。

恋爱婚姻

2月14日是西方传统的情人节，王志文一大早就买了一束玫瑰花，等候在女友的楼下，然后两个人开始了浪漫的一天。"送玫瑰是表达爱情的一种经典方式，"王志文说，"在这个节日送玫瑰，表示了我对女朋友深深的爱，她也非常感动。"

情人节"登陆"中国只不过是最近几年的事情，而这个"西洋节"却已在年轻人中间迅速地流传开来。一束玫瑰或者一盒巧克力，往往能给心上人带来很大的惊喜，这对讲究含蓄的中国人来说，确实是一场情感世界的革命。大学生李云觉得，情人节是一年中最浪漫的一天。她说："在求爱的方式上，中国人含蓄，西方人开放。情人节给了年轻人一个非常好的表白的机会。"南京市一家花店，在情人节期间买进了几百束玫瑰花，几个小时内就全卖完了。店主小林说："买玫瑰花的大多是年轻人，而且有不少还是女孩子。"看来，中国女孩子在追求爱情上也主动起来了。

在求爱的方式上，中国人含蓄，西方人开放。情人节给了年轻人一个非常好的表白的机会。

中国人的恋爱、婚姻，在几千年的封建社会里，一直受到许多限制。青年男女不能自由恋爱，他们的婚姻要由父母决定，讲究的是门当户对。社会地位高的、有钱人家的儿子，要娶有钱人家的女儿。社会地位低的、穷人的女儿，只能嫁给穷人的儿子。结婚以前，男女双方不能见面，更不能说话。结婚以后，不管有没有感情都不能离婚。如果妻子死了，丈夫可以再结婚。

但是如果丈夫死了，妻子即使很年轻也不能再结婚。因此，在旧中国，家庭一直是非常"稳定"的，但是，这种稳定需要牺牲个人的感情。

从二十世纪中期开始，父母决定婚姻的情况有了根本的改变，青年人可以自由恋爱、自由结婚了，但是千百年流传下来的传统婚姻观念还存在。找对象时，还必须看对方的社会地位；结婚后，不幸福也不敢或不能离婚，怕别人笑话、看不起；老年人恋爱会受到子女和周围人的反对。不同的人仍然在用不同的方式压抑着自己的感情。

进入20世纪90年代以后，随着中国经济改革和对外开放带来的社会和思想进步，人们的婚恋观念也开放起来。他们再也不用压抑自己的感情，再也不必受外力的影响，而可以勇敢地追求爱情和幸福了。婚姻的主要功能不再是为家族"传宗接代"。人们追求的理想婚姻，更强调感情的融洽，更讲究家庭夫妻关系的平等。人们对婚姻的期望值也远远高于上一代人。如果婚后的现实与婚前的期望产生不可调和的矛盾，他们多数选择离婚，而不愿意继续凑合下去。婚姻观念的变化，不但表现在年轻一代身上，中国老人也由以前的"从一而终"到现在愿意考虑再次结婚，他们的爱情观也开始与年轻人相接近。◆

戀愛婚姻

　　2月14日是西方傳統的情人節，王志文一大早就買了一束玫瑰花，等候在女友的樓下，然後兩個人開始了浪漫的一天。"送玫瑰是表達愛情的一種經典方式，"王志文說，"在這個節日送玫瑰，表示了我對女朋友深深的愛，她也非常感動。"

　　情人節"登陸"中國只不過是最近幾年的事情，而這個"西洋節"卻已在年輕人中間迅速地流傳開來。一束玫瑰或者一盒巧克力，往往能給心上人帶來很大的驚喜，這對講究含蓄的中國人來說，確實是一場情感世界的革命。大學生李雲覺得，情人節是一年中最浪漫的一天。她說："在求愛的方式上，中國人含蓄，西方人開放。情人節給了年輕人一個非常好的表白的機會。"南京市一家花店，在情人節期間買進了幾百束玫瑰花，幾個小時內就全賣完了。店主小林說："買玫瑰花的大多是年輕人，而且有不少還是女孩子。"看來，中國女孩子在追求愛情上也主動起來了。

　　中國人的戀愛、婚姻，在幾千年的封建社會裡，一直受到許多限制。青年男女不能自由戀愛，他們的婚姻要由父母決定，講究的是門當戶對。社會地位高的、有錢人家的兒子，要娶有錢人家的女兒。社會地位低的、窮人的女兒，只能嫁給窮人的兒子。結婚以前，男女雙方不能見面，更不能說話。結婚以後，不管有沒有感情都不能離婚。如果妻子死了，丈夫可以再結婚。但是如果丈夫死了，妻子即使很年輕也不能再結婚。因此，在舊中國，家庭一直是非常"穩定"的，但是，這種穩定需要犧牲個人的感情。

從二十世紀中期開始，父母決定婚姻的情況有了根本的改變，青年人可以自由戀愛、自由結婚了，但是千百年流傳下來的傳統婚姻觀念還存在。找對象時，還必須看對方的社會地位；結婚後，不幸福也不敢或不能離婚，怕別人笑話、看不起；老年人戀愛會受到子女和周圍人的反對。不同的人仍然在用不同的方式壓抑著自己的感情。

進入20世紀90年代以後，隨著中國經濟改革和對外開放帶來的社會和思想進步，人們的婚戀觀念也開放起來。他們再也不用壓抑自己的感情，再也不必受外力的影響，而可以勇敢地追求愛情和幸福了。婚姻的主要功能不再是為家族"傳宗接代"。人們追求的理想婚姻，更強調感情的融洽，更講究家庭夫妻關係的平等。人們對婚姻的期望值也遠遠高於上一代人。如果婚後的現實與婚前的期望產生不可調和的矛盾，他們多數選擇離婚，而不願意繼續湊合下去。婚姻觀念的變化，不但表現在年輕一代身上，中國老人也由以前的"從一而終"到現在願意考慮再次結婚，他們的愛情觀也開始與年輕人相接近。◆

A 段落的主题句 The Topic Sentence of a Paragraph

In addition to grasping the general idea of an article, it is also important to be able to identify the topic sentence of a paragraph, which states its main idea. A paragraph may contain more than one important idea supported by details and facts. However, some paragraphs may have no stated topic sentence at all, but rather imply the main idea.

Being able to read a text and separate the most important ideas from less important supporting ideas is a useful reading skill. The second paragraph in this reading doesn't seem to have a stated topic sentence. Read Paragraph 2 again and write a topic sentence for it on your own.

Topic sentence for Paragraph 2:

_____

_____

B 支援主题的细节 Supporting Details

While the topic sentence is a general statement, all the other sentences in the paragraph are typically specific details, facts, statistics, or examples used to explain, describe, extend, or support this main-idea sentence.

Below is the topic sentence of Paragraph 3:

中国人的恋爱、婚姻，在几千年的封建社会里，一直受到限制。

Now read Paragraph 3 again and find the details that are used to support the topic sentence (note: you don't need to copy every word):

1 青年男女的恋爱

_____

2 他们的婚姻

_____

3 结婚以前

_____

4 结婚以后

_____

5 如果妻子死了

_____

6 如果丈夫死了

_____

C 阅读技巧练习 Reading Skill Practice

Write out the topic sentences of Paragraphs 4 and 5, and then list their supporting details.

Paragraph 4

Topic Sentence: _____

Supporting details:

1 _____

_____

2 _____

_____

3 _____

_____

Paragraph 5

Topic Sentence: _____

Supporting details:

1 _____

_____

2 _____

_____

3 _____

_____

词汇与句型

A 一大早 in the early morning

"大" can be used with time words as an adverb to add emphasis.

1 情人节这天，王志文一大早就买了
一束玫瑰花，等候在女友的楼下。

On Valentine's Day, Wang Zhiwen bought a bundle of roses
in the early morning and waited downstairs at his
girlfriend's apartment building.

2 什么？你想跟那个明星结婚？
真是大白天说梦话！

What? You want to marry that movie star?
You must be daydreaming!

3 按照春节的传统，大年夜应该全家一起
吃团年饭。大年初一就开始拜年了。

According to the tradition of Chinese New Year, the whole
family should have the reunion dinner together on New Year's
Eve; then on New Year's Day, people start to exchange New
Year's greetings.

B 讲究 (v.) be particular about, strive for

1 这对讲究含蓄的中国人来说，确实是
一场情感世界的革命。

To the Chinese people, who have always paid great attention
to restrained and reserved manners, this is indeed a revolution
in their emotional world.

2 在我父母家不必讲究礼节，
他们都是很随和的人。

Don't worry about formalities at my parents' place.
They are both easygoing.

3 王阿姨吃饭是很讲究的，她只吃少油，
少盐，无糖，无味精的有机食品。

Aunt Wang is quite particular about what she eats; it must be
organic food with little oil, little salt, no sugar, and no MSG.

C 追求 seek, pursue, court (someone)

1 虽然追求丽丽的人很多，但她至今
没有找到理想的男朋友。

Though Lily has many suitors, she hasn't found her
Mr. Right yet.

2 做生意不能只追求利润；树立良好的
信誉对长远利益更重要。

In business, one cannot exclusively seek profit. Rather, building
a good reputation is more important in the long run.

3 人的一生是为了什么？有人追求财富，
有人追求权力，有人追求爱情，有人
追求真理。你呢？

What is the purpose of life? Some people go for wealth;
some run after power; some pursue love; some seek truth.
How about you?

D 凑合 makeshift, make do, offhand, improvise

1 他们多数选择离婚，而不愿意继续
凑合下去。

The majority of them choose divorce, unwilling to go on
with the make-do marriage.

2 离电影开始没多长时间了，咱们凑合
吃点快餐吧。

Not much time left before the movie starts. Let's just get some
fast food to eat.

3 —电影好看吗？ — 还凑合。

– How was the movie? – Just so-so.

4 我忘带演讲稿了，看来只好现场
凑合着说了。

I left my lecture notes behind. Guess I'll have to improvise.

E 以往 vs. 以前

以往 and 以前 both indicate a time "before." They are sometimes interchangeable (see Sentence 1). However, 以前 can be used with another word or phrase to indicate "before a certain point of time" (e.g., 毕业前 before graduation, 一年前 a year ago), while 以往 cannot be used in this way. The table below shows their different collocations:

词语搭配
（以前 vs. 以往）

	以前	以往
一年～	✓	
毕业～	✓	
结婚～	✓	
上大学～	✓	
回国～	✓	
～的日子	✓	✓
比～好得多	✓	✓

1 中国女孩子在追求爱情上比以往任何
时候都要主动了。（"以前"也可以）

Chinese girls have become more active in pursuing love than ever before.

2 以往的事情已经过去了，不要再提了。
（"以前"也可以）

The past is past. Don't mention it again.

3 他们三个月以前才认识，现在已经
结婚了。（"以往"不可以）

They only got to know each other three months ago, but now they are already married.

F 表白 (v.) express, profess, vindicate, justify oneself

1 情人节给了年轻人一个非常好的<u>表白</u>
爱情的机会。

Valentine's Day provides young people with a good
opportunity to express their love.

2 我们看一个人，不是根据他的<u>表白</u>，
而是根据他的行动。

We don't judge a person by what he says but by what he does.

3 听了他深情的<u>表白</u>，丽丽不知道该
怎么办才好。

Hearing his affectionate confessions of love to her, Lily didn't
know what to do.

The common semantic property of 表白 and 表达 is 表
(to express), but 表白 places more emphasis on "clarify,
make clear." It's used more on occasions for (deep) feelings and
emotions, with human beings as its subjects. 表白 can be used
as a noun, but 表达 cannot.

4 这件礼物虽小，但<u>表达</u>了我们对你的
感谢。（⊗ 表白）

This is a little gift, but it's a token of our gratitude to you.

5 我们看一个人，不是根据他的<u>表白</u>，
而根据他的行动。（⊗ 表达）

We judge a person not by his words but by his actions.

G 再也不 not any more, not any longer

1 他们<u>再也不</u>用压抑自己的感情，<u>再也不</u>
必受外力的影响，而可以勇敢地追求爱
情和幸福了。

They don't have to constrain their feelings or be influenced by
external forces any more. They can now openly pursue their
true love and happiness.

2 我<u>再也</u>不喝这种烈酒了！

I will never drink this kind of strong liquor again!

3 自从发现他说谎 (shuōhuǎng) (lie) 以后，
她<u>再也</u>不相信他了。

Ever since she found out that he was lying to her, she never
trusted him again.

H 不再 no longer, no more

1 婚姻的功能<u>不再</u>是为家族"传宗接代"。

The function of marriage is no longer to bear children to carry
on the family name.

2 在就业方面，当今的流行语已<u>不再</u>是
"政府分配你做什么，你就做什么"，
而是"你选择什么"。

In terms of employment, today's popular saying is no longer
"do whatever the government assigns you to do," but "do what
you choose to do."

3 我<u>不再</u>开车上学了，而是每天骑自行车
上学，既健康又环保。

I no longer drive to school but bike there every day, which is
not only healthy but also friendly to the environment.

I 比较：看来，看起来，看样子，看上去

These phrases are like the English expressions "it looks like...," "it
seems that...," and "it appears..." They are used to make tentative
inferences or judgments on the basis of something/someone's
outer appearance. In some cases they are interchangeable, as in
Sentence 1:

1 天这么黑，<u>看来</u>要下雨。（天这么黑，
<u>看起来</u>／<u>看样子</u>／<u>看上去</u>要下雨。）

It's so dark now. It looks like it's going to rain.

2 今天的作业真多啊，<u>看来</u>（<u>看起来</u>／
<u>看样子</u>）今天晚上我又睡不成觉了。

There is so much homework to do today. Looks like I won't
get any sleep again.

3 从目前的业务<u>看来</u>，我们很可能要再聘
一位销售员。

   Judging from the present business situation, it seems that we probably need to hire another salesperson.

4 在小李<u>看来</u>，没有什么比找到一份理想
的工作更让他高兴的了。

   It seems to Xiao Li that there would be nothing more delightful than finding an ideal job.

The differences among these expressions are that 看来 can be used with prepositional phrases such as "从……看来" and "在……看来" (Sentences 2, 3, and 4), while the others cannot:

5 从目前的业务<u>看来</u>，我们很可能要再聘
一位销售员。（⊗看起来／⊗看样子／
⊗看上去）

看上去 is mainly used in situations when an inference is drawn only by objective visual observation. (Therefore, it is generally not used when the subject is a first person pronoun.)

6 <u>看上去</u>他还不到二十岁。（看起来／
看样子）

7 <u>看起来</u>王先生对美国人的婚恋观念非常
了解。（⊗看上去）

8 <u>看起来</u>／<u>看样子</u>今天晚上我又睡不成
觉了。（⊗看上去）

J 不管……都 no matter..., regardless...

This construction expresses: 1) the determination of the subject to take a certain action regardless of whatever event happens, 2) that a certain situation or condition remains unchanged despite any interference. 不管 is used to introduce the cited event or interference. The constituent following 不管 must be rendered in the form of a question, either as an "alternative question" or a "question word question," but not in the form of a regular "吗" question. In other words, the immediate constituent following 不管 must include one of these words: 谁, 什么, 怎么, 哪儿, 多么, or "VP 不／没 VP."

Furthermore, 不管 must be used in conjunction with 都 or 也 to indicate that there are no exceptions. Similar expressions are 无论……都…… and 不论……都…….

1 结婚以后，<u>不管</u>有没有感情<u>都</u>不能离婚。

   After getting married, they couldn't divorce no matter whether they loved each other or not.

2 我们公司聘人看能力，不看关系。<u>无论</u>
是谁，想进我们公司<u>都</u>得先经过考试。

   Our company employs personnel by ability, not relying on connections. Whoever wants to work in our company must first take a test.

3 <u>不论</u>别人怎么看不起她的工作，
她<u>还是</u>每天照样去快餐店上班。

   Regardless of how others look down on her job, she still goes to work at the fast food restaurant every day.

K 即使……也 even if..., still...

即使 is used in the first clause to express an extreme supposition (often a counterfactual condition). 也 in the second clause stresses that the action/result stated in this clause will not change regardless of the supposition. Similar expressions are 哪怕……也…… and 就是……也……, which are more colloquial in style.

1 如果丈夫死了，妻子<u>即使</u>很年轻<u>也</u>
不能再结婚。

   If the husband dies, the wife cannot remarry even if she is very young.

2 这是个大秘密。<u>哪怕</u>最好的朋友，
你<u>也</u>不能说。

   This is a big secret. You cannot tell anyone, even your best friend.

3 明天要交作业，今晚我<u>就是</u>不睡觉
<u>也</u>要把它写完。

   The paper is due tomorrow. I have to finish it, even if I don't get any sleep tonight.

语法

A 方位补语的引申义
Extended meaning of directional complements

There are fourteen commonly used compound directional complements: 上来, 下来, 进来, 出来, 回来, 过来, 起来, 开来, 上去, 下去, 进去, 出去, 回去, and 过去. They are usually used after verbs (as complements) to indicate the direction of the action. However, many of these directional compounds have extended meanings that are not exactly "directional," but rather metaphorical, indicating the starting, continuing, or changing aspects of actions or states. In this sense, they can also be used after adjectives. Examples from Lesson 8 are 开来, 起来, 下来, and 下去:

A1 V/adj. + 开来 indicating the action of spreading, becoming widespread

1 而这个"西洋节"却已在年轻人中间迅速地流传开来。

But this Western festival has quickly spread in popularity among young people.

A2 V/adj. + 起来 indicating the start of an action or state

1 中国女孩子在追求爱情上也主动起来了。

Chinese girls are starting to take more initiative in pursuing love.

2 人们的婚恋观念也开放起来。

People's ideas of love and marriage also became more liberated.

A3 V/adj. + 下去 indicating the continuation of an action/state (from now to the future)

1 他们多数选择离婚，而不愿意继续凑合下去。

The majority of them would choose divorce rather than continuing the make-do marriage.

A4 V/adj. + 下来

1 Indicating the continuation of an action/state (from the past to now):

但是千百年流传下来的传统婚姻观念还存在。

But there still exist those traditional views of marriage that had been handed down thousands of years ago.

2 Indicating a change from an active/positive state to a static/negative state:

回到家后，他的心情才慢慢地平静下来。

Only after he came home did he gradually calm down.

B "受／受到"的用法

The original meaning of 受／受到 is "to receive," which implies a passive meaning as opposed to "giving," so it can be used to express the passive tone in Chinese. 受／受到 is usually followed by a disyllabic nominalized verb that belongs to a closed list of words of abstraction (限制 "restrict," 影响 "influence," or 关注 "notice," etc.), and it is often translated into the passive voice in English as "to be restricted" or "to be noticed."

受 states a general situation and can be modified by 很 or 不, whereas 受到 indicates a more specific event during a particular time frame (in either the past or the future) and can be used with 没(有) or 了 (but not 很 or 不).

1 他觉得一个人跟谁恋爱结婚应该不受限制。

In his opinion, a person shouldn't be restricted as to whom he/she can love and marry.

2 政府的节能政策很受群众欢迎。

The government's energy-saving policy is well received by the people.

(The government's energy-saving policy is very popular among the people.)

3 水污染使附近居民的正常生活<u>受到</u>了很大的影响。

Water contamination has impacted the everyday life of nearby residents.

4 他的这本新书没有<u>受到</u>好评。

His new book was not well received (did not receive favorable reviews).

5 老太太担心她的再婚会<u>受到</u>儿女们的反对。

The old lady is worried that her remarrying might be objected to by her children.

C 介词"于"的用法

于 (prep.) is a classical word that is still used frequently in modern written Chinese. It is a preposition used before a noun, pronoun, or noun phrase in order to form a phrase that introduces a place, time, position, direction, object, recipient, etc., of an action (or a state). The English translation of 于 varies according to the English conventional use of prepositions. The position of this prepositional phrase is usually after the verb, while most modern prepositional phrases in Chinese are more often placed before the verb (see the following examples with comparisons in modern Chinese).

C1 于 phrase used after a verb

1 广东位<u>于</u>中国南部。（比较：广东<u>在</u>中国南部。）

Guangdong is situated in the southern part of China.

2 赵先生1981年毕业<u>于</u>清华大学。（比较：赵先生1981年<u>从</u>清华大学毕业。）

Mr. Zhao graduated from Tsinghua University.

3 这位数学家生<u>于</u>1882年。（比较：这位数学家是1882年生的。）

The mathematician was born in 1882.

4 经验来源<u>于</u>实践。（比较：经验是<u>从</u>实践中来的。）

Experience comes from practice.

When the 于 phrase is used to indicate time, it can sometimes be placed before a verb. For example:

5 来信已<u>于</u>昨日收到。

The letter was received yesterday.

C2 于 phrase used after an adjective

1 人们对婚姻的期望值也远远<u>高于</u>上一代人。（比较：人们对婚姻的期望值也<u>比</u>上一代人高很多。）

The value that Chinese people now place on marriage is much higher than that of the earlier generation.

2 中国人口远远<u>多于</u>日本（人口）。

The Chinese population is much larger than that of Japan.

3 友谊<u>贵于</u>黄金。

Friendship is more precious than gold.

4 这种住房政策<u>有利于</u>低收入家庭。

This kind of housing policy is beneficial to low-income families.

D 不可…… in word formation

不可 literally means "not able." It can be used with verbs to form compound words (typically four-character compounds) that have become idiomatic expressions. They are very expressive, and usually used in the written style. The following are some common examples:

- <u>不可</u>调和 incompatible, irreconcilable
- <u>不可</u>避免 inevitable, unavoidable
- <u>不可</u>救药 incorrigible, incurable
- <u>不可</u>缺少 indispensable
- <u>不可</u>告人 unspeakable, secret, hidden
- <u>不可</u>思议 unbelievable, unimaginable

A 语音

Write the following underlined Chinese characters in *pinyin*. Pay special attention to their different pronunciations in different contexts.

机<u>会</u>（　　）　　　<u>会</u>计 （　　）

<u>调</u>和（　　）　　　强<u>调</u>（　　）

<u>多</u>数（　　）　　　<u>数</u>一下（　　）

<u>中</u>间（　　）　　　看<u>中</u> （　　）

<u>强</u>调（　　）　　　<u>勉</u>强 （　　）

B 词汇与句型

B1 词语搭配 Match the following words by considering their appropriate collocations. (There may be multiple possible collocations, but each word can be used only once.)

Group One (Verb + Object)		Group Two (Noun + Noun)	
1 限制	＿＿幸福	1 经典	＿＿观念
2 压抑	＿＿爱情	2 封建	＿＿关系
3 追求	＿＿含蓄	3 传统	＿＿地位
4 表白	＿＿自由	4 社会	＿＿方式
5 讲究	＿＿感情	5 夫妻	＿＿社会

B2 Provide the informal counterparts of the following formal expressions.

等候＿＿＿　　妻子＿＿＿　　或 ＿＿＿

迅速＿＿＿　　丈夫＿＿＿　　子女＿＿＿

由A至B＿＿＿　因此＿＿＿　　仍然＿＿＿

选择＿＿＿　　时 ＿＿＿　　高于＿＿＿

如果＿＿＿　　婚后＿＿＿　　与＿＿＿

相爱＿＿＿　　不可＿＿＿　　即使＿＿＿

B3 近义词用法区别练习

1 表达／表白

虽然他一再＿＿＿，可是没人相信他。

这束玫瑰＿＿＿了他对女朋友深深的爱情。

2 看起来／看来

这种工作＿＿＿很容易，可是要做得好还真难。

在老王＿＿＿，孩子的婚姻不应该受到家长的限制。

3 不管／即使

＿＿＿他的儿女反对，他也一定要跟这位老奶奶结婚。

＿＿＿下多大的雨，我们都要去。

4 受／受到

西方的"情人节"很＿＿＿中国年轻人的欢迎。

中国的教育事业在文化大革命期间曾经＿＿＿很大的损害。

B4 用指定的句型完成下面对话

1 问：住房制度改革以前，在中国
  不能买房子？

  答：不可以，_____
  _____

  （即使……也……）

2 问：你今天为什么这么高兴？

  答：因为_____
  _____

  （再也不……了！）

3 问：她父母好像很不喜欢她那个
  当普通工人的男朋友吧？

  答：是啊，可是她说_____
  _____

  （不管……都……）

4 问：你打算怎样去找工作？

  答：我先上招聘网站把简历投了，
  _____
  _____

  （然后……）

5 问：为什么结婚以前我说什么他都
  同意，可结婚以后情形就大不
  一样了？

  答：_____
  _____

  （看来……）

C 语法

C1 选词填空 Fill in the blanks with the most appropriate
"不可……" compounds from the list provided.

a 不可调和   d 不可思议
b 不可缺少   e 不可避免
c 不可告人   f 不可救药

1 阳光、空气和水是所有生命_____
  的养料。

2 你们之间并没有_____的矛盾，
  为什么一定要离婚呢？

3 面对媒体的报道，这家公司的沉默
  背后一定有_____的秘密。

4 尽管朋友们一再帮助他，他还是不改，
  真是_____！

5 如今大学生毕业后都_____地
  面临就业的压力。

6 这些中学生所承受的学习压力之大
  是_____的。

C2 用适当的词语填空
  a 下来   b 下去   c 开来   d 起来

1 为什么中式情人节没能流行_____？

2 大部分古代的建筑都完整地保存
  _____了。

3 我们离婚吧，我不想这样凑合
  _____了。

4 那谣言 (rumor) 在公司里慢慢流传
  _____。

5 他的话还没说完，大家就都笑
  _____了。

6 即使有再大的困难，我也要坚持
  _____。

7 这是古代流传_____的一个神话故事。

8 火车慢慢停_____了。

9 人都走了，大楼里安静_____了。

10 你不能再瘦了。再瘦_____你就只剩下骨头了。

C3 用"于"组成的词填空

a	有利于	i	来源于
b	成立于	j	有害于
c	等于	k	低于
d	生于	l	属于
e	高于	m	位于
f	对于	n	由于
g	至于	o	关于
h	少于	p	处于

1 _____他来说，这次恋爱只是一场游戏。

2 这本书的内容，我一直记得。_____书的作者，我却早就忘记了。

3 这位老人_____1930年。

4 这家公司_____2005年。

5 很多成语_____历史故事。

6 即使女大学生找到工作，她们的薪水也远远_____男生。

7 吸烟_____健康。

8 国家利益_____一切。

9 如果不向先进国家学习，我们将永远_____落后地位。

10 _____健康原因，他父亲提前退休了。

11 十五加十三_____多少？

12 老师要我们讨论_____年轻人婚恋观变化的问题。

13 地球是_____我们大家的，应该受到我们的保护。

14 新鲜空气_____健康。

15 河南_____黄河以南。

16 到我们公司来工作吧。我们保证月薪不_____五千元。

D 综合

D1 英译汉

1 There are people buying roses everywhere. It looks like Valentine's Day has become increasingly popular in China.

_____

_____

_____

2 After returning from studying abroad, she is no longer as reserved as she was before, but has become much more cheerful and outgoing.

_____

_____

_____

3 She thought her parents might look down upon her new boyfriend, who was just an ordinary worker. To her surprise, they liked him the first time they met him. （看不起、没想到）

_____

_____

_____

4 His income is way below average. (adj. 于)

_____

_____

_____

5 *A Dream of Red Mansions* (红楼梦) is one of the classics of Chinese literature.

_____

_____

_____

6 Although she didn't state it openly, we could detect the implicit critical tone.

_____

_____

_____

7 问: Excuse me, how can I get to the Museum of Modern Art?

答: Go down the street, and then turn right at the second cross street.

_____

_____

_____

D2 短文填空 Fill in the blanks to complete the story on the right.

a 传统   i 巧克力
b 情人节   j 主动
c 玫瑰   k 西方
d 来自   l 惊喜
e 经典   m 爱上
f 恋爱   n 观念
g 爱情   o 追求
h 心上人   p 相爱

中国情人节 —— 七夕[1]

每年的2月14日是_____情人节。这是个浪漫的日子，近年来在中国非常流行。_____花和_____是最_____的表白方式。很多年轻人想尽办法为_____带来_____，有人甚至选择在这一天求婚 (propose)。

最近，中国人又推出了中国自己的_____："七夕节"。这个节日_____于一个古代的传说：美丽的织女 (Zhīnǚ) (Weaver Girl) 是天帝 (Celestial Emperor) 的女儿，她_____了人间的牛郎 (Cowherd)，就偷偷来到人间，与牛郎结成了夫妻，还生了一对可爱的小儿女。但是天帝不赞成他们自由_____，就把他们分隔在银河 (Milky Way) 两岸，牛郎在河东，织女在河西，每年七夕才准他们见一次面。但是他们仍然深深_____，千百年来一直没有改变。所以，牛郎织女的故事被认为是中国人最理想的_____故事。

[1] The seventh evening of the seventh moon in the lunar calendar.

可是七夕节在年轻人中的影响力，比西方情人节小得多了。虽然媒体和商界大力宣传，还是没有什么人关注这个节日。因为有人认为中国情人节代表的是_____的情感世界，已不再吸引大胆而开放的现代男女，他们的_____是"爱，就要_____争取"。不过，如今在一些大城市，牛郎织女相会的七夕变成了单身男女相识交友的好日子。有七夕交友活动能吸引上千人，这给单身男女创造了一个了解、_____异性的好机会。

D3 按照这篇文章的意思，下面的说法对不对？(T/F)

1 _____ 中国传统的情人节在每年的二月，是个很浪漫的日子。

2 _____ 七夕就是中国自己的情人节。

3 _____ 在年轻人看来，西方情人节不如中国自己的情人节浪漫。

4 _____ 中国自己的情人节来源于一个古老的神话。

5 _____ 牛郎织女的爱情表现了中国现代年轻人的爱情观。

6 _____ 每年只见一次面的爱情很难被现代的年轻人接受。

7 _____ 七夕没有受到很多人关注是因为媒体和商界只重视宣传西方情人节。

8 _____ 在一些大城市，很多单身男女在七夕交友活动中互相认识交朋友。

短文（一）
"三高"、"三低"和"三手"

今天是阿玲第一次带男朋友回家，可是见过面以后，老张夫妇并不太满意。张太太还记得三年前"面试"大女儿阿文的男朋友，那时他已经得到了美国的博士学位，而且自己开了公司，人也长得又高又帅。可是，现在二女儿怎么会喜欢这样的男生？他只不过是一个普通的公司职员，话不多，长得很平常，而且只比阿玲高一点儿，看起来以后女儿连高跟 (high heel) 鞋也不能穿了。

阿玲听了妈妈的话后，大笑起来："妈，现在是什么年代了，您还想着'三高'男生？现在流行的是'三低'男生。"

老张问道："什么'三高'、'三低'？"

阿玲回答说："大姐结婚时最流行'三高'男生：个子高、学历高、收入高。可是那些条件都只是外在 (external, extrinsic) 的，恐怕他们的脾气 (píqi) (temperament, disposition) 比谁都坏，忙起事业来家里的事情都不管，而且你也不知道他们一天到晚在外面做什么。现在呀，最流行'三低'……"

老张太太好奇 (hàoqí) (curious) 起来："'三低'？让我猜猜。血压 (xuèyā) (blood pressure) 低、负担低……"

阿玲笑得更厉害了:"妈,您还是老看法。'三低'是姿态 (zītài) (attitude, pose) 低、风险 (fēngxiǎn) (risk) 低、束缚 (shùfù) (restriction) 低。这样的男生呀,懂得尊重女性,会做家务事,不在外头随便交朋友,又会给老婆自由和空间。我可不想嫁给'三高'男生去做家庭主妇,跟'三低'男生过日子才幸福。"

这时,正在上大学的小女儿阿新走进房间:"爸妈、二姐,你们听没听说过最新的'三手'男生?我要找的是'三手':帮手 (helper)、携手 (xiéshǒu) (hand in hand, collaborate)、牵手 (qiānshǒu) (hold hands, involve)。我们在事业和家庭上互相帮助,互相理解,携手合作,相亲相爱 (xiāng qīn xiāng ài) (love each other) 手牵手走过一生!这才是最理想的爱情!"

老两口半天没说出话来,现在的年轻人,想法真是不一样啊!

E1 回答下面问题

1 老张夫妇三个女儿选择对象的观点有什么不同?

_____

_____

2 这三种观点表现出中国女性在恋爱婚姻观念上怎样的变化?

_____

_____

3 这些变化的原因是什么?

_____

_____

E2 根据短文内容,选择最佳答案回答问题

1 "三低"指的是:

a 身材低、姿态低、血压低

b 姿态低、风险低、负担低

c 束缚低、姿态低、风险低

d 血压低、风险低、个子低

2 三女儿阿新最可能被下面哪位男生吸引?

a 小赵:电影演员,28岁,高大英俊。

b 小钱:硕士,30岁,高级职员,收入好,事业心强。

c 小孙:21岁,同校同学,一起参加登山俱乐部,一起准备出国考试。

d 小李:公司普通职员,28岁,工作稳定,为人诚实可靠,性格好。

3 "三高"男生不再流行的原因:

a 女性不再像以前那样看重男性的外在条件。

b "三高"男生往往不懂体贴太太和照顾家庭。

c 女性期待在两性关系中有更重要的地位。

d A、B、C 都对。

4 老张太太不太介意男方的什么?

a 身材相貌

b 学位学历

c 工作事业

d 脾气性格

5 根据短文,以下哪项是最佳答案?

a 大女儿阿文的恋爱观是:恋爱关系以男性为中心。

b 二女儿阿玲的恋爱观是:恋爱关系以女性为中心。

c 三女儿阿新的恋爱观是:恋爱关系以双方的互动 (interaction) 为中心。

d 以上都正确。

6 以下哪项最好地说明了这篇短文的主题？

a 随着时代的发展，女性的择偶标准也不断变化。

b 老张夫妇对恋爱婚姻的看法已经过时了。

c 老张夫妇对大女儿的男朋友最满意。

d 现在的女大学生最喜欢"三手"男生。

短文 (二)
爱情和婚姻

柏拉图 (Plato) 曾经问他老师苏格拉底 (Socrates)："什么是爱情？"苏格拉底叫他到玉米 (corn) 地里去，摘 (zhāi) (pick) 一根最大的玉米回来，但只能摘一次，而且只准向前走，不准回头。结果柏拉图两手空空的回来了。老师问他为什么。他说："每次见到很大的玉米时，本来想摘，可是因为不知道前面是不是还有更好的，所以就放弃了；等到玉米地走完时，才发现后面的玉米都不如以前见到的好。原来玉米地里最大的玉米早就被我错过 (miss) 了，所以我什么也没摘到。"

老师说："这就是爱情。"

又有一天，柏拉图问苏格拉底，什么是婚姻？老师叫他到树林里，砍 (kǎn) (cut) 一棵最大最漂亮的树回来。可是条件跟前次一样，只能砍一次，而且只准向前走，不准回头。这次柏拉图带了一棵普普通通，不是很漂亮的树回来了。老师问他为什么？他说："因为有了上一次的经验，当我走完了大半个树林还两手空空时，看到这棵树不算太差，就把它砍下来，恐怕错过。"

老师说："这就是婚姻。"

E3 根据短文内容，完成下面表格

	爱情	婚姻
理想	摘最大的玉米 （比喻：最理想的爱情）	
结果	两手空空回来	
原因	不知道前面是不是还有更好的	
寓意 (moral lesson)	人们对爱情的期望过高使人们常常错过真正的爱情	

E4 回答下面问题

1 柏拉图问苏格拉底两个什么问题？

_____

_____

2 苏格拉底让柏拉图做两件什么事？
这两件事有什么共同的条件和不同
的结果？

_____

_____

_____

3 产生这两个不同的结果的原因是什么？

_____

_____

4 根据短文中苏格拉底的观点，爱情与
婚姻有什么共同之处和不同之处？

_____

_____

E5 根据短文内容，选择最佳答案

1 在短文中，"玉米"和"树"分别指：

a 田地 (field) 和森林 (forest)

b 学生和老师

c 男人和女人

d 爱情和婚姻

2 为什么柏拉图没摘到玉米？

a 玉米地里没有大的玉米。

b 他错过了那片玉米地。

c 他总以为前面可能还有更好
的玉米。

d 玉米地里的玉米都没有他
想象中那样大。

3 以下哪个选项最好地说明了柏拉图
砍树时和摘玉米时的不同心态？

a "可能还有更好的。"/"千万别
错过，选个差不多的就可以了。"

b "这个不一定是最好的。"/"这个
一定是最好的！"

c "宁可错过，也不能错选。"/
"宁可错选，也不能错过。"

d "只有一次机会，我要好好考虑。"/
"反正不止一次机会，错了可以
再选。"

4 苏格拉底认为爱情_____，
婚姻_____。

a 一生多次；一生一次

b 是婚姻的起点；是恋爱的终点

c 使人两手空空；使人满载而归 (return
with fruitful results)

d 是不切实际 (unrealistic) 的期望；是
现实主义 (realistic) 的选择

5 关于爱情与婚姻，以下哪项不符合
短文内容？

a 柏拉图是爱情与婚姻方面的专家。

b 苏格拉底用比喻的方式让柏拉图
明白什么是爱情和婚姻。

c 苏格拉底认为，那些一心追求理想
爱情的人，最后往往没有什么结果。

d 苏格拉底认为，婚姻就是在一个
比较合适的时候选一个不算太差
的伴侣。

6 以下哪项最好地说明了这篇短文的
主题？

a 砍树和摘玉米都应该早一点做决定。

b 柏拉图根据摘玉米的经验学会了
砍树。

c 苏格拉底不相信理想的爱情，只
相信现实的婚姻。

d 爱情和婚姻不同之处在于爱情是
理想的，而婚姻是现实的。

F1 Evaluate the following infographic and discuss the questions in pairs or small groups.

女性重视的对方条件
1 领导才能
2 收入
3 幽默感
4 聪明
5 工作技能
6 事业成功

男性重视的对方条件
1 长相
2 性格热情温柔
3 持家能力
4 善于打扮
5 社交能力
6 会体贴人

摘自《世界周报》
Source: World News Weekly

1 北美的女性和男性在找对象时所重视的条件有什么不同？你觉得这个调查结果反映了真实的情况吗？

2 还有别的因素你会考虑吗？

3 请列出你找对象时觉得最重要和最不重要的条件（可参考上表）。

最重要的

a _____

b _____

c _____

最不重要的

a _____

b _____

c _____

4 在你们的国家，一个人结不结婚很重要吗？什么年龄是最合适的结婚年龄？

5 结婚是两个人的事情还是两家人的事情？父母有没有权利管孩子的婚姻？

6 生孩子重要不重要？什么年龄最适合生孩子？一对夫妇应该有多少个孩子？

7 夫妇可不可以是最好的朋友？你认不认识这样的夫妇？他们为什么做到这样？

8 什么样的爱情是真正的爱情？世界上有没有无条件的爱？

F2 Presentation Topic: 什么是真正的爱情

作文题：任选一题（450-550字）

a 我所追求的爱情

b 我所向往的婚姻

c 我为什么不想结婚

Write an essay expressing your opinion on love and marriage. Select one topic from the list above. Write topic sentences for your paragraphs and support them with facts and examples. Use expressions you learned from this lesson.

一则征婚启事和应征者

- 什么人会用征婚这种方式来找对象？

- 征婚有什么优势？有什么问题？

- 除了网络上可以征婚以外，还有别的征婚方式吗？

- 你会用征婚这种方式找对象吗？说说你的原因。

- 你知道哪些跟"征婚"有关的词汇？

This lesson's reading is about an online "personal ad" (or more literally, "marriage-seeking ad"). Additional passages discuss dating and marriage more broadly. While traditional Chinese values continue to influence society, three decades of combustive economic growth have reshaped the landscape of love and marriage. New trends are starting to change the social norms involved in courtship and dating in China, which will have a significant impact on the shape and dynamics of romantic relationships for generations to come.

9
第九课

生词

自学生词

Match each new word with its English translation by deducing the word's meaning from its characters.
(The first one is done for you).

| 年薪 | 未婚 | 男子汉(漢) | 话题(話題) | 反问(問) |
| 一连(連)串 | 短信 | 平淡 | 共同 | 自信 |

1 平淡 _____ ordinary, plain

2 _____ self-confident, confident

3 _____ together, jointly

4 _____ a series of, a chain of

5 _____ short message, text message

6 _____ a real man, true man

7 _____ unmarried

8 _____ ask (a question) in reply

9 _____ annual salary

10 _____ topic, subject of conversation

成语和惯用语

成语／惯用语	单字解释	意思
1 兴致勃勃 *xìng zhì bó bó* 她<u>兴致勃勃</u>地讨论起创业的话题来了。	兴(興)致 interest, excitement, mood to enjoy 勃勃 exuberant, vigorous, full of vitality	Full of zest or enthusiasm
2 有所作为 *yǒu suǒ zuò wéi* 我喜欢在事业上<u>有所作为</u>的男子汉。	有所 have (a) certain degree (of), to some extent 作为(為) accomplishment	Have (a certain) accomplishment, accomplished

	简体	繁体	拼音	词性	英文
1	征	徵	*zhēng*	v.	solicit
2	启事	啟	*qǐshì*	n.	notice, announcement
3	应征	應徵	*yìngzhēng*	v.	respond to an ad or solicitation
4	登		*dēng*	v.	publish (in a newspaper)
5	企业家	業	*qǐyèjiā*	n.	entrepreneur
6	余	餘	*yú*	v./n.	have a surplus; surplus
7	楼房	樓	*lóufáng*	n.	multi-storied building
8	社交		*shèjiāo*	n.	social intercourse
9	秘书	書	*mìshū*	n.	secretary
10	伴侣	侣	*bànlǚ*	n.	companion, mate, partner
11	优越	優	*yōuyuè*	adj.	superior, advantageous
12	吸引		*xīyǐn*	v.	attract
13	勉强	強	*miǎnqiǎng*	v.	do or manage with difficulty
14	冒		*mào*	v.	emit, give off, send out
15	细	細	*xì*	adj.	thin, fine, slender
16	汗珠		*hànzhū*	n.	bead of sweat
17	冒险	險	*màoxiǎn*	v.o.	take an adventure, take a risk
18	愿	願	*yuàn*	v.	be willing to, want to
19	出场	場	*chūchǎng*	v.o.	appear on the scene
20	盼望		*pànwàng*	v.	look forward to
21	围巾	圍	*wéijīn*	n.	scarf
22	神秘		*shénmì*	adj.	mysterious, mystical
23	特长	長	*tècháng*	n.	special aptitude, specialty
24	酒量		*jiǔliàng*	n.	capacity for liquor
25	匿名		*nìmíng*	attr.	anonymous, anonymity
26	才能		*cáinéng*	n.	talent, ability, capacity
27	热恋	熱戀	*rèliàn*	v.	be passionately in love

第一读：掌握课文大意

Skim the reading; then select the option below that best captures its main idea.

a 从一则征婚启事及应征者看人们的婚恋观

b 三位女应征者对婚姻的看法

c 一个征婚者的故事

第二读：细节和理解

A Read the text again carefully and answer the following questions.

1 在百合网上征婚的是一个什么样的人？

_____

_____

2 他对征婚对象有什么要求？

_____

_____

3 为什么他没想到会有那么多人应征？而且有大学生？

_____

_____

4 A姑娘是个什么样的人？是什么吸引她来应征的？

_____

_____

5 B姑娘长得怎么样？她的性格怎么样？她喜欢什么样的人？

_____

_____

6 C姑娘有什么特别的地方？她为什么要用这种方式跟征婚者见面？

_____

_____

7 你觉得征婚者会选哪一位姑娘？为什么？

_____

_____

B Choose the best inference from the three possible choices. Underline the clue(s) that helped you choose.

1 没想到，才过了三天，就收到了约四百封信，而且有不少是大学生写来的。

a 农民征婚能收到大学生的应征信是一件很不平常的事情。

b 农民征婚三天就收到四百封大学生的应征信是一件很不平常的事情。

c 农民征婚三天就收到四百封应征信是一件很不平常的事情。

2 征婚者勉强回答着，头上却已冒出细细的汗珠……

a 征婚者出汗是因为天气太热。

b 征婚者出汗是因为不好意思。

c 征婚者出汗是因为心情很激动。

3 征婚者反问道："你不怕我太喜欢冒险吗？我虽然有房子，但那是我冒险借钱买的。"

a 征婚者想知道应征姑娘是不是怕他太冒险。

b 征婚者想知道这位姑娘是不是怕冒险。

c 征婚者想知道姑娘前面说的话是不是真的。

一则征婚启事和应征者

"百合网"[1]上海网站最近登出了一则征婚启事：

"某男，三十四岁，农民企业家，年薪五十万以上，在农村有四百余平米楼房，在本市也有一套120平米的住房。欲寻家住本市，会社交，能作秘书工作，长相较好，有高中以上文化水平，二十四至二十八岁的未婚姑娘为伴侣。"

没想到，才过了三天，征婚者就收到了约四百封应征信，而且有不少是大学生写来的。下面介绍其中三位姑娘的情况：

A姑娘最先来与征婚者见面。她说："我去年商业大学毕业，你优越的条件非常吸引我，但更重要的是，我喜欢在事业上有所作为

的男子汉，并愿意用我所学到的知识去帮助他。"接着，她兴致勃勃地讨论起创业的话题来了。她向征婚者提出一连串企业管理方面的问题，征婚者勉强回答着，头上却已冒出细细的汗珠……

B姑娘今年二十六岁，眼睛又大又圆，说话非常痛快。她说："我正在上网络大学，还有一年就毕业了。我喜欢冒险，不愿平平淡淡过一辈子，希望我的伴侣也是个冒险家。我想，一个农民企业家，敢到大上海来找伴侣，就是一种冒险，这就是我所要追求的。"征婚者反问道："你不怕我太喜欢冒险吗？我虽然有房子，但那是我冒险借钱买的。"B姑娘说："我们可以努力工作，共同还这笔钱。"

1 Baihe Online is a famous dating website in China.

某男 34岁

农民企业家，年薪五十万以上，在农村有四百余平米楼房，在本市也有一套120平米的住房。

欲寻家住本市，会社交，能作秘书工作，长相较好，有高中以上文化水平，二十四至二十八岁的未婚姑娘为伴侣。

　　C姑娘的出场最有意思。一天中午，征婚者忽然收到一条短信，上面写着："十四日晚八时上海咖啡馆见。"发短信的人没留名字。征婚者正感到奇怪，第二条短信又来了："非常盼望见到你，请到38号桌，戴红围巾的姑娘等你。"同样，还是没有名字。到了那天，征婚者终于见到了这位神秘的姑娘。

　　她说："我是某大学的学生，今年毕业，对公共关系非常感兴趣。你不是要找一位会社交、能作秘书工作的伴侣吗？我想我一定可以。"
征婚者问："你还有什么特长？"
姑娘自信地回答："会说英语、日语，会用电脑，会跳舞，字写得不错，酒量也还行，可以了吗？"
"你怎么会想到'匿名邀请'这个主意呢？""据我所知，你的条件优越，有许多姑娘来应征，所以，我就想出了这个主意，来显示一下我的社交才能。其实，我也想试试自己的能力，谢谢你给了我一次实践的机会。"

　　现在，征婚者已经找到了自己满意的女朋友，正在热恋中。◆

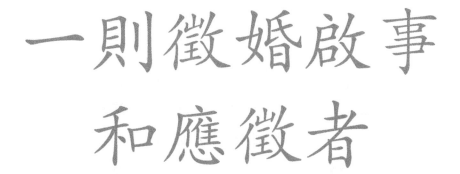

一則徵婚啟事和應徵者

"百合網"上海網站最近登出了一則徵婚啟事：

"某男，三十四歲，農民企業家，年薪五十萬以上，在農村有四百餘平米樓房，在本市也有一套120平米的住房。欲尋家住本市，會社交，能作秘書工作，長相較好，有高中以上文化水平，二十四至二十八歲的未婚姑娘為伴侶。"

沒想到，才過了三天，徵婚者就收到了約四百封應徵信，而且有不少是大學生寫來的。下面介紹其中三位姑娘的情況：

A姑娘最先來與徵婚者見面。她說："我去年商業大學畢業，你優越的條件非常吸引我，但更重要的是，我喜歡在事業上有所作為的男子漢，並願意用我所學到的知識去幫助他。"接著，她興致勃勃地討論起創業的話題來了。她向徵婚者提出一連串企業管理方面的問題，徵婚者勉強回答著，頭上卻已冒出細細的汗珠……

B姑娘今年二十六歲，眼睛又大又圓，說話非常痛快。她說："我正在上網絡大學，還有一年就畢業了。我喜歡冒險，不願平平淡淡過一輩子，希望我的伴侶也是個冒險家。我想，一個農民企業家，敢到大上海來找伴侶，就是一種冒險，這就是我所要追求的。"徵婚者反問道："你不怕我太喜歡冒險嗎？我雖然有房子，但那是我冒險借錢買的。"B姑娘說："我們可以努力工作，共同還這筆錢。"

C姑娘的出場最有意思。一天中午，徵婚者忽然收到一條短信，上面寫著："十四日晚八時上海咖啡館見。"發短信的人沒留名字。徵婚者正感到奇怪，第二條短信又來了："非常盼望見到你，請到38號桌，戴紅圍巾的姑娘等你。"同樣，還是沒有名字。到了那天，徵婚者終於見到了這位神秘的姑娘。她說："我是某大學的學生，今年畢業，對公共關係非常感興趣。你不是要找一位會社交、能作秘書工作的伴侶嗎？我想我一定可以。"徵婚者問："你還有什麼特長？"姑娘自信地回答："會說英語、日語，會用電腦，會跳舞，字寫得不錯，酒量也還行，可以了嗎？""你怎麼會想到'匿名邀請'這個主意呢？""據我所知，你的條件優越，有許多姑娘來應徵，所以，我就想出了這個主意，來顯示一下我的社交才能。其實，我也想試試自己的能力，謝謝你給了我一次實踐的機會。"

　　現在，徵婚者已經找到了自己滿意的女朋友，正在熱戀中。◆

阅读技巧

A 篇章关联词 Discourse Connectors/Connectives

Discourse connectors help the reader follow the direction of a writer's thought. They are like signposts that guide travelers along the road. Look at the following sentences:

1 我喜欢喝咖啡，它有时候让我睡不着觉。(?)

2 我喜欢喝咖啡，但是它有时候让我睡不着觉。

3 我喜欢喝咖啡，虽然它有时候让我睡不着觉。

Sentence 1 seems a little odd since the two ideas (expressed by the two clauses) do not connect in a logical way.

Sentences 2 and 3 make more sense because the two connectors indicate the contrast between ideas.

A discourse is more than just a collection of loose sentences. These sentences should be clearly connected so that readers can follow along. Being able to recognize and use these connectors will greatly enhance your skills in both reading and writing. In the previous lessons, we have introduced some of these connectors (e.g., cause-effect, contrast-comparison, temporal sequence).

B 常用篇章关联词 Commonly Used Discourse Connectors

The table below summarizes the most "commonly used" discourse connectors. There are undoubtedly connectors that you may know which are not listed here, and you will certainly learn more of them in your future study. You should pay close attention to their usage, as they are very important in expressing and understanding meanings beyond the sentence level.

篇章功能 Discourse Function	篇章关联词 Discourse Connectors	
Listing	首先／第一 first 另外、此外 also, besides	其次／第二 next/second 第三、最后 third, finally
Temporal Sequencing	最初／起初 in the beginning, at first 同时 at the same time, meanwhile 从那以后 since then, from that time on 将来／以后／今后 in the future, from now on	后来 later on 接着 following on, going on, proceeding 现在／目前 now, currently, presently
Addition (further information)	而且 (not only)...but also, also 此外／除此以外 besides, in addition 另外 besides	再说 in addition, furthermore 更重要的是 what's more important
Cause-Effect/Result	因此／因而 therefore 于是 therefore, thereupon, hence	结果 as a result
(Un)expected Result	果然／果真 just as expected	没想到 unexpectedly
Comparison and Contrast	同样 in the same way 与此相反 on the contrary, conversely	相比之下 in comparison
Transition	可是、但是、不过 but	然而、而 however, nevertheless
Example	比方说、比如、例如 for example	就拿……来说 take... as an example
Emphasis	真的、确实、的确 really, indeed	
Giving Facts	其实、实际上、事实上 actually, in fact 实话说 to tell you the truth, honestly speaking	
Reasoning	这说明 this indicates 毫无疑问 undoubtedly	由此可见 evidently
Condition	要是／如果 if 不管 no matter	只要 as long as, provided

第九课 · 一则征婚启事和应征者 · 课文 191

篇章功能 Discourse Function	篇章关联词 Discourse Connectors	
Concession	虽然 although 即使 even if	尽管 even though
Specification	关于、至于、对于 as to, as for, with regard to 就……来说／而言 as far as... is concerned	
Generalization	一般来说 generally speaking, in general	
Conclusion and Summary	一句话、总而言之 in one word, in summary	
Restatement	也就是说 which means	换一句话说 in other words

C 阅读技巧练习 Reading Skill Practice

1　Read this lesson's article again. As you read, notice how the discourse connectors guide you along, helping you to see how one detail leads to the next. Mark all of them down by underlining or circling them.

2　Write down the discourse connectors and their functions in the following table. Check your answers with your classmates.

篇章关联词	篇章功能

词汇与句型

A 应 responding to

1 如果你在报纸上看到一则征婚启事，你会不会去应征？

If you saw a personal ad in a newspaper, would you respond to it?

2 我们公司今天面试了二十多个应聘者。

Our company interviewed more than twenty applicants today.

3 随着出国旅游的人越来越多，各种国际旅行社应运而生。

As more people travel abroad, all sorts of international travel agencies have come into being.

B 登 publish in a newspaper or magazine

1 她写的文章登在《中国日报》上了。

Her article was published in *China Daily*.

2 你在报纸上登过征婚启事吗？

Have you published any personal ads in the newspaper?

3 我们登了一则招聘会计的广告。

We posted an employment advertisement for accountants.

C 冒 emit, give off, risk, be covered with

1 着火的房子冒出大量的烟。

The burning house is emitting a large amount of smoke.

2 你愿不愿意跟一个喜欢冒险的人结婚？

Would you want to marry a risk-taker?

3 我今天没带雨伞，放学后只好冒雨走回家。

I didn't bring an umbrella today. I had to walk home in the rain after school.

D 吸引 attract, appeal

1 什么样的电影最吸引你？

What kind of movie appeals to you most?

2 我被中国传统文化深深吸引。

I am deeply drawn to traditional Chinese culture.

3 我觉得这个工作最吸引人的地方是薪水高。

I think the most appealing part of this job is its high salary.

E 痛快 straightforward, very happy, to one's heart's content

1 我喜欢跟说话痛快的人交朋友。

I like to make friends with those who speak straightforwardly.

2 昨天我们在迪士尼 (Díshìní) 乐园玩得很痛快。

We had a lot of fun at Disneyland yesterday.

3 考完了以后，我真想痛痛快快地睡几天觉。

After the exams, I really want to take a few days off and sleep to my heart's content.

F 具有 have, possess

具有 is used only in written Chinese. The object of 具有 must be an abstract noun with two or more syllables, and that abstract noun often has a modifier.

1 应征者必须具有高中以上文化水平。

The applicant must have more than a high school level education.

2 1972年中美上海公报具有伟大的历史意义。

The 1972 Sino-American Shanghai Joint Communiqué has great historical significance.

3 这种广告对年轻人具有很强的吸引力。

This kind of commercial is very appealing to young people.

G 恋 be in love, date

1 听说那对热恋的情侣是通过征婚启事认识的。

It is said that those two, who are passionately in love, met through a personal ad.

2 没人能忘得了自己的初恋。

Nobody can forget his/her first love.

3 在过去的三年中，他一直暗恋着那位韩国姑娘。

In the past three years, he has been secretly in love with that Korean girl.

4 他和他中学时的恋人结婚了。

He married his high school sweetheart.

H 一连串 a succession of, a series of

1 那个学生问了老师一连串的问题。

The student asked the teacher a series of questions.

2 一连串的事故使公司今年的利润大大减少。

A string of accidents caused great financial losses for the company this year.

3 我们学校篮球队今年取得了一连串的胜利。

Our school's basketball team had a succession of victories this year.

I 道 say, speak, talk

道 can be used as a verb, meaning "speak, say, talk, express in words," in literary works or idiomatic expressions. It is often used with another verb (e.g., 笑, 回答, 问, 解释) to indicate the manner of speaking.

1 姑娘笑道："如果我不用这个办法，你不会注意到我的。"

The girl said with a smile, "If I hadn't used this method, you wouldn't have noticed me."

2 他大声回答道："我就是你要找的人。"

He answered loudly, "I'm the one you're looking for."

3 "'道'就是'说'的意思"，老师解释道。

"Dao means to speak," the teacher explained.

Can you match the following?

a 能说会道   _____ congratulate

b 道谢   _____ have a silver tongue

c 道歉   _____ thank

d 道喜   _____ apologize

J 匿名 anonymous, anonymity

1 经理上周接到好几封提意见的匿名信。

The manager received several anonymous complaint letters last week.

2 一位匿名作者写了一篇批评文章。

An anonymous author wrote a critical article.

3 三年以来，他一直匿名支付那个学生的学费。

In the past three years, he has been paying the student's tuition fees anonymously.

K 接着 go on with, carry on with

1 你说完了，我接着说几句。

I'll add a few words when you finish.

2 姑娘先介绍了自己的情况，接着就问了他一连串的问题。

The girl first introduced herself, then asked him a whole series of questions.

3 今天上午我和老王看了三十多份简历，接着我们又讨论了明天面试的计划。

Lao Wang and I reviewed thirty-some résumés this morning. After that, we discussed interview plans for tomorrow.

L 不是……吗? Isn't it…? Don't…? Haven't…?

1 你不是想知道那位神秘的姑娘是谁吗?
就是我。

Don't you want to know who that mysterious girl is? It's me.

2 你不是已经去了日本吗? 怎么又回来了?

Didn't you already go to Japan? How come you are back now?

3 你很想找一位上海姑娘做伴侣,不是吗?

You really want to find a Shanghainese girl to be your wife, don't you?

M 正在……中 in the process/course of

The construction 正在 + VO + 中 is normally used in written Chinese to express that an action is in progress. The verb used in this construction is normally a process verb of two syllables.

1 农民企业家和他的女朋友正在热恋中。

The peasant entrepreneur and his girlfriend are passionately in love now.

2 那个村子经过七级地震后,现在正在
重建中。

After suffering a magnitude 7 earthquake, the village is now in the midst of rebuilding.

3 到西北地区去帮助农民的计划正在
讨论中。

The plan to go help the peasants in the Northwest is under discussion.

天生女汉子

四川成都　　23岁

跳舞　瑜伽　旅行　美食

绝对的女汉子不解释。不喜欢
自拍,不喜欢宅男。希望我的
另一半愿意和我一起周游世界,
建立一个温馨和睦的小家庭。

东湖探险家

湖北武汉　　26岁

健身　旅行　烹饪　看书

典型的文艺青年。性格成熟稳重,
幽默风趣。会体贴照顾人,喜欢
学外语、做西餐。希望我和未来
的女朋友能在事业上一起奋斗,
给未来的小朋友做个好榜样。

语法

A 广告语言中的书面词语: 本、未、者、某、余、欲、为

A1 本 is a demonstrative pronoun that indicates or singles out the entity it refers to. It can be translated as "this," but it expresses the idea of "one's own" or "native."

1 本课主要介绍当代中国人对恋爱和婚姻的看法。

This lesson mainly introduces contemporary Chinese people's opinions regarding love and marriage.

2 从他的口音我听出来他不是本地人。

From his accent I could tell that he is not a local (a person born in this place).

3 本人是清华大学的研究生。

I (this person) am a graduate student at Tsinghua University.

A2 未 is an adverb that goes before a verb. It is equivalent to 没有 in colloquial Chinese.

1 代表团去香港的日期未定，因此无法买机票。

The departure date of the delegation to Hong Kong has not yet been decided. Therefore, we cannot book the airline tickets.

2 这几栋维修过的公寓楼价格还未作调整。

The prices of those renovated apartment buildings have not been readjusted.

3 校园门口手拿鲜花的那位姑娘是房老师的未婚妻。

The young woman at the school gate with flowers (lit. holding) in her hands is Teacher Fang's fiancée.

A3 者 is a suffix that can be added to a noun, verb or adjective to form a noun and be roughly translated as "……的人."

- 作者　　　　　author, writer
- 记者　　　　　reporter, journalist
- 读者　　　　　reader
- 应聘者　　　　applicant
- 教育工作者　　educator
- 音乐爱好者　　music lover

A4 某 refers to an unspecified person or entity. Sometimes it can be duplicated when referring to a certain person or institute.

1 听说他毕业于某某名牌大学。

It is said that he graduated from a certain well-known university.

2 她男朋友毕业后被东北某地一家公司聘用。

After graduation, her boyfriend was hired by a company somewhere in the Northeast.

3 在某种程度上我同意他的看法。

I agree with him to a certain degree.

A5 余 more than; have a surplus; surplus

1 本人从事教育工作二十余年，从未见过这样优秀的学生。

I have never seen such an outstanding student during my twenty-odd years' career in education.

2 一则征婚广告有四百余人应聘，征婚者条件一定非常优越。

One personal ad attracted more than 400 responses. This person must have excellent qualifications.

3 中国人吃年夜饭时一定要有鱼，意思是希望"年年有鱼(余)"。

Chinese people must have fish for the banquet on New Year's Eve. It symbolizes "having surplus every year."

A6 欲 want, hope, wish, desire

1 某女，32岁，硕士学历，未婚。<u>欲</u>寻条件相当的国内外男子为伴。

Female, 32, M.A. degree, single, seeking compatible male (domestic or abroad).

A7 为 (wéi) be, as

1 我们都同意选他<u>为</u>班长。

We all agreed to elect him as the class president.

2 大家都亲切地称他<u>为</u>老大哥。

Everybody affectionately calls him "old brother."

3 他希望找一位三十岁以下的未婚姑娘<u>为</u>伴侣。

He wants to find an unmarried girl under 30 to be his wife.

B The nominalization function of 所

所 can be used as a grammatical particle before a verb to form a noun phrase (i.e. to nominalize the verb). The following examples from the text illustrate the different usages of the 所 + verb phrases:

1 <u>据我所知</u>，你的条件优越，有许多姑娘来应征。

According to what I know, there are many girls responding because of your excellent qualifications.

2 ……，并愿意用<u>我所学到的</u>知识去帮助他。

… and I would like to help him with the knowledge I have learned.

3 这就是<u>我所要追求的</u>。

This is what I am pursuing.

4 我喜欢在事业上<u>有所作为</u>的男子汉。

I like men who are accomplished in their careers.

B1 所 + (monosyllabic) V

This kind of usage is usually in idiomatic phrases, with a strong literary flavor. Although there is no object after the verb, it is understood from the context, as with the nominalized "……的" phrase.

1 据我所知：根据我(所)知道的

According to what I know

2 个人所得：个人(所)得到的

What one earns/gains

3 所见所闻：(所)见到的和听到的

What one has seen and/or heard

4 各尽所能：各人尽量做自己能做的

Each does whatever he/she can

5 前所未有：以前从来没有过的

Something that has never happened before

B2 所 + V + 的 + (N)

In this structure, 所 + V + 的 is used as a relative clause to modify the noun that follows it. If the noun is not stated, it is understood from the context.

1 我愿意用<u>我所学到的</u>知识去帮助他。

I am willing to help him with the knowledge I have learned.

2 我们应该重视<u>大家所提的</u>意见。

We should pay attention to the opinions various people put forward.

3 这就是<u>我所要追求的</u>。

This is what I am pursuing.

4 <u>他所得到的</u>比失去的多。

He gained more than what he lost. (i.e., what he gained is more than what he lost.)

B3 有所 + (disyllabic) V

有所 is an adverbial to the verb, meaning "to some extent; somewhat."

1 我喜欢在事业上<u>有所作为</u>的男子汉。

I like men who are accomplished in their careers.

2 这个孩子又聪明又勤奋，将来一定<u>有所作为</u>。

The kid is both smart and diligent. He will surely accomplish something in the future.

3 吃了王医生开的中药以后，他父亲的病<u>有所好转</u>。

His father is getting better after taking the Chinese medicine prescribed by Dr. Wang.

Chinese punctuation marks came into use relatively recently, as the ancient forms of the language had no punctuation at all. Most Chinese punctuation marks are similar in use to their Western equivalents, as they were directly imported from Western typography.

One difference is in size: they are full-width instead of half-width, which means that each punctuation mark takes up the same space as one Chinese character.

The following are the most frequently used punctuation marks and their equivalents in English. Pay special attention to those marked with an asterisk to indicate their difference from English:

	Chinese Punctuation	Chinese Term	English Punctuation	Function
1	。	句号 (jùhào)*	.	Marks the completion of a sentence
2	，	逗号 (dòuhào)	,	Separates clauses, phrases, or items in a series
3	？	叹号 (wènhào)	?	Marks an interrogative sentence
4	！	号 (tànhào)	!	Indicates strong feeling
5	" " ' '	引号 (yǐnhào)	" " ' '	Quotes speech or indicates irony
6	（ ）	括号 (kuòhào)	( )	Contains optional or additional material in a sentence
7	：	冒号 (màohào)	:	Introduces an explanation or series of examples
8	；	分号 (fēnhào)	;	Separates independent clauses
9	——	破折号 (pòzhéhào)*	—	Indicates a sudden break in thought, sets off parenthetical material (note: double dash)
10	......	省略号 (shěngluèhào)*	...	Indicates an omission of a word or phrase (note: 6 dots)
11	、	顿号 (dùnhào)*	N/A	Separates words in a list (e.g., 一、二、三 or 你、我、她)
12	《 》 〈 〉	书名号 (shūmínghào)*	N/A	Indicates the title of a book or an article (e.g., 《高级中文》)

Of all the marks above, the most important are the 句号 (period) and 逗号 (comma). In written Chinese, 逗号 is used more frequently than in English, since Chinese is a language with less morphology and no case markers. A subordinate clause or coordinate clause is sometimes connected without any conjunctions in a sentence. 逗号 becomes an important cue for long Chinese sentence parsing. 逗号 is also used to indicate where a slight pause should be made for clarity and for catching one's breath when reading aloud or reciting a long sentence.

练习

A 语音

Write the following underlined Chinese characters in *pinyin*. Pay special attention to their different pronunciations in different contexts.

应征（　　　）　　　　应该（　　　　）

勉强（　　　）　　　　强大（　　　　）

特长（　　　）　　　　长大（　　　　）

酒量（　　　）　　　　测量（　　　　）

B 词汇与句型

B1 词语搭配 Match the following words by considering their appropriate collocations.

Group One
(Verb + Object)

1　发　　　　_____广告
2　吸引　　　_____汗
3　冒　　　　_____特色
4　讨论　　　_____短信
5　登　　　　_____注意
6　具有　　　_____问题

Group Two
(Adj. + Noun)

1　优越的　　_____生活
2　热恋的　　_____男子汉
3　匿名的　　_____条件
4　自信的　　_____情侣
5　平淡的　　_____汗珠
6　细细的　　_____来信

B2 选词填空

a 共同　　　　h 接着
b 登　　　　　i 热恋
c 冒险　　　　j 一连串
d 应征　　　　k 道
e 吸引　　　　l 匿名
f 勉强　　　　m 特长
g 具有　　　　n 优越

1　这份工作条件_____，招聘广告才_____了三天，就已收到一百多封_____信。

2　你把所有的钱都投资在股票 (stock) 里，实在是太_____了。

3　他回答_____："没关系，我们_____努力工作，一定可以尽快还清银行贷款。"

4　面试的时候，招聘人仔细地看我的简历，_____又问了我_____的问题。

5　这个工作虽然年薪很高，_____一定的_____力。可是不适合我，因为不能发挥我的_____。

6　听说那对_____中的情侣是通过网上交友认识的。

7　那位企业家由于小时候家里太穷，_____读到了初中毕业。现在她一直_____资助失学儿童。

B3 选词填空

a	兴致勃勃	e	门当户对
b	有所作为	f	脸红心跳
c	平平淡淡	g	传宗接代
d	痛痛快快	h	从一而终

1 他很像你，追求成功，喜欢冒险，希望在事业上_____，不愿意过_____的生活。你们应该会很谈得来。

2 等我把所有的考试考完了以后，一定要_____地玩几天！

3 下课后，同学们_____地来到体育场，观看足球比赛。

4 以前，很多人找对象的时候很重视对方的社会地位和家庭背景，他们要求对方跟他们_____。

5 随着妇女地位的提高，她们的家庭职责不再只是_____，如果家庭生活不幸福，她们也不必要_____，维持那种凑合婚姻。

6 她是个勇敢的女孩。当着全校几千个人讲话_____不_____，_____不_____。

B4 用所给句式或词完成句子

1 问：你们的孩子对这里的生活适应得怎么样？

　答：不错！他们_____。

　（才……就……）

2 问：是你的老师推荐你来申请这个工作的吗？

　答：不是，_____。

　（是……的）

3 问：为什么每年都有这么多人移民到美国来？

　答：_____。

　（……，更重要的是……）

4 问：考试总算考完了，今天晚上我们做什么呢？

　答：_____！

　（不是……吗？那……）！

5 问：昨天你们在城里都做了些什么？

　答：我们先去参观了博物馆，_____。

　（……，接着……）

C 语法

C1 汉译英

1 <u>我所认识的人</u>都反对我跟她结婚。

_____

_____

2 他现在<u>所需要的</u>就是一个会说英语、日语，会用电脑的秘书。

_____

_____

3 近几年来这个城市的环境<u>有所改善</u>。

_____

_____

4 回国以后，他将自己在国外的<u>所见所闻</u>写成了一篇报道。

_____

_____

C2 用正确的标点符号填空 Fill in the blanks with correct punctuation marks.

1 这些日商评价说_____简直是一大奇观_____

2 我好不容易才说服他陪你去晚会_____为什么你又不要他去了_____

3 70年代末_____中国开始实行计划生育政策_____一个家庭只能生一个孩子_____

4 我认为中国人坐车难_____看病难_____住房难等问题的原因是人口太多_____

5 由于高考在六月举行_____很多家长和学生把这个月称为_____黑色的六月_____

6 为了鼓励个人及家庭购买私房_____政府采取了一些措施_____一是提供购房补助_____帮助居民买房_____二是调整贷款制度_____让他们可以借钱买房_____三是兴建更多面积小价格低的经济型住房_____让他们买得起房_____

7 性情活泼_____好学上进_____善良热情_____这就是我_____一名普通的中学教师_____

8 你看过中国小说_____西游记_____没有_____

9 只要上了重点大学_____就能当医生_____律师_____电脑工程师_____CEO_____

C3 英译汉

1 Just as I was beginning to feel puzzled, the phone rang. It was he who called to explain the situation that day.

_____

_____

_____

2 To gain more experience, I decided to risk working in that newly established small company.

_____

_____

_____

3 Yesterday morning I mailed fifty résumés. After that I went on to send out a hundred e-mails to various companies.

_____

_____

_____

4 She thought her parents might look down upon her new boyfriend, who was just an ordinary worker. To her surprise, they liked him the first time they met him.

_____

_____

_____

5 Aren't you that famous peasant entrepreneur?

_____

6 Our company is going to hire a PR manager. The ideal applicant should have excellent social skills, intermediate computer proficiency, and 2–4 years of relevant experience in PR and business management.

_____

_____

_____

D 综合

D1 短文填空 (each word can be used multiple times)

a 本	d 某	g 为	j 之
b 未	e 余	h 觅	
c 者	f 欲	i 达	

中国人征婚启事30年变化

从1981年"新中国第一条征婚广告"诞生至今，征婚启事已经走过了30多年的历程。从下面不同时期的征婚启事，我们可以看出不同时期的社会婚姻观念。

1984年的一则征婚启事：张建国，男，_____矿务局煤矿工人，27岁，党员，文学爱好_____，不抽烟喝酒。求心地善良，能料理家务，有正式工作的女子_____妻。

1987年的一则征婚启事：_____女，32岁，身高1.65米，长相俊美，大专学历，月收入200元，婚后单位可分房。_____寻学历条件相当 (match)、有所作为的国内外男子_____知音。

1995年的一则征婚启事：_____男，33岁，身高1.68米，离婚有一七岁男孩，私车跑运输，日入百_____元，住房180平方米。觅_____市清秀健康的_____婚女子为伴。

2007年的一则征婚启事：男，37岁，MBA，在_____合资企业行政部担任部门经理，月薪_____数万元。有房有车。_____25岁以下，通情达理，性格温和女子一起开创美好未来。

2014年的一则征婚启事：有房、有车、有存款；无周末、无假期、_____男友；2014年，决心给幸福一个交代，找到我的 Mr. Right，_____人王如冰，85后房产营销经理。

1 80年代初人们征婚时比较注重什么？
2000年以后呢？

_____

_____

_____

2 这五则征婚启事中的男女在征婚时的
要求有什么不同？

_____

_____

_____

3 这几则征婚启示反映了三十年来中国
的社会婚姻观念的哪些变化？

_____

_____

_____

D3 短文填空

a	更重要的是	g	痛快
b	具有	h	盼望
c	有所作为	i	兴致勃勃
d	优越	j	结婚
e	吸引人	k	一连串
f	共同	l	作为

相亲

我的表妹文文，长得很漂亮，眼睛又大又圆，说话做事都很_____。她大学毕业以后一直在外地工作，是个高级会计师。可是今年二十八岁了，还没_____。平常因为工作很忙，很少回家。但过年时是一定得回来的。

文文并不特别_____回家。因为她知道，回家过年将要面对什么。所以不到大年三十，她绝不进家门。

不过，她妈也有办法。大年三十不好安排，但过年的"相亲 (blind date) 会"，一定从正月初一开始，一直排到初六。

其实，就是大年三十那天，对文文来说也不轻松。我妈三姐妹，亲戚们加起来二十多口，吃团年饭时，热闹非常！_____亲戚，每人都"有资格"关心文文，都可以对文文的终身大事提出"建议"，就连文文三岁的小侄女 (zhínǚ) (niece) 也会问她："姑姑 (gūgu) (aunt)，什么时候才能见到姑爹 (gūdiē) (husband of aunt) 啊？"

大年初一开始，文文妈就_____地带着文文上各亲戚家拜年，当然，每个亲戚家年前已接受一个_____的"任务"。比方说，去年我就给文文介绍了我同事的儿子。听说那男生在大学工作，条件很_____。初一那天，我同事让他儿子到我们家"拜年"，当然文文妈跟文文也"正好"来了。一坐下，文文妈就问了那男生_____的问题。问完后她跑到厨房跟我说，那男生根本不是31岁，而是33岁。_____，他虽然在大学工作，却只是一个图书馆管理员，并不_____什么特别的才能。文文也说那男生没有什么_____的地方。我家的"相亲会"就这样失败了。

出门时，文文妈鼓励我，要我继续为文文介绍男朋友。今年春节又将来到了，作为文文家的亲戚，我将继续努力，争取在文文的相亲大事上_____。

D4 按照这篇文章的意思，下面的说法对不对？(T/F)

1 _____ 过年时文文并不太想回家，因为工作太忙了。

2 _____ 文文总是等到大年三十才回家。

3 _____ 文文的妈妈为文文的婚事很着急。

4 _____ 由于文文没结婚，家人和亲戚们对文文的压力很大。

5 _____ 连文文三岁的小侄女都很关心她的婚事。

6 _____ 文文妈带着文文上各亲戚家拜年，主要是为了相亲。

7 _____ 文文妈对"我"介绍的那个男生不满意。

8 _____ 文文到"今年春节"还没有找到合适的男朋友。

E 阅读

短文（一）
相亲角

每到周末，上海人民公园的相亲角就挂满了各种征婚启事和青年男女的照片。每一张启事所列明的要求，都往往是年龄、身高、学历、收入、或户口这样的外部条件。替孩子相亲的家长们聚集在公园里，在几百张征婚广告前反复挑选，互相交流。

江阿姨为了29岁的女儿，已经在"相亲角"坚持3年了。她每周都会来公园替女儿相亲。她先把写满女儿征婚信息的广告挂在最显眼的位置，然后看看树上的其他相亲广告有没有合适人选。环绕一周后，就会坐在树下与同样是来代儿女相亲的老人聊天。这样的周末生活成了江阿姨的习惯，也成了她的精神寄托。

有时碰到其他家长，江阿姨会主动上前，探问对方的信息。"你儿子今年多大了？哪个学校毕业的？你家住在哪里？"这些看似简单的问话，实际上都包含着丰富的内容。比方说，"你家住哪里"这样的问题，目的在于以居住的小区和地段，推测对方家庭的经济实力。

在中国很多大城市的公园里，都有这种相亲角。相亲双方都是以结婚为目的的。父母之间所谓的"合适"对象，其实就是各种条件的对等。在这里，浪漫总是败给现实。相亲从很大程度上已经变成了一种交易。

E1 根据短文内容，选择最佳答案回答问题

1 "相亲角"指的是：

　a 一个有很多人的公园

　b 一个父母给孩子找对象的地方

　c 一种现代征婚广告

　d 一个热闹的交易场所

2 去相亲角的人，大多是：

　a 年轻的男女恋人

　b 年老的父母

　c 做交易的生意人

　d 大学学生家长

3 根据短文内容，下面哪句话是正确的？

　a 在相亲角征婚的人一般都比较重视外部条件。

　b 中国的父母特别关心儿女的婚姻问题。

　c 代儿女相亲的老人聊天都是有目的的。

　d 在公园的相亲角相亲比较浪漫。

4 为什么说"相亲从很大程度上已经变成了一种交易"？

　a 因为相亲人的首要标准，往往是对等的经济条件，而不是爱情。

　b 因为父母们问的问题很巧妙。

　c 因为代儿女相亲的父母常常互相交流信息。

　d 因为公园里人太多，相亲角就成了交易会。

<u>短文（二）</u>

非诚勿扰[1]

《非诚勿扰》是一个人气很高的电视相亲节目，24位女孩子站成一排，挑选上台的男人——男人能不能留在台上，得看有没有女孩子为他留灯。

每个男人的出场方式尽管各有不同，但假如这个男人是个"成就男"，他一定会在第一时间让你知道：在他的个人短片中，一定会出现他开的名车，假如他有房，他一定会在房前的草坪前漫步；假如他有钱，他一定会给你展现他那些昂贵的爱好——比如收藏，或是骑马；至少，他也要让你看到他拿一杯红酒，站在窗前<u>若有所思</u> (as if lost in thought)，红酒是一种象征，象征一种有品质的生活。

《非诚勿扰》的相亲短片，更像是一个产品广告，这使"成就男"比那些骑自行车挤公交上班，爱好只限于跑步和上网的男人更容易<u>胜出</u> (win)。难怪当一位爱骑自行车的男<u>嘉宾</u> (guest) 向女嘉宾求爱时，女嘉宾却说："我宁愿坐在<u>宝马</u> (BMW) 里哭，也不坐在你的自行车后面笑。"

---

[1] 非诚勿扰 (fēi chéng wù rǎo) (If You Are the One, lit. "not sincere, don't bother") is a popular Chinese dating show that first aired on January 15, 2010, and has become the most-viewed dating show in the Chinese-speaking world. The show has twenty-four female contestants, most of whom are regulars, and one male hoping to win their hearts. The women get to question the potential suitor and decide whether or not they want to date him. The show's popularity and social commentary has drawn the attention of academics and foreign media. In 2011, the government stepped in to regulate the show's format to de-emphasize factors such as financial wealth.

E2 根据短文内容，选择最佳答案回答问题

1 关于《非诚勿扰》，以下哪项不符合
短文内容：

  a 《非诚勿扰》是一个电视征婚节目。

  b 《非诚勿扰》是一个很受人欢迎
的电视相亲节目。

  c 《非诚勿扰》的男嘉宾都是"成
就男"。

  d 《非诚勿扰》的相亲短片都像推
销产品的广告。

2 根据短文，"成就男"一般都：

  a 在自我介绍短片中展现自己的财富

  b 喜欢喝红酒

  c 喜欢骑自行车

  d 有一样的出场方式

3 根据短文，"成就男"让你看到他拿一
杯红酒是因为：

  a 他很喜欢喝红酒。

  b 他在为昂贵的红酒做广告。

  c 他觉得喝红酒能体现高贵身份。

  d 他不喜欢喝白酒。

4 "我宁愿坐在宝马里哭，也不坐在你
的自行车后面笑。"意思是：

  a "我喜欢坐在宝马车里哭。"

  b "坐在自行车后面很好笑。"

  c "我选择虽然不幸福但是有钱的
婚姻。"

  d "我选择虽然没有很多钱但是夫妻
相爱的婚姻。"

E3 根据短文内容，回答下列问题

1 什么样的人可以称得上是"成就男"？

_____

_____

2 "宝马车"代表什么？自行车呢？

_____

_____

3 为什么说《非诚勿扰》的相亲短片，
更像是一个产品广告？

_____

_____

_____

4 在一个电视相亲节目里能选到
真爱吗？

_____

_____

5 你会去参加电视征婚节目吗？
为什么？

_____

┌─────────────────────────────┐
F 口语
└─────────────────────────────┘

F1 讨论问题

1 除了网络、报纸、电台、电视征婚以
外，还有什么其它的征婚方式？它们
各有什么利弊？

2 你相信"一见钟情"(love at first sight) 吗？

3 人为什么要结婚？你觉得所有的人都
应该结婚吗？为什么？

4 假如你必须跟一个你非常爱可是很穷的人或者是你不爱可是非常有钱的人结婚，你会选哪一个？为什么？

5 一个人的恋爱结婚跟父母有没有关系？

6 你会在什么时候把你的男／女朋友介绍给你的父母？为什么？

　a 刚开始约会时

　b 恋爱了一段时间以后

　c 等到恋爱关系确定了以后

7 要是你父母不喜欢你的男／女朋友，你怎么办？

F2 小组活动（两人一组）

1 下面是人们选择伴侣时一般要考虑的几个因素。请跟你的同伴讨论，看对你们来说哪个因素最重要？请用数字（1-8）把他们按重要性排列。最重要的用1，最不重要的用8。

Eight factors that people generally consider when choosing a partner are listed below. Please discuss with a classmate and rank the factors from 1 to 8, with 1 being the most important factor for you when choosing a partner, and 8 being the least important.

＿＿＿性格	＿＿＿长相
＿＿＿收入	＿＿＿兴趣
＿＿＿学历	＿＿＿年龄
＿＿＿家庭背景	＿＿＿生活习惯

2 如果你觉得还有重要的因素没有列出来，请加上，并用数字也注上重要性。

3 跟别的小组讨论，比较你们的答案，看看你们的观点有什么不同。

F3 辩论

Research both sides of the following topic. The class will be divided into two sides. Each side will take turns presenting their arguments.

辩论题：父母应该代子女征婚吗？

支持方：父母年纪大有经验，可以帮助年轻人做决定

Helpful arguments:

相爱是两个人的事，结婚是两个家庭的事。在结婚这件事情上，中国的父母代子女征婚，是因为父母对婚姻的感悟要比子女深刻许多、看人更准确，可以预防子女脑袋过热选错人。另外，家人作陪可以显示对相亲的重视程度，提高双方交往的诚意。如果相亲成功，子女不用担心父母不同意双方的交往。

反对方：子女的婚姻应该由子女做主

Helpful arguments:

婚姻是子女一辈子的事，应该由子女自己做主。家长、子女两代人观念不同，对婚姻看法会不同，看人的着重点也不同，容易产生分歧。而且父母亲在场，有可能给相亲者造成心理压力，破坏浪漫气氛。

G 写作

作文题：我对网恋的看法（450-550字）

Use the new vocabulary and discourse connectors you have learned in this lesson to write an essay of 450–550 characters expressing your opinion of online dating.

Discourse connectors:

Listing

首先／第一，其次／第二，另外／此外，第三，最后

Addition

而且，再说，此外，更重要的是

Transition

可是，但是，然而，而

Example

比方说，比如，就拿……来说

Reasoning

这说明，由此可见

Conclusion and summary

一句话，总而言之

Useful words and expressions:

优越	吸引	具有	匿名	接着
本	某	神秘	冒险	
兴致勃勃		有所作为		
不是……吗				

家庭妇女

阅读前讨论

- 你喜欢大家庭还是小家庭？为什么？

- 父母应不应该管孩子？怎样管才合理？

- 什么样的家庭是理想的家庭？家庭成员之间的关系应该怎么样？

- 如果你做了家长，你会在什么地方跟你的父母做得不一样？

- 你知道哪些跟"家庭"有关的词汇？

This lesson is about the transformation of the Chinese family system in general, as well as the changes in women's status within it. The one-child policy has achieved the intended outcome of controlling China's rapid population growth. Yet it has inadvertently caused the Chinese family system to transform from an extended household to the contemporary nuclear unit. The status of women, who were traditionally subservient to the interests of their families, has also evolved unexpectedly. Many women have gained the confidence to reassess their personal value as individuals, and some now choose to live independently.

10

第十课

生词

自学生词

Match each new word with its English translation by deducing the word's meaning from its characters.
(The first one is done for you).

儿(兒)女   儿孙(兒孫)   如今   黄昏恋(戀)   儿孙满(兒孫滿)堂   独(獨)生子女

一家之主   自由自在   喜好   谈(談)起   生养(養)   单(單)身

1 <u>独生子女</u> only child

2 _____ have many children and grandchildren

3 _____ children and grandchildren, descendants

4 _____ like, be fond of

5 _____ nowadays, now

6 _____ unmarried or single person

7 _____ free as the wind, lighthearted

8 _____ mention, speak of

9 _____ twilight romance, romance of the elderly

10 _____ head of the household

11 _____ sons and daughters, children

12 _____ have and raise children

主要生词

	简体	繁体	拼音	词性	英文
1	福气	氣	*fúqi*	n.	good luck, good fortune
2	典型		*diǎnxíng*	n./adj.	model; typical
3	年长	長	*niánzhǎng*	adj.	senior
4	长辈	長輩	*zhǎngbèi*	n.	elder generation, elders, seniors
5	权力	權	*quánlì*	n.	power, authority
6	有权	權	*yǒuquán*	v.o.	have the right/power to, be entitled to
7	掌管		*zhǎngguǎn*	v.	be in charge of, administer
8	钱财	錢財	*qiáncái*	n.	wealth, money
9	孙辈	孫輩	*sūnbèi*	n.	grandchildren
10	晚辈	輩	*wǎnbèi*	n.	younger generation, juniors

	简体	繁体	拼音	词性	英文
11	服从	從	*fúcóng*	v.	obey, follow
12	责任	責	*zérèn*	n.	duty, responsibility
13	持家		*chíjiā*	v.o.	keep house, run one's household
14	自豪		*zìháo*	adj.	proud
15	统管	統	*tǒngguǎn*	v.	govern, reign
16	允许	許	*yǔnxǔ*	v.	permit, allow, grant
17	保护	護	*bǎohù*	v.	protect
18	独立	獨	*dúlì*	v./adj.	(become) independent
19	积极	積極	*jījí*	adj.	positive, active, enthusiastic
20	整整		*zhěngzhěng*	adj.	whole, full
21	群体	體	*qúntǐ*	n.	colony, community, group
22	经营	經營	*jīngyíng*	v.	manage, run
23	属于	屬於	*shǔyú*	v.	belong to
24	减	減	*jiǎn*	v.	subtract, reduce, decrease
25	皇帝		*huángdì*	n.	emperor
26	顶	頂	*dǐng*	v.	sustain, support, hold up
27	整		*zhěng*	adj.	whole, complete
28	维护	維護	*wéihù*	v.	protect, uphold, defend
29	权威	權	*quánwēi*	n.	authority
30	晚年		*wǎnnián*	n.	old age, one's later years
31	太极拳	極	*tàijíquán*	n.	tai chi
32	黄昏		*huánghūn*	n.	dusk
33	贵族	貴	*guìzú*	n.	nobleman, aristocrat
34	状态	狀態	*zhuàngtài*	n.	state, condition
35	享受		*xiǎngshòu*	v.	enjoy (rights, benefits, etc.)
36	孤独	獨	*gūdú*	adj.	lonely, solitary, lonesome
37	闷	悶	*mèn*	adj.	bored, depressed
38	城堡		*chéngbǎo*	n.	castle

课文

第一读：掌握课文大意

Skim the reading; then select the option below that best captures its main idea.

a 中国传统家庭与现代家庭的比较

b 中国的家庭结构、家庭观念和妇女地位的改变

c 中国妇女在家庭中的地位

第二读：细节和理解

Read the text again carefully and answer the following questions.

1 中国的传统家庭结构是什么样子的？

_____

_____

2 在中国的传统家庭中，谁最有权利？谁最没有权利？

_____

_____

3 传统家庭中的家长有些什么权力？

_____

_____

4 妇女在传统家庭中的主要责任是什么？

_____

_____

5 妇女在家庭中的地位从什么时候开始改变？

_____

_____

6 中国政府什么时候开始积极推行独生子女政策？这个政策的结果怎么样？

_____

_____

7 独生子女家庭结构的模式和传统家庭的模式有什么不同？

_____

_____

8 说说现代的小家庭是什么样子。

_____

_____

9 "小皇帝"指的是谁？是什么意思？

_____

_____

10 现代家庭中的老年人跟以前有什么不同？

_____

_____

11 为什么有些职业妇女想过单身贵族的生活？

_____

_____

家庭妇女

在中国，几代人住在一起的大家庭存在了几千年。在这种典型的大家庭中，最年长的男性是最有权力的一家之主。这位家长不仅有权掌管全家的钱财，而且有权决定儿女及孙辈的婚姻和前途。在这样的大家庭里，女人是没有地位的。她们只能服从长辈，服从丈夫，甚至服从儿子。女人的责任就是为大家庭生养、持家。哪个女人生的儿子多，她对大家庭的贡献就大；哪个大家庭儿孙多，家长就觉得自豪。传统的中国人以"儿孙满堂"为最大的福气。

二十世纪中期，这种传统的家庭结构和妇女地位开始发生变化。家长不再像以前那样统管一切，他们大多数开始允许孩子自由恋爱、自由选择前途。妇女也开始有了地位，她们不仅受到一夫一妻制的保护，还走出家门，参加工作，并逐渐在经济上独立。

七十年代末，中国政府开始积极推行独生子女政策，三十年后的今天，中国有了整整一代独生子女群体。传统的家庭结构和家庭观念大大改变，儿孙满堂的

> 传统的家庭结构和家庭观念大大改变，儿孙满堂的大家庭模式变成了以独生子女为中心的小家庭模式。

大家庭模式变成了以独生子女为中心的小家庭模式。如今，特别在大城市里，传统的大家庭几乎找不到了。年轻夫妇不再和老年人住在一起，而是独立经营属于自己的三口之家。离婚率的逐年增加，又使不少三口之家继续减至"两口之家"。每个新的小家庭中，有一个"小皇帝"，成为全家生活的中心。而"小皇帝"的妈妈们，地位也提高了。有的妈妈甚至从"妇女能顶半边天"提高到"妇女顶起整片天"，还当上了"家长"。老年人也不再努力维护自己的家长权威，而去追求新的晚年生活——跳舞、打太极拳、读老年大学，有的甚至谈起黄昏恋来。

近些年来，家庭观念继续变化。一些职业女性认为单身贵族才是理想的生活状态。她们觉得做母亲为子女从早忙到晚，完全没有自己的生活。因此，她们决定不结婚、不成家，连孩子都不要，完全享受属于自己的自由自在的生活。有人担心她们会不会生活太孤独，她们说，工作那么忙，哪有时间孤独？再说，实在闷了，身边还有其他单身贵族，随便约几个朋友出来玩不就好了？她们的理想生活，就是住在安全的"个人城堡"里，能够掌握自己的时间，培养自己的兴趣，满足自己的需要，不必忍受另外一个人的坏习惯，更不必做什么事都得考虑另外一个人的心情和喜好。

随着社会的发展，中国的家庭结构、家庭观念和妇女地位都在不断变化之中。◆

家庭　婦女

　　在中國，幾代人住在一起的大家庭存在了幾千年。在這種典型的大家庭中，最年長的男性是最有權力的一家之主。這位家長不僅有權掌管全家的錢財，而且有權決定兒女及孫輩的婚姻和前途。在這樣的大家庭裡，女人是沒有地位的。她們只能服從長輩，服從丈夫，甚至服從兒子。女人的責任就是為大家庭生養、持家。哪個女人生的兒子多，她對大家庭的貢獻就大；哪個大家庭兒孫多，家長就覺得自豪。傳統的中國人以"兒孫滿堂"為最大的福氣。

　　二十世紀中期，這種傳統的家庭結構和婦女地位開始發生變化。家長不再像以前那樣統管一切，他們大多數開始允許孩子自由戀愛、自由選擇前途。婦女也開始有了地位，她們不僅受到一夫一妻制的保護，還走出家門，參加工作，並逐漸在經濟上獨立。

　　七十年代末，中國政府開始積極推行獨生子女政策，三十年後的今天，中國有了整整一代獨生子女群體。傳統的家庭結構和家庭觀念大大改變，兒孫滿堂的大家庭模式變成了以獨生子女為中心的小家庭模式。如今，特別在大城市裡，傳統的大家庭幾乎找不到了。年輕夫婦不再和老年人住在一起，而是獨立經營屬於自己的三口之家。離婚率的逐年增加，又使不少三口之家繼續減至"兩口之家"。每個新的小家庭中，有一個"小皇帝"，成為全家生活的中心。而"小皇帝"的媽媽們，地位也提高了。

有的媽媽甚至從"婦女能頂半邊天"提高到"婦女頂起整片天"，還當上了"家長"。老年人也不再努力維護自己的家長權威，而去追求新的晚年生活——跳舞、打太極拳、讀老年大學，有的甚至談起黃昏戀來。

近些年來，家庭觀念繼續變化。一些職業女性認為單身貴族才是理想的生活狀態。她們覺得做母親為子女從早忙到晚，完全沒有自己的生活。因此，她們決定不結婚、不成家，連孩子都不要，完全享受屬於自己的自由自在的生活。有人擔心她們會不會生活太孤獨，她們說，工作那麼忙，哪有時間孤獨？再說，實在悶了，身邊還有其他單身貴族，隨便約幾個朋友出來玩不就好了？她們的理想生活，就是住在安全的"個人城堡"裡，能夠掌握自己的時間，培養自己的興趣，滿足自己的需要，不必忍受另外一個人的壞習慣，更不必做什麼事都得考慮另外一個人的心情和喜好。

隨著社會的發展，中國的家庭結構、家庭觀念和婦女地位都在不斷變化之中。◈

阅读技巧

A 中文论说文的结构 Structure of the Chinese Expository Essay

An essay is not just a composition of sentences and paragraphs. Beyond these two important components, there is an overarching structure or organization that holds the entire essay together. Expository essays in Chinese are organized differently from those in English. While the English expository essay generally uses the deductive method, the Chinese expository essay typically employs the inductive method, only sometimes using the deductive method.

Normally, the deductive method moves from the main point of the article to supporting details, whereas the inductive method starts from a number of specific examples and ends with the main topic statement. Chinese essays also have other distinctive characteristics that differ from the typical English style. The following is a brief summary of the organizational styles of Chinese expository writing used in previous lessons. This knowledge will guide you to read more effectively, saving you time and energy when searching for main ideas or sorting out key sentences in a Chinese expository essay.

Lessons 3 and 4 use the deductive method. Both essays start by stating the main point of the topic, then narrow it down to specific cases and examples. Each paragraph focuses on a particular aspect or specific point, and expounds on a new or independent subject.

Lessons 2, 6, and 8 use the inductive method (moving from separate examples to the author's opinion or generalization). These kinds of essays are often more difficult to understand, as the beginning paragraph does not state the overall point. Instead, specific observations or examples are introduced in the initial paragraph, followed by other examples and leading up to a statement of the author's position or conclusion in the last one or two paragraphs.

Inductive arguments can be organized in a variety of ways. The essay may be completely inductive, in which case the author saves his or her position for the end; or partially inductive, in which case the author's position is introduced in the middle of the argument.

Finally, many expository essays are written in the traditional style, which requires beginning a piece with an introductory element, called 引论 (*yǐnlùn*) in Chinese, that may or may not appear directly relevant to the piece as a whole. 引论 may be in the form of a short story, a proverb, a poem, or even a statistical survey. For example, the 引论 of Lessons 2 and 8 are both short stories, but Lesson 6 cites an online survey regarding the graduate students' professional preferences.

B 阅读技巧练习 Reading Skills Practice

The main reading in Lesson 10 is organized according to the inductive method. The format is similar to that of Lessons 2, 6, and 8, with the exception that this essay does not have a 引论, and instead begins with a piece of specific information. Complete the following exercise to see how this lesson is organized. For each paragraph, there are two statements. In the exercise below, select the statement that sums up the corresponding paragraph.

1 第一段
   a 中国传统大家庭中长辈的权力
   b 中国传统大家庭的结构和妇女的地位

2 第二段
   a 中国传统大家庭的结构和妇女地位改变的原因
   b 中国传统家庭结构和妇女地位的初期改变

3 第三段
   a 现代家庭的结构和妇女的地位
   b 独生子女小家庭的模式

4 第四段
   a 职业妇女理想生活的新模式
   b 家庭观念的改变对职业妇女的新影响

5 最后：作者从上面四段特点的讨论中归纳 (*guīnà*) (induce) 出来的结论是什么？

_____

_____

词汇与句型

A 掌管 control and administer, be in charge of
统管 administer or manage in an overall manner

Both of these words carry the meaning of management and administration. 掌管 emphasizes the subject's power and control over things, whereas 统管 emphasizes that the subject is in charge of all aspects of a certain project.

1 一家之主不仅有权掌管全家的钱财，而且有权决定儿女及孙辈的婚姻和前途。

The head of the household has the power not only to control the finances of the whole family, but also to decide the children's and grandchildren's marriages and life paths.

2 在古希腊 (Xīlà) 神话中，雅典娜 (Yǎdiǎnnà) 是掌管智慧、技艺和战争的女神。

In Greek mythology, Athena is the goddess in charge of wisdom, crafts, and warfare.

3 家长不再像以前那样统管一切，他们开始允许孩子自由恋爱、自由选择前途。

Parents no longer control everything as before; they have begun to allow their children to choose partners as well as life paths for themselves.

4 人力资源部统管着全厂职工的档案 (dàng'àn)。

The Department of Human Resources administers all the workers' files in this factory.

B 一夫一妻制 monogamy

1 在一夫多妻制的封建社会，妇女的社会地位非常低。

In feudal society, when polygamy was dominant, women's social status was very low.

2 现代社会一夫一妻制是主流。但一夫多妻制在某些地区仍然存在。

Monogamy is the mainstream in modern society. But polygamy still exists in some places.

3 在这个国家，实行一夫一妻制只不过是十年前的事情。

It was just ten years ago that monogamy was introduced into this country.

C 推行 promote, enforce, implement

1 七十年代末，政府开始积极推行独生子女政策。

In the late seventies, the government began to actively enforce the one-child policy.

2 我们正在本市大力推行更完善的垃圾回收体系。

We are making great efforts to promote better recycling systems in our city.

3 随着教育改革的推行，越来越多的学校采用了先进的教育模式。

With the implementation of educational reform, more and more schools adopted advanced educational models.

D 群体 group, population, community

1 中国的独生子女群体被普遍认为是被宠坏的一代。

The only-child population in China is widely considered to be a spoiled generation.

2 城市青年女性是一个极具特色的消费群体，她们最容易接受新的消费观念。

Urban young women are a very distinctive consumer group. They are the most ready to embrace novel ideas of consumption.

3 这部纪录片引起了社会对弱势 (ruòshì) 群体更多的关注。

This documentary attracted social attention to disadvantaged groups.

E 模式 mode, model, style

1 中国家庭从大家庭模式逐渐转变为以独生子女为中心的小家庭模式。

Family structures in China gradually changed from the extended family mode with many children and grandchildren to the nuclear family mode centered on the only child.

2 设计这个项目不需要根据任何固定模式，这为设计者提供了更大的自由。

The design of this project is not based on any set model, which allows more freedom for the designers.

3 我们公司的管理模式还需要进一步改革和完善。

Our company's management framework needs further reformation and improvement.

F 经营 run, operate, manage, build up

1 年轻夫妇不再和老年人住在一起，而是独立经营属于自己的三口之家。

Young couples no longer live with elders, but run their own family of three independently.

2 我叔叔经营一家快餐店，最近好像在招人，你可以去试试。

My uncle runs a fast-food restaurant. He seems to have been hiring recently. You can give it a try.

3 美满的婚姻需要用真诚的爱来细心经营。

A happy marriage needs to be managed attentively with devotion and love.

G 顶 hold up, stand up to

1 这里的妇女走路时喜欢把重物顶在头上。

Women here like to carry heavy things on their heads while walking.

2 "妇女能顶半边天"是中国妇女解放运动时期的一句流行语。

"Women can hold up half the sky" was a popular saying of the Women's Liberation Movement in China.

3 任务虽重，他们两个也顶下来了。

The workload was heavy, but the two of them coped with it just fine.

H 哪 + V……? How...? (A rhetorical question)

1 工作那么忙，哪有时间孤独？

I am so busy with work; how would I have time to feel lonely?

2 他刚失恋，哪有心情来参加聚会（or 派对）？

He just broke up with his significant other. How could he be in the mood to party?

3 您是长辈，这么重的体力活儿哪能让您干？我来！

You are a senior. How can I let you do such heavy labor? Let me do it!

I 不就……了？ Wouldn't it be…?
(A rhetorical question)

1 实在闷了，身边还有其他单身贵族，
随便约几个朋友出来玩<u>不就</u>好<u>了</u>？

If I feel really lonely, I'll just hang out with other single friends. Wouldn't that be good enough?

2 在报纸上发一则征婚启事<u>不就</u>行<u>了</u>？

Why don't you just print a personal ad in the newspaper?

3 你们小两口开一个联合账户<u>不就</u>
方便<u>了</u>？

Wouldn't it make things more convenient for you two as a couple to just open a joint account?

J 甚至 even, so much so that

1 女人是没有地位的，只能服从长辈，
服从丈夫，<u>甚至</u>服从儿子。

Women didn't have any status. They could only obey their parents, their husbands, or even their sons.

2 你有任何理由生我的气，<u>甚至</u>解雇我，
但请一定先听我解释。

You have every right to be mad at me, or even fire me, but please hear my explanation first.

3 为了准备高考，她忙得<u>甚至</u>（连）觉也
睡不了。

Because of her preparations for the college entrance exam, she didn't even have time to sleep.

语法

A 书面语 "之"

A1 Modifier + 之 + (monosyllabic) noun

As a function word from classical Chinese, 之 can be used between a modifier and a noun. Its meaning and function are similar to the modern Chinese particle 的, but 之 is only used formally, and mostly in idiomatic expressions. For stylistic reasons, the noun following 之 is usually a monosyllabic word. The following examples illustrate the differences between 之 and 的:

1 一家之主：一个家庭的主人

Master of the house

2 三口之家：三口人的家庭

A family of three people

3 无价之宝：没有价钱（可以买到）的宝物

Priceless treasure

4 二分之一：两份中的一份，一半

Half of ...

A2 之 + localizer

之 is also used with the localizers 前, 后, 内, 外, 间, 中, 上, and 下 to form compound localizers that indicate relative positions or time. They are usually used in a formal context. In an informal context, 之 can be omitted. Some of these expressions (之前, 之后, 之内, 之外) also have informal counterparts such as 以前, 以后, 以内, and 以外.

1 随着社会的发展，中国的家庭结构、家庭观念和妇女地位都在不断变化之中。

With societal development, China's family structure, family values, and gender norms are all in the process of continual change.

2 这种情况两年之前也曾发生过。

3 三天之后，经理终于同意了这个计划。

4 我们必须在一年之内学完这两本书。

5 除了老王之外，没人能做好这件事。

6 领导也不能高居于群众之上。

7 在社会压力之下，很多感情并不好的夫妻也只好凑合着过日子。

8 三个海岛之中，绿岛是最美的。

9 朋友之间还有什么不可说的吗？

B 书面语 "以"

B1 以 as a preposition 以 + N + V(O)

以 is one of the most important and commonly used function words in classical Chinese. In modern Chinese, it has retained its functions mostly in a formal context. 以 is mainly used as a preposition before a noun (or noun phrase) to indicate the means or reason by which an action occurs. Its interpretation varies according to the context of the sentence:

1 这份订单客户要求以支票支付。

The customer has asked to pay for this order by check.

2 这个国家的经济正在以惊人的速度发展。

The country's economy is developing at amazing speed.

3 他以博学多才闻名于全校。

He is famous throughout the school for his wide-ranging academic achievements.

Many set phrases (成语) with 以 are composed in this pattern (以 + N + VO). For example:

- 以毒攻毒 combat poison with poison (repay evil with evil)
- 以少胜多 defeat the many with the few
- 以权代法 replace law with one's power (in handling legal cases)

B2 以 A 为 B: to take A to be B, to consider/regard A as B

以 A 为 B is originally a pattern in classical Chinese, and it is still in active use in modern formal writing. The entire construction 以 A 为 B can be translated as "把／拿／用 A 当／作 B" in spoken Chinese, and as "to take/consider A to be B" in English.

1 传统的中国人<u>以</u>"儿孙满堂"<u>为</u>最大的福气。

Traditionally, Chinese people regarded "a house full of offspring" as the greatest blessing.

2 大家庭模式变成了<u>以</u>独生子女<u>为</u>中心的小家庭模式。

The extended family mode changed into the nuclear family mode centered on the only child.

3 我们的调查报告应该<u>以</u>事实<u>为</u>根据。

The conclusion of our investigative report should be based on fact.

C 表示强调的方法 Ways to express emphasis/focus

In Chinese, there are many ways to focus on or emphasize a certain element in a sentence to make that element prominent. The following list summarizes some basic ways to express emphasis/focus. Most examples are from this lesson.

C1 是…… 的

Emphasizing the time, place, manner, etc. of a past event/action: 是 is placed before the emphasized element, and 的 is usually placed at the end of the sentence.

1 在传统的大家庭里，女人<u>是</u>没有地位<u>的</u>。

2 我们<u>是</u>昨天离开<u>的</u>。

3 林小姐<u>是</u>来北京学音乐<u>的</u>。

C2 连…… 都／也

Using an "extreme" example to further explain or comment on the previously mentioned situation: 连 is placed before the emphasized element. 都／也 must be used.

1 她们决定不结婚、不成家，<u>连</u>孩子<u>都</u>不要。

2 他失业了，穷得<u>连</u>吃饭的钱<u>都</u>没有。

C3 Interrogatives + 都／也

Showing indefinite indication, emphasizing "no exception" in statements: 都／也 must be used. 也 is usually used for negative sentences.

1 更不必做什么事<u>都</u>得考虑另外一个人的心情和喜好。

2 他不开心，哪儿<u>也</u>不想去。

C4 就 + V

Emphasizing the ideas of "only, right, just, or precisely": 就 is placed before the emphasized verb, and is stressed in reading.

1 女人的责任<u>就</u>是为大家庭生养、持家。

2 我家<u>就</u>在市图书馆对面。

C5 是 + V

Emphasizing that the case that follows is true: The function is like the emphatic "do" in English. 是 is placed before the emphasized verb or adjective, and is stressed.

1 我<u>是</u>喜欢他，但他并不知道。

2 她的身体<u>是</u>不好。

3 她<u>是</u>没去过这个地方。

C6 反问句 Rhetorical questions (哪儿……？ 不是……吗？ 不就……了？)

Using rhetorical questions to refute a certain case that is not consistent with the facts, or emphasizing certainty: The negative form is to emphasize an affirmative meaning, and vice versa.

1 工作那么忙，<u>哪</u>有时间孤独？

2 <u>谁</u>不想得第一名？

3 你<u>不是</u>跟她说好了<u>吗</u>？她怎么还没来呢？

C7 双重否定 Double negation

Negation + negation = emphasized affirmation: 不 and 没有 may occur in the same sentence to form a double negation.

1 你是他的好朋友，<u>不能不去</u>。

2 只要有决心，世界上<u>没有做不到的</u>事情。

D 修辞手法：排比
Rhetorical devices: parallelism

Parallelism is a pattern of repeated sentence structure. When parallelism is used, several parts of a sentence or several sentences are expressed similarly. Parallelism adds balance and rhythm and, most importantly, emphasis to the sentence, creating expectation, excitement, and climax. It is often used for emotive and persuasive effects in writing and public speaking.

Compare the following sentences:

1 在这样的大家庭里，女人是没有地位的，只能<u>服从长辈，服从丈夫，甚至服从儿子</u>。

2 在这样的大家庭里，女人是没有地位的，只能<u>服从长辈、丈夫，甚至儿子</u>。

A woman in this kind of traditional extended family had no status. All she could do was obey the senior members of the family, obey her husband, or even obey her son.

The meanings of 1 and 2 seem to be the same in English. However, with the parallel structure (the repeated verb phrase 服从…), Sentence 1 is much more effective in depicting the oppressed status of women in the traditional family system. The following is another example of parallelism from this lesson:

3 她们的理想生活，就是住在安全的"个人城堡"里，能够<u>掌握自己的时间，培养自己的兴趣，满足自己的需要</u>，<u>不必忍受另外一个人的坏习惯</u>，<u>更不必做什么事都得考虑另外一个人的心情和喜好</u>。

Their ideal life is to stay in their secure "private castle," where they can control their own time, cultivate their own interests (hobbies), and satisfy their own needs. They don't have to tolerate another person's bad habits, and they don't have to consider another person's mood or preference whenever they want to do something.

练习

A 语音

Write the following underlined Chinese characters in *pinyin*. Pay special attention to their different pronunciations in different contexts:

长辈（　　）　　　家长（　　）

长江（　　）　　　年长（　　）

喜好（　　）　　　好像（　　）

几乎（　　）　　　几个（　　）

B 词汇与句型

B1 词语搭配 Match the following words by considering their appropriate collocations.

Group One
(Verb + Object)

1 掌握　　　____家庭

2 选择　　　____地位

3 建立　　　____对象

4 服从　　　____钱财

5 提高　　　____长辈

Group Two
(Verb + Noun)

1 参加　　　____变化

2 维护　　　____自豪

3 发生　　　____工作

4 做出　　　____贡献

5 感到　　　____利益

B2 选词填空 Choose the most appropriate words from the list below to fill in the blanks. (Note: each word may be used more than once.)

a 长辈　　　　b 晚辈　　　　c 儿孙辈

在中国，尊重_____是一种传统美德。所以_____在_____面前说话得非常注意。要是_____对老人说话太随便，就会被认为是没有礼貌。

a 网恋　　　　　　　d 恋爱
b 黄昏恋　　　　　　e 失恋
c 初恋　　　　　　　f 热恋

1 问：你知道小王又有男朋友了吗？
  答：怎么会不知道呢？从眼睛可以看出_____中的女人嘛！听说她是在网上认识这位男朋友的。

2 问：真的吗？我可不相信_____。你怎么知道这个人不是在骗你呢？

  答：哎呀！你这个人太保守 (conservative) 了！现在的_____模式已经不是以前的老一套了，连老人都在谈_____了！

3 问：我不是保守，我是关心小王。你知道她刚刚_____不久。为了她的_____失败，她难过了那么久。我真怕看到她再受伤害。你说是不是？

a	自豪	e	家庭	i	甚至
b	儿孙满堂	f	几乎	j	推行
c	三口之家	g	模式		
d	结构	h	几世同堂		

在过去数千年的时间里，中国人的
_____普遍存在三世同堂、四世同堂
_____五世同堂的现象。能够在晚年
享受_____的福气，_____是所有中国
人的心愿。因此，家长们常常以自己的
大家庭而特别_____。20世纪80年代以
来，人们的家庭观念发生了很大变化。中
国家庭_____也渐渐缩小。加上20世纪70
年代末中国政府_____计划生育政策后，
出现了第一代独生子女，由夫妻和一个
孩子三口人组成的"核心家庭" (héxīn jiātíng)
(nuclear family) 逐渐成为城市家庭_____的
主流 (mainstream)。中国家庭已经从传统的
_____的大家庭，渐渐转向_____的
"核心家庭"。

B3 选择填空

1 我们应该有自己的想法，不要随便
   听从_____名人。
   a 权利　　b 权力　　c 权威

2 在中国传统的大家庭中，家长有
   _____掌管全家的钱财。
   a 权利　　b 权力　　c 权威

3 投票选举是每个公民的_____。
   a 权利　　b 权力　　c 权威

4 在传统的婚姻中，_____夫妻有没有
   感情，都不能离婚。
   a 尽管　　b 不管　　c 不仅

5 在传统的婚姻中，_____夫妻没有
   感情，也不能离婚。
   a 尽管　　b 不管　　c 不仅

C1 The following sentences all include set phrases (成语) with the "以 + N + V + N" structure. Infer the meaning of these 成语 based on their context by matching them with the English meanings in the list below.

1 我们公司聘人主要是看品质和才能，
   绝不会<u>以貌取人</u>。

2 她一想到因病去世的孩子，心里就
   非常难过，经常<u>以泪洗面</u>。

3 你必须<u>以诚待人</u>，别人才会以诚
   相报。

4 父母教育孩子，不要用强迫的方法，
   应该多讲道理，<u>以理服人</u>。

5 数万人上街游行，要求参加G20会议
   的各国领导人<u>以人为本</u>，解决贫困、
   就业和环境变化等问题。

成语	Meaning
a 以诚待人	_____ have a tearful face, swim in tears
b 以泪洗面	_____ human-oriented, people-oriented
c 以理服人	_____ judge/select people by their appearance
d 以貌取人	_____ convince people by reasoning
e 以人为本	_____ treat people with all sincerity

把下列句子改写成强调句（强调划线部分）， 每句至少用两种句型

例：家长的话，她一定得听。

a 家长的话，她哪能不听？（反问句）

b 家长的话，她不得不听。（双重否定）

c 家长的话，她是一定得听的。（是…的）

1 他最近很忙。

 a ＿＿＿＿＿＿＿＿＿＿＿＿＿＿＿

 （是）

 b ＿＿＿＿＿＿＿＿＿＿＿＿＿＿＿

 （连……都……）

2 我知道这件事情，只是不想告诉别人。

 a ＿＿＿＿＿＿＿＿＿＿＿＿＿＿＿

 ＿＿＿＿＿＿＿＿＿＿＿＿＿＿＿

 （双重否定）

 b ＿＿＿＿＿＿＿＿＿＿＿＿＿＿＿

 ＿＿＿＿＿＿＿＿＿＿＿＿＿＿＿

 （哪儿）

3 今天的会很重要，她应该来。

 a ＿＿＿＿＿＿＿＿＿＿＿＿＿＿＿

 ＿＿＿＿＿＿＿＿＿＿＿＿＿＿＿

 （双重否定）

 b ＿＿＿＿＿＿＿＿＿＿＿＿＿＿＿

 ＿＿＿＿＿＿＿＿＿＿＿＿＿＿＿

 （是……的）

4 我姐姐没有跟他去看电影。

 a ＿＿＿＿＿＿＿＿＿＿＿＿＿＿＿

 （哪儿）

 b ＿＿＿＿＿＿＿＿＿＿＿＿＿＿＿

 （是……的）

5 你们应该请一位专家来解决这个问题。

 a ＿＿＿＿＿＿＿＿＿＿＿＿＿＿＿

 ＿＿＿＿＿＿＿＿＿＿＿＿＿＿＿

 （就）

 b ＿＿＿＿＿＿＿＿＿＿＿＿＿＿＿

 ＿＿＿＿＿＿＿＿＿＿＿＿＿＿＿

 （不就……了？）

D 综合

D1 英译汉

1 As the head of the household, you have the responsibility to tackle the problem.

 ＿＿＿＿＿＿＿＿＿＿＿＿＿＿＿

 ＿＿＿＿＿＿＿＿＿＿＿＿＿＿＿

2 With the increase in their income, the Yu family's life has improved a lot; they paid off the entire mortgage for their house last year, and even managed to buy a small car this year.

 ＿＿＿＿＿＿＿＿＿＿＿＿＿＿＿

 ＿＿＿＿＿＿＿＿＿＿＿＿＿＿＿

 ＿＿＿＿＿＿＿＿＿＿＿＿＿＿＿

3 I want to write an essay on the topic of environmental issues. （以……为……）

 ＿＿＿＿＿＿＿＿＿＿＿＿＿＿＿

 ＿＿＿＿＿＿＿＿＿＿＿＿＿＿＿

4 I am proud of living in such a beautiful country. （以……而……）

 ＿＿＿＿＿＿＿＿＿＿＿＿＿＿＿

 ＿＿＿＿＿＿＿＿＿＿＿＿＿＿＿

5 That government of the people, by the people, for the people, shall not perish from the earth. (Use "parallel structure")

_____

_____

6 Along with people's rapidly changing attitude towards the traditional family, the divorce rate has increased day by day.

_____

_____

7 In many areas of the world today, very often it is still the husband, not the wife, who controls the family's financial affairs and their children's future.
（掌管、决定）

_____

_____

8 She has changed too much during the past five years. I could hardly recognize her the last time we met.
（几乎）

_____

_____

9 Many government officials are only interested in pursuing power and protecting their own positions. Some of them will even abuse their power for their own benefit.
（维护）

_____

_____

D2 短文填空

a 自由自在　　h 模式
b 责任　　　　i 父母
c 典型　　　　j 孩子
d 属于　　　　k 后代
e 反对　　　　l 夫妇
f 状况　　　　m 享受
g 传宗接代

丁克家庭

"丁克"就是 DINK (Dual Income, No Kids)，就是"双收入无子女"的意思。20世纪80年代之后，这种家庭_____在中国逐渐流行。目前，选择"丁克家庭"的_____已经突破60万，主要集中在北京、天津、上海、广州等大城市。

王文和罗小红已经结婚12年了，还没有要孩子的打算。最初决定"丁克"的时候，两人都刚刚大学毕业。新婚的小夫妻，只想充分_____完全_____他们自己的二人世界。他们说工作压力太重，收入也不是很高，没有生孩子的条件。虽然双方父母都不赞成他们的想法，但听到他们所说的理由，也就暂时不说他们了。

8年以后，王文和小红在事业上都很成功，经济_____也好了。他们分期付款买了房，还买了车。这时候，_____说话了："现在不是有条件了吗？怎么还不要孩子？不生孩子，结婚干什么呢？"实在没有办法，王文和小红只好向父母实说，他们已经决定永远不要_____。

双方父母一起坚决＿＿＿＿＿＿，特别是王文的父母，只有这么一个儿子，这样做那王家不就没有＿＿＿＿＿＿了吗？王文却明确表示，"我们结婚不是为了＿＿＿＿＿＿，是因为相爱才结婚，是为了过我们想过的幸福生活才结婚。"

像王文夫妇这样＿＿＿＿＿＿的丁克夫妻往往属于"三高"阶层（高学历，高职位，高收入）。他们不接受中国传统婚姻生活中传宗接代的观念，而选择过高质量的、＿＿＿＿＿＿＿的"两人世界"生活。他们的理由是：

一、为人父母的＿＿＿＿太重大，受不了；

二、不能为了孩子放弃自己的事业；

三、孩子会影响夫妻的二人世界；

四、没有能力给孩子提供最好的教育不如不生；

五、将来如果婚姻不稳定，会伤害孩子。

D3 按照上面这篇文章的意思，下面的说法对不对？(T/F)

1 ＿＿＿＿丁克家庭是中国新出现的一种家庭模式。

2 ＿＿＿＿中国农村也有很多丁克家庭。

3 ＿＿＿＿丁克夫妻选择这种家庭模式是因为没有生孩子的条件。

4 ＿＿＿＿王文和小红的父母不能理解丁克一族的想法。

5 ＿＿＿＿丁克夫妻一般都比较重视自我。

6 ＿＿＿＿丁克夫妻一般都上过大学。

7 ＿＿＿＿对于丁克夫妻来说，生育已不再是婚姻家庭最重要的目的。

8 ＿＿＿＿丁克夫妻太重视他们的二人世界。

9 ＿＿＿＿丁克夫妻可能对自己的婚姻没有信心。

10 ＿＿＿＿丁克家庭能被越来越多的人接受，说明人们的家庭观念有所改变。

E 阅读

短文（一）
独身女性

王爱玲大学毕业三年多了，有一份很好的工作，也曾经交过几个男朋友，但她说自己不会结婚。 她认为男性分两种：一种是很优秀但是把自己看得很重要的男人；她不能嫁给这种男人，因为这种男人太自大 (zìdà) (self-important)，而她自己个性 (gèxìng) (personality) 也太强，一定合不来 (hébulái) (be unable to get along)。另一种男人性格很好，很听女人的话，生活上会对你照顾得很好。这种男人，她也不能嫁，因为跟这种男人结婚，虽然生活会比较稳定，但他没有什么主见，日子一定会很没有意思。所以，她觉得：浪漫的婚姻不稳定，稳定的婚姻不浪漫。

有报道说，在中国对一些月薪在5000元至15000元的女性进行的调查发现，这些女性中独身者高达50.2%，一家投资公司的独身女性甚至高达75.3%。她们选择独身的原因基本有五种：

一、经济独立，不必依靠男性占48.3%；

二、对感情不信任，占23.4%；

三、太优秀，找不到更优秀的男士，占12.2%；

四、事业太忙，占6.5%；

五、其它占9.6%。

可以看出，经济独立是高收入女性独身的主要原因。她们不必依靠男性，不用通过婚姻来获得稳定的生活。她们更重视的是自己的感觉，对感情的不信任也是高收入女性独身的主要原因。而且，不少像王爱玲这样的女性，不是找不到对象，而是她们的要求太高了，因为她们不愿意选择一种平凡 (píngfán) (ordinary) 的婚姻生活。不管是什么原因，这些独身女性们已经走出了中国女性的传统规范 (guīfàn) (norm)，而去寻找自己喜爱的生活方式。

E1 根据短文内容，选择最佳答案回答问题

1 王爱玲对婚姻有什么看法？

a 嫁给性格温和 (gentle) 的男人，婚姻才会幸福。

b 浪漫的婚姻不稳定，稳定的婚姻不浪漫。

c 浪漫的婚姻比稳定的婚姻好。

d 平凡的婚姻总比不结婚好。

2 王爱玲对男性有什么看法？

a 男性分两种：一种很自大，一种个性太强。

b 男性分两种：一种很浪漫，一种很稳定。

c 她不想嫁给没有主见的男性，因为她希望男性事业成功。

d 她不想嫁给自大的男性，因为自大的人不好相处。

3 对月薪在5000元至15000元的女性进行的调查发现，这些女性中独身者高达

a 75.3%

b 23.4%

c 48.3%

d 50.2%

4 对高收入女性的调查表明，她们选择独身的最主要原因是：

a 对情感不信任和忙于事业

b 经济独立和自身条件太优秀

c 忙于事业和对婚姻要求太高

d 经济独立和对情感不信任

5 下面哪句话不符合短文内容？

a 王爱玲是一位个性很强的女性。

b 王爱玲对婚姻的要求很高，不愿意过平凡的婚姻生活。

c 王爱玲走出了中国女性的传统规范。

d 王爱玲以前交过几个男朋友，曾经考虑过结婚。

6 这篇短文主要说明了什么？

a 现代女性选择独身的原因

b 现代女性选择独身的结果

c 现代女性选择独身的方法

d 现代女性选择独身的影响

按照这篇文章的意思，下面的说法对不对？(T/F)

1 _____ 王爱玲的婚姻观受到她父母的影响。

2 _____ 现代女性越来越看重自己的感觉，选择自己喜欢的生活方式。

3 _____ 根据调查，在某投资公司中，大约四分之三（3/4）的女性选择独身。

4 _____ 现代女性越来越少依赖男性。

5 _____ 现代女性的<u>安全感</u> (sense of security) 主要来自家庭生活。

短文（二）
从人口普查数据看中国家庭的变化

中国家庭的变化首先是在家庭<u>规模</u>(size) 上。从人口<u>普查</u> (census) 数据看来：1982年中国家庭平均人口为4.43人；1990年下降到3.97人，2000年继续下降到3.44人。而到2005年，全国户均人口为3.13人，其中城镇平均每户家庭人口为2.97人，农村为3.27人。

家庭模式多样化成为中国现代家庭的另一个重要特征。在北京、上海等大城市，这种现象更加突出。据2002年的统计数据，这两个城市的一人户和二人户相加的数字超过了全部家庭总数的35%，北京一代户占所有家庭的30.93%，上海为35.18%；一代户和一人户、二人户的增长，在很大程度上说明，除"核心家庭"外，其他小家庭模式，如"丁克 (DINK) 家庭"、"独身家庭"、"单亲家庭"等，也正在中国城乡出现。

随着家庭观念和模式的改变，在更加注重个人价值观念的影响下，中国人的婚姻家庭观念也正发生着变化，并对社会发展产生了很大的影响。

中国的结婚率在1981年达到最高峰 (20.8‰) 之后，开始逐渐下降。选择性独身和晚婚是导致结婚率下降的主要原因。婚龄推迟和独身增多又影响到生育率下降。在上海，不断下降的生育率已使人口进入<u>负</u> (negative) 增长。

E3 扫描：用短文中的信息填写下列表格

Scanning: Find the information from the passage to fill in the tables below.

家庭规模变化
(家庭平均人口统计)

1982年	
1990年	
2000年	
2005年	

家庭模式多样化(2002 年统计数字)

	一代户 比例	一人户＋ 二人户比例	三人以上 户比例
北京			
上海			

E4 根据短文内容回答下面的问题

1 最近人口普查数据表明，中国家庭规模：

a 越来越大

b 越来越小

c 越来越复杂

d 越来越多样化

2 下面哪句话是对的？

a 北京的一人户超过了全部家庭总数的35%。

b 北京的二人户超过了全部家庭总数的35%。

c 北京和上海的一人户相加超过了全部家庭总数的35%。

d 北京的一人户和二人户相加超过了全部家庭总数的35%。

3 一人户和二人户比例增加是因为：

a 独生子女政策的推行

b 核心家庭的增长

c "丁克(DINK)家庭"、"独身家庭"、"单亲家庭"的出现

d 结婚率下降

4 家庭规模和模式的改变，与____有关。

a 人们更加注重个人价值观念

b 中国人的婚姻家庭观念变化

c 中国社会发展

d 以上都是

5 下面哪一项不是生育率下降的原因？

a 核心家庭增长

b 结婚率下降

c 婚龄推迟

d 独身增多

F 口语：讨论问题

F1 你的家庭是什么样的家庭？你们家有什么跟别人家不一样的地方？

F2 在你们家谁最有权威？有没有每个人都需要服从的规矩？这些规矩是谁定的？

F3 在你们家谁照顾孩子？谁做家务事？

F4 要是你遇到问题，你会找家里人帮助吗？你一般会找谁？

F5 跟家人在一起的时候，最让你高兴的是什么？你最不喜欢的是什么？

F6 你觉得父母应不应该管孩子？孩子的哪些方面需要父母管？哪些方面不需要？

F7 谈谈你对大家庭、核心家庭、丁克家庭、独身家庭、单亲家庭、同性恋家庭的看法。说说它们各有什么好处和坏处。

F8 你们国家的现代家庭模式也有变化吗？这些变化好还是不好？为什么？

F9 对你来说，什么样的家庭是最理想的家庭？

F10 妇女在你们国家的社会地位、家庭地位怎么样？

G 写作

作文题：什么是理想的家庭？ （500-600字）

Use the new vocabulary and sentence patterns you have learned in this lesson to write an essay of 500–600 characters expressing your opinion of the "ideal family." Use either the inductive or deductive method of organizing an expository essay to express your ideas. The following structures you learned in this lesson can also help you with your writing:

1 Emphatic expressions

2 Parallel structures

Vocabulary Index
Chinese - English

拼音	简体	繁体	词性	英文	课数
ài	唉		intj.	sigh	5
báilǐng	白领	領	n.	white-collar (worker)	7
bānbù	颁布	頒	v.	issue, publish	4
bānfā	颁发	頒發	v.	issue, award (certificate, medal)	2
bànlǚ	伴侣	侶	n.	companion, mate, partner	9
bǎohù	保护	護	v.	protect	10
bǎoshí	宝石	寶	n.	precious stone, gem	5
bǎozhàng	保障		v./n.	safeguard; protection, guarantee	6
bǎozhèng	保证	證	v.	pledge, guarantee, assure	7
bàozhà	爆炸		v./n.	explode; blast, explosion	1
bèipò	被迫		v.	be forced, be compelled	4
běnkē	本科		n.	undergraduate	4
bǐlì	比例		n.	ratio, proportion	2
biànhuàn	变换	變換	v.	vary, alternate	7
biǎobái	表白		v.	express or state clearly	8
biéshù	别墅		n.	villa	3
bóshì	博士		n.	Ph.D., doctoral degree	4
bǔzhù	补助	補	v./n.	subsidize; subsidy	3
bùkān	不堪		v./adv.	cannot stand; extremely	1
bùyóude	不由得		adv.	can't help	5
bù zhī bù jué	不知不觉	覺	i.e.	unconsciously, unknowingly	5
cáifù	财富	財	n.	wealth	6
cáinéng	才能		n.	talent, ability, capacity	9
cǎiqǔ	采取	採	v.	adopt, carry out	3
cǎiyòng	采用	採	v.	adopt, use	3
càidān	菜单	單	n.	menu	7
cānyǐn	餐饮	飲	n.	food and drink	7
chājià	差价	價	n.	price difference	7
chāyì	差异	異	n.	differentiation, difference	6
chángshì	尝试	嘗試	v.	attempt, try	7
chāoguò	超过	過	v.	surpass, exceed	1

拼音	简体	繁体	词性	英文	课数
chāoshí	超时	時	v.	go overtime	1
chēxiāng	车厢	車廂	n.	carriage, compartment	1
chéngbǎo	城堡		n.	castle	10
chéngdù	程度		n.	extent, level, standard, degree	4
chéng qiān shàng wàn	成千上万	萬	i.e.	thousands of, millions of	1
chíjiā	持家		v.o.	keep house; run one's household	10
chōngmǎn	充满	滿	v.	be full of	6
Chóngqìng	重庆	慶	p.n.	large city in Sichuan Province	1
chōuyàng	抽样	樣	v./n.	sample	2
chūchǎng	出场	場	v.o.	appear on the scene	9
chūshēng	出生		v.	be born	2
chūzhōng	初中		n.	junior high school	4
chuántǒng	传统	傳統	n./adj.	tradition; traditional	2
chuán zōng jiē dài	传宗接代	傳	i.e.	(have a son to) carry on the family name, continue the ancestral line	8
chuǎn	喘		v.	breathe rapidly, gasp for air	5
chuāngtái	窗台	臺	n.	windowsill	5
chuàng	创	創	v.	begin, initiate, establish	7
chuàngyè	创业	創業	v.o.	start an undertaking	6
chuàngzào	创造	創	v.	create	5
chūnyùn	春运	運	attr.	Spring Festival travel season	1
cí	辞	辭	v.	resign, dismiss, decline	6
cǐwài	此外		conj.	besides, in addition, furthermore	2
cóng yī ér zhōng	从一而终	從 終	i.e.	be faithful to one's husband (or be faithful to one's master)	8
còuhe	凑合	湊	v.	make do (with), passable, improvise	8
cùjìn	促进	進	v.	promote, advance, accelerate	6
cuòshī	措施		n.	measure, step	3
dádào	达到	達	v.	reach, achieve, attain	2
dáfù	答复	復	v.	answer, reply	7
dǎzhàng	打仗		v.o.	fight a war	1
dàduō	大多		adv.	mostly	8
dàtīng	大厅	廳	n.	lobby, hall	1
dàzhuān	大专	專	n.	junior college, technical college	4

拼音	简体	繁体	词性	英文	课数
dàikuǎn	贷款	貸	n./v.o.	loan, mortgage	3
dàiyù	待遇		n.	salary, benefit, treatment	4
dānshēn	单身	單	adj.	unmarried, single	10
dǎnliàng	胆量	膽	n.	courage, guts, nerve	6
dāngdì	当地	當	n.	local	7
dēng	登		v.	publish (in a newspaper or magazine)	9
dēnglù	登陆	陸	v.o.	land, disembark	8
děnghòu	等候		v.	wait, await	8
dītóu	低头	頭	v.o.	hang or lower one's head	5
dìwèi	地位		n.	position, status	4
diǎnxíng	典型		n./adj.	model; typical	10
diànmíng	店名		n.	name of a store	7
diàochá	调查	調	v./n.	investigate; investigation, survey	2
dīnglínglíng	叮呤呤		ono.	ringing sound	5
dǐng	顶	頂	v.	sustain, support, hold up	10
dìngdān	订单	訂單	n.	order form	7
dìnggòu	订购	訂購	v.	order (goods)	7
dúlì	独立	獨	v./adj.	(become) independent	10
dúmùqiáo	独木桥	獨 橋	n.	single-plank bridge	4
dúshēngzǐnǚ	独生子女	獨	n.	only child	10
dǔ	堵		v.	block, suffocate	1
duǎnxìn	短信		n.	short message, text message	9
duī	堆		v./n.	pile up; pile, heap	5
duì	对	對	m.	pair, couple	2
duìwu	队伍	隊	n.	team, profession, troops, army	4
érnǚ	儿女	兒	n.	sons and daughters, children	10
érsūn	儿孙	兒孫	n.	children and grandchildren, descendants	10
ér sūn mǎn táng	儿孙满堂	兒孫滿	i.e.	have many children and grandchildren	10
fāhuǒ	发火	發	v.o.	get angry, lose one's temper	5
fǎlǜ	法律		n.	law	3
fǎnwèn	反问	問	v.	ask (a question) in reply	9
fàncài	饭菜	飯	n.	rice and other dishes, meal	7
fángdìchǎn	房地产	產	n.	real estate, realty	3

拼音	简体	繁体	词性	英文	课数
fàngqì	放弃	棄	v.	abandon, give up	7
fēizhǎng	飞涨	飛漲	v.	shoot up, rise dramatically	3
fèipǐn	废品	廢	n.	waste product, reject	6
fēnchéng	分成		v.	divide (into)	4
fēnfēn	纷纷	紛	adv.	one after another	3
fēnpèi	分配		v.	distribute, allocate	3
fēnggé	风格	風	n.	style, manner	7
fēngjiàn	封建		adj./n.	feudal; feudalism	8
fēngwèi	风味	風	n.	special flavor	7
fúcóng	服从	從	v.	obey, follow	10
fúdù	幅度		n.	range, scope, extent	2
fúqi	福气	氣	n.	good luck, good fortune	10
fùdān	负担	負擔	v./n.	burden; load	3
gǎijìn	改进	進	v.	improve	7
gǎishàn	改善		v.	improve	3
gǎndòng	感动	動	v.	move, touch (emotionally)	8
gǎnkǎi	感慨		v./n.	sigh with emotion	6
gāofēng	高峰		n.	peak	1
gāokǎo	高考		n.	college entrance examination	4
gāoyú	高于	於	i.e.	superior to, higher than	8
gōngchéngshī	工程师	師	n.	engineer	5
gōngfáng	公房		n.	state-owned housing	3
gōngmín	公民		n.	citizen	2
gōngnéng	功能		n.	function	3
gōngshāng	工商		n.	industry and commerce	4
gōngyù	公寓		n.	apartment	3
gōngzhèng	公正		adj.	just, fair	3
gòngtóng	共同		adv.	together, jointly	9
gòngxiàn	贡献	貢獻	v./n.	contribute; contribution	6
gūdú	孤独	獨	adj.	lonely, solitary, lonesome	10
gǔlì	鼓励	勵	v.	encourage, urge	3
guàhào	挂号	掛號	v.	register (at a hospital)	1
guānniàn	观念	觀	n.	notion, thought, concept	2

拼音	简体	繁体	词性	英文	课数
guānzhù	关注	關	v.	pay close attention to	2
guǎnlǐ	管理		v./n.	manage, administer; management, administration	4
guǎngdà	广大	廣	adj.	broad, numerous	3
guī	归	歸	v.	belong to	3
guìzi	柜子	櫃	n.	cupboard, cabinet	5
guìzú	贵族	貴	n.	nobleman, aristocrat	10
guǒrán	果然		conj.	really, indeed, as expected	7
guòhòu	过后	過後	adv.	afterwards, later	7
hāqian	哈欠		n.	yawn	5
hánxù	含蓄		adj.	implicit, veiled, reserved	8
hànzhū	汗珠		n.	bead of sweat	9
hángyè	行业	業	n.	trade, profession, industry	6
háohuá	豪华	華	adj.	luxurious, extravagant	3
hǎobùróngyì	好不容易		adv.	with great difficulty, finally	1
héfàn	盒饭	飯	n.	box lunch	7
hòuchēshì	候车室	車	n.	waiting room, waiting lounge	1
hùjūn	户均	戶	attr.	per household	3
huādiàn	花店		n.	florist	8
huà	划	劃	v.	draw or mark a line	4
huàtí	话题	話題	n.	topic, subject of conversation	9
huáiyí	怀疑	懷	v.	doubt, suspect, distrust	7
huánbǎo	环保	環	attr.	environmental protection	6
huángdì	皇帝		n.	emperor	10
huánghūn	黄昏		n.	dusk	10
huánghūnliàn	黄昏恋	戀	n.	twilight romance, romance of the elderly	10
huīfù	恢复	復	v.	recover, restore, reinstate	4
huíshōu	回收		v.	collect to be recycled	6
hūnliàn	婚恋	戀	n.	marriage and courtship	8
huòdé	获得	獲	v.	obtain, acquire	6
jīguān	机关	機關	n.	office	6
jīhū	几乎	幾	adv.	almost, nearly	6
jījí	积极	積極	adj.	positive, active, enthusiastic	10
jīliè	激烈		adj.	intense, acute, fierce	4

拼音	简体	繁体	词性	英文	课数
jíshí	及时	時	adj.	timely, prompt	7
jíshǐ	即使		conj.	even if, even though	8
jǐ	挤	擠	v./adj.	shove, push; crowded	1
jìtuō	寄托	託	v.	place (hope, feeling, etc.) on	4
jiāzhǎng	家长	長	n.	parents, head of a family	4
jiāzú	家族		n.	clan, family	8
jià	价	價	n.	price	7
jià	嫁		v.	marry (a man)	8
jiàgé	价格	價	n.	price	3
jiàwèi	价位	價	n.	price level	7
jiàzhí	价值	價	n.	value	7
jiǎn	减	減	v.	subtract, reduce, decrease	10
jiǎnlì	简历	簡歷	n.	résumé	6
jiǎnpiào	检票	檢	v.o.	check tickets	1
jiànzào	建造		v.	construct, build	3
jiànzhù	建筑	築	n.	architecture, building	6
jiāngjìn	将近	將	adv.	close to, almost	1
jiǎngjiu	讲究	講	v.	pay attention to, strive for	8
jiāodiǎn	焦点	點	n.	focus, focal point, central issue	2
jiāoliú	交流		v.	exchange, communicate	6
jiāolǜ	焦虑	慮	adj.	agitated, anxious	6
jiāotōng	交通		n.	traffic	1
jiējìn	接近		v.	be close to, approximate	8
jiēshòu	接受		v.	accept, take on, undertake	2
jiégòu	结构	結構	n.	structure, composition	2
jīnróng	金融		n.	finance, banking	4
jǐnjiēzhe	紧接着	緊 著	adv.	immediately, right after	5
jīngdiǎn	经典	經	n./adj.	classics; classical	8
jīng pí lì jìn	精疲力尽	盡	i.e.	exhausted, worn out	5
jīngxǐ	惊喜	驚	n.	pleasant surprise	8
jīngyíng	经营	經營	v.	manage, run	10
jǐngzhōng	警钟	鐘	n.	alarm bell	2
jìngzhēng	竞争	競爭	v./ n.	compete; competition	4

拼音	简体	繁体	词性	英文	课数
jiǔliàng	酒量		n.	capacity for liquor	9
jiùyè	就业	業	v.o.	obtain employment	6
jūmín	居民		n.	resident, inhabitant	3
jūzhù	居住		v.	reside, dwell	3
jú	局		n.	bureau	3
jùhào	句号	號	n.	period, full stop	4
jùjí	聚集		v.	gather, get together	1
kāifāshāng	开发商	開發	n.	developer	3
kāifàng	开放	開	adj.	open-minded	8
kē	颗	顆	m.(n.)	small particles	5
kēmù	科目		n.	school subject or course	5
kèhù	客户	戶	n.	client, customer	7
kěndìng	肯定		adv.	definitely, undoubtedly	6
kǒuwèi	口味		n.	taste	7
kuàicān	快餐		n.	fast food	7
kuānchǎng	宽敞	寬	adj.	spacious, roomy	3
kuòdà	扩大	擴	v.	broaden, expand	3
làngfèi	浪费	費	v.	waste	6
làngmàn	浪漫		adj.	romantic	8
lǎobǎixìng	老百姓		n.	ordinary people	3
lǎobǎn	老板	闆	n.	boss	6
lǎolíng	老龄	齡	attr.	old age	2
líhūn	离婚	離	v.o.	divorce	8
lìrùn	利润	潤	n.	profit, profit return	6
liǎnhóng xīntiào	脸红心跳	臉紅	v.p.	blush with shame or shyness	7
línshí	临时	臨時	adj.	temporary	1
liúchuán	流传	傳	v.	circulate, spread	8
liúlèi	流泪	淚	v.o.	shed tears	7
liúliàng	流量		n.	volume of flow, rate of flow	1
liúxíng	流行		adj.	popular, fashionable	6
liúxué	留学	學	v.	study abroad	4
lóufáng	楼房	樓	n.	multi-storied building	9
lùtú	路途		n.	road, journey	5

拼音	简体	繁体	词性	英文	课数
lǜ	率		n.	rate, proportion, ratio	2
lǜdēng	绿灯	綠燈	n.	green light	1
lǜshī	律师	師	n.	lawyer	5
mǎnzú	满足	滿	v.	satisfy	7
máodùn	矛盾		n.	conflict, contradiction	8
mào	冒		v.	emit, give off, send out	9
màoxiǎn	冒险	險	v.o.	take an adventure, take a risk	9
méiguī	玫瑰		n.	rose	8
mén dāng hù duì	门当户对	門當戶對	i.e.	be well-matched in social and economic status for marriage	8
ménzhěn	门诊	門診	n.	outpatient service	1
mèn	闷	悶	adj.	bored, depressed	10
mǐ	米		n.	meter	3
mìshū	秘书	書	n.	secretary	9
miǎnfèi	免费	費	v.o.	free of charge	4
miǎnqiǎng	勉强	強	v.	do or manage with difficulty	9
miànjī	面积	積	n.	area, square measure	3
miànlín	面临	臨	v.	be faced with	2
miànshí	面食	麵	n.	food made of wheat	7
miànxiàng	面向		v.	face, be geared to the needs of, cater to	3
miáoshù	描述		v.	describe	6
mùguāng	目光		n.	look, sight, vision	5
nán shàng jiā nán	难上加难	難	i.e.	make a difficult situation even more difficult	1
nánzǐhàn	男子汉	漢	n.	real man, true man	9
nàozhōng	闹钟	鬧鐘	n.	alarm clock	5
nìmíng	匿名		attr.	anonymous, anonymity	9
niándài	年代		n.	decade, time, era	2
niánxiàn	年限		n.	fixed number of years	2
niánxīn	年薪		n.	annual salary	9
niánzhǎng	年长	長	adj.	senior	10
páxíng	爬行		v.	crawl	1
páiduì	排队	隊	v.	line up	1
pànwàng	盼望		v.	look forward to	9
pèitào	配套		v.	form a complete set	3

拼音	简体	繁体	词性	英文	课数
pèngbì	碰壁		v.o.	be rebuffed	7
pīn	拼		v.	go all out in work	5
pìnqǐng	聘请	請	v.	hire	7
píngdàn	平淡		adj.	ordinary	9
píngfāng	平方		n.	square	3
pòlàn	破烂	爛	n.	junk, scrap	6
qīdài	期待		v.	anticipate, expect	5
qījiān	期间	間	n.	period, duration	1
qīwàng	期望		v./n.	hope, expect; expectation	8
qíquán	齐全	齊	adj.	complete, well-stocked	3
qǐchū	起初		adv.	at first, in the beginning	7
qǐshì	启事	啟	n.	notice, announcement	9
qǐyèjiā	企业家	業	n.	entrepreneur	9
qiān jūn wàn mǎ	千军万马	軍萬馬	i.e.	thousands of soldiers and horses (a big army)	4
qiáncái	钱财	錢財	n.	wealth, money	10
qiántú	前途		n.	future	4
qiángdiào	强调	強調	v.	stress, emphasize	8
qiāo	敲		v.	knock, strike, beat	2
qiǎokèlì	巧克力		n.	chocolate	8
qīnzì	亲自	親	adv.	personally, in person	7
qīngchén	清晨		n.	early morning	5
qīngshàonián	青少年		n.	youth, teenager	4
qínggǎn	情感		n.	emotion, feeling	8
qíngrén	情人		n.	lover, sweetheart	8
qíngrénjié	情人节	節	p.n.	Valentine's Day	8
qióngrén	穷人	窮	n.	poor people	8
qiú'ài	求爱	愛	v.o.	woo, court	8
qiúzhí	求职	職	v.o.	apply for a job	6
qǔ	娶		v.	marry (a woman)	8
quán	权	權	n.	power, rights	3
quánlì	权力	權	n.	power, authority	10
quánwēi	权威	權	n.	authority	10
qúntǐ	群体	體	n.	colony, community, group	10

拼音	简体	繁体	词性	英文	课数
rèliàn	热恋	熱戀	v.	be passionately in love	9
rèmén	热门	熱門	adj.	popular, hot	4
réncái	人才		n.	person with ability	4
réncì	人次		n.	person-time	1
rénjūn	人均		attr.	per capita, per person	3
rénkǒu	人口		n.	population	2
rénmínbì	人民币	幣	n.	RMB, Chinese currency	1
rén shān rén hǎi	人山人海		i.e.	mountains and seas of people	1
rìyì	日益		adv.	more and more	6
róngqià	融洽		adj.	harmonious	8
róngyù	荣誉	榮譽	n.	honor, glory, credit	2
rúcǐ	如此		pron.	so, such, like this	1
rújīn	如今		adv.	nowadays, now	10
rúxià	如下		v.	as follows	6
rùxué	入学	學	v.o.	enter a school, be enrolled in, matriculate	4
shāngpǐn	商品		n.	commodity, goods	3
Shàngdì	上帝		p.n.	God	5
shàngshēng	上升		v.	rise, ascend	2
shàngzhǎng	上涨	漲	v.	rise, go up	3
shèjiāo	社交		n.	social intercourse	9
shèshī	设施	設	n.	installation, facility	3
shénmì	神秘		adj.	mysterious, mystical	9
shēngjí	升级	級	v.o.	go up (in grade, etc.)	7
shēngxué	升学	學	v.o.	enter a higher school	5
shēngyǎng	生养	養	v.	have and raise children	10
shēngyù	生育		v./n.	give birth to; childbearing	2
Shèngjīng	圣经	聖經	p.n.	Bible	5
shībài	失败	敗	v./n.	fail, lose; failure, loss	6
shīfàn	师范	師範	n.	teachers' college, normal school	4
shīqù	失去		v.	lose, miss	6
shītiáo	失调	調	v./adj.	lose balance; unbalanced	2
shīzī	师资	師資	n.	teaching staff	4
shíxíng	实行	實	v.	carry out, implement	2

拼音	简体	繁体	词性	英文	课数
shízài	实在	實	adv.	indeed, as a matter of fact	3
shìjì	世纪	紀	n.	century	2
shìxiān	事先		adv.	in advance, beforehand	7
shōují	收集		v.	collect, gather	7
shōurù	收入		n.	income, revenue	3
shǒuxiān	首先		adv.	first, first of all	2
shǒuxuǎn	首选	選	n.	first choice	6
shòu	受		v	get, receive, suffer	4
shūjià	书架	書	n.	bookshelf	5
shūshì	舒适	適	adj.	comfortable, cozy	3
shǔyú	属于	屬於	v.	belong to	10
shù	束		m.	bundle, bunch	8
shùliàng	数量	數	n.	quantity, amount	2
shuāngfāng	双方	雙	n.	both sides, two parties	8
shuāngxiàng	双向	雙	adj.	two-way, bidirectional	4
shuìmèng	睡梦	夢	n.	deep sleep, slumber	5
shuòshì	硕士	碩	n.	master, master's degree	4
sī	丝	絲	m.	thread	5
sīfáng	私房		n.	privately owned house	3
sòngcān	送餐		n.	delivery	7
sùdù	速度		n.	speed, pace	3
sùliào	塑料		n.	plastic	6
sùzhì	素质	質	n.	innate quality	2
suízhe	随着	隨著	prep.	along with, in the wake of	2
sūnbèi	孙辈	孫輩	n.	grandchildren (generation)	10
sǔnhài	损害	損	v./ n.	harm, injure; damage	4
sǔnshī	损失	損	n./v.	loss; damage	1
suǒ	锁	鎖	n.	lock	5
tàijíquán	太极拳	極	n.	tai chi	10
tánlùn	谈论	談論	v./n.	talk about, discuss; discussion	2
tánqǐ	谈起	談	v.	mention, speak of	10
tècháng	特长	長	n.	special aptitude, specialty	9
tèsè	特色		n.	salient feature, characteristic	7

拼音	简体	繁体	词性	英文	课数
tíqián	提前		v.	shift to an earlier time	1
tiān zhī jiāo zǐ	天之骄子	驕	i.e.	God's favored one, an unusually privileged person	6
tiáohé	调和	調	v.	mediate, reconcile	8
tiáozhěng	调整	調	v./n.	adjust; adjustment	3
tiǎozhàn	挑战	戰	v./n.	challenge	2
tiěfànwǎn	铁饭碗	鐵飯	n.	iron rice bowl, secure job	6
tōngxíng	通行		v.	pass through	1
tǒngguǎn	统管	統	v.	govern, reign	10
tǒngjì	统计	統計	n./v.	statistics, census; gather statistics	1
tóu hūn nǎo zhàng	头昏脑胀	頭 腦脹	i.e.	dizzy, feel one's head swimming	5
tūpò	突破		v.	break through	7
tuīxiāo	推销	銷	v.	promote (goods)	7
tuīxíng	推行		v.	carry out, implement	5
wàilì	外力		n.	outside or external force	8
wǎnbèi	晚辈	輩	n.	younger generation, juniors	10
wǎnnián	晚年		n.	old age, one's later years	10
wǎngluò	网络	網絡	n.	(computer) network	6
wǎngzhàn	网站	網	n.	website	6
wéihù	维护	維護	v.	protect, uphold, defend	10
wéijīn	围巾	圍	n.	scarf	9
wéixiū	维修	維	v.	maintain, repair	3
wèi	未		adv.	not	1
wèihūn	未婚		attr.	unmarried	9
wōniú	蜗牛	蝸	n.	snail	1
wúbǐ	无比	無	adv.	incomparably, unparalleled	2
wúchērì	无车日	無車	n.	Car-Free Day	1
wúnài	无奈	無	adj.	helpless	5
wúsuǒwèi	无所谓	無 謂	i.e.	(do) not care, be indifferent	6
xīshēng	牺牲	犧	v.	sacrifice	8
xīyáng	西洋		adj.	the West, the Occident	8
xīyǐn	吸引		v.	attract	9
xǐhào	喜好		v.	like, be fond of	10

拼音	简体	繁体	词性	英文	课数
xǐyuè	喜悦		adj./n.	happy, joyous; happiness	2
xì	细	細	adj.	thin, fine, slender	9
xiàjiàng	下降		v.	descend, drop, fall, decline	2
xiànzhì	限制		v.	restrict, limit, confine	3
xiāngtián	香甜		adj.	fragrant and sweet, sound (sleep)	5
xiángxì	详细	詳細	adj.	detailed, elaborate	7
xiǎngshòu	享受		v.	enjoy (rights, benefits, etc.)	10
xiǎochī	小吃		n.	snacks	7
xiàoyuán	校园	園	n.	campus, schoolyard	4
xiězìlóu	写字楼	寫 樓	n.	office building	7
xīnjiàn	新建		v.	newly built	3
Xīnlàngwǎng	新浪网	網	p.n.	Sina News website	6
xīnlǐ	心理		n.	psychology, mentality; mental	6
xīnshàngrén	心上人		n.	sweetheart, heart's desire	8
xìnxī	信息		n.	information	7
xīngjiàn	兴建	興	v.	build, construct	3
xīngqǐ	兴起	興	v.	rise, spring up	4
xìngbié	性别	別	n.	gender	2
xìng zhì bó bó	兴致勃勃	興	i.e.	full of zest or enthusiasm	9
xuéchéng	学成	學	v.	complete study	4
xuélì	学历	學歷	n.	educational background	4
xuéwèi	学位	學	n.	academic degree	4
xùnsù	迅速		adj.	rapid, speedy	3
yā	压	壓	v.	press, push down	5
yāyì	压抑	壓	v.	constrain, inhibit, depress	5
yánjiūshēng	研究生		n.	graduate student	4
yánzhòng	严重	嚴	adj.	serious	3
yáo	摇	搖	v.	shake, wave, rock	5
yáoyuǎn	遥远	遙遠	adj.	distant, remote, far away	5
yèwù	业务	業務	n.	business	7
yìjiāzhīzhǔ	一家之主		n.	head of the household	10
yìkǒuqì	一口气	氣	adv.	in one breath, without a break	5
yìliánchuàn	一连串	連	n.p.	series of, a chain of	9
yìxìliè	一系列		attr.	series of	4

拼音	简体	繁体	词性	英文	课数
yì	亿	億	num.	hundred million	1
yìwù	义务	義務	n.	duty, obligation	4
yīng	婴	嬰	n.	infant, baby	2
yíngyǎng	营养	營養	n.	nutrition	7
yìng yùn ér shēng	应运而生	應運	i.e.	emerge in response to the proper time or opportunity	3
yìngzhēng	应征	應徵	v.	respond to an ad or solicitation	9
yōngdǔ	拥堵	擁	adj.	crowded, jammed	1
yōngjǐ	拥挤	擁擠	adj.	crowded, packed	1
yǒng	涌	湧	v./n.	(of water or clouds) gush, surge	6
yǒnggǎn	勇敢		adj.	brave, courageous	8
yòngrén	用人		v.o.	employ people	4
yōu	忧	憂	v.	be worried, be concerned, worry	2
yōuhuì	优惠	優	n.	favor, discount	7
yōuxiù	优秀	優	adj.	outstanding, excellent	5
yōuyuè	优越	優	adj.	superior, advantageous	9
yóu cǐ ér lái	由此而来	來	i.e.	(it) comes/originated from this (cause or source)	5
yǒuquán	有权	權	v.o.	have the right/power to, be entitled to	10
yǒu suǒ zuò wéi	有所作为	為	i.e.	have (a certain) accomplishment, accomplished	9
yú	余	餘	v./n.	have a surplus; surplus	9
yǔ	与	與	conj.	and	1
yùjì	预计	預計	v.	estimate, calculate in advance	2
yùqī	预期	預	v.	expect, anticipate, predict	2
yuàn	愿	願	v.	be willing to, want to	9
yǔnxǔ	允许	許	v.	permit, allow, grant	10
zàicì	再次		adv.	second time, once more	8
zàishēng	再生		v./attr.	regrow, reproduce, recycle	6
zàochéng	造成		v.	bring about, cause	3
zébèi	责备	責備	v.	accuse, blame	7
zérèn	责任	責	n.	duty, responsibility	10
zéyè	择业	擇業	v.o.	select a career	6
zhǎ	眨		v.	(of eyes) blink, wink	5
zhǎngbèi	长辈	長輩	n.	elder generation, elders, seniors	10

拼音	简体	繁体	词性	英文	课数
zhǎngguǎn	掌管		v.	be in charge of, administer	10
zhāopìn	招聘		v.	advertise job offers, recruit employees	6
zhāoshēng	招生		v.o.	recruit students	6
zhèn	阵	陣	m.	short period, a spell	5
zhēng	征	徵	v.	solicit	9
zhēngqǔ	争取	爭	v.	strive for	3
zhěng	整		adj.	whole, complete	10
zhěngzhěng	整整		adj.	whole, full	10
zhèngcè	政策		n.	policy	2
zhèngshì	正式		adj.	formal, official	2
zhèngshū	证书	証書	n.	certificate, diploma	2
zhīmíng	知名		adj.	well-known, famous	7
zhí	值		n.	value, worth	8
zhídé	值得		v.	be worth, deserve	2
zhì	制		v./n.	make; system	3
zhìdù	制度		n.	system	3
zhìyú	至于	於	prep.	as for	3
zhōngshēn	终身	終	n.	lifetime	6
zhōngzhuǎn	中转	轉	v.	transfer, change hands	7
zhòng nán qīng nǚ	重男轻女	輕	v.o.	value male more than female	2
zhú	逐		adj.	one by one	4
zhújiàn	逐渐	漸	adv.	gradually	4
zhǔdòng	主动	動	adj.	active, voluntary	8
zhǔxiū	主修		v.	major, specialize	4
zhùfú	祝福		v./n.	wish happiness to; blessing, benediction	2
zhùzhái	住宅		n.	residence, dwelling	3
zhuānmén	专门	專門	adj.	special, specialized	7
zhuǎnháng	转行	轉	v.	change profession	4
zhuànqǔ	赚取	賺	v.	earn, make a profit	7
zhuàngtài	状态	狀態	n.	state, condition	10
zhuīqiú	追求		v.	seek, pursue, court (a person)	8
zìháo	自豪		adj.	proud	10

拼音	简体	繁体	词性	英文	课数
zìxìn	自信		adj.	self-confident, confident	9
zì yóu zì zài	自由自在		adj.	free as the wind, light-hearted	10
zìzhǔ	自主		v.	of one's own will	6
zǒudào	走道		n.	aisle	1
zú	族		n.	ethnicity, race, a group of people with common features	4
zuìzhōng	最终	終	adv.	finally, at last	1

Vocabulary Index
English - Chinese

英文	简体	繁体	拼音	词性	课数
abandon, give up	放弃	棄	fàngqì	v.	7
academic degree	学位	學	xuéwèi	n.	4
accept, take on, undertake	接受		jiēshòu	v.	2
accuse, blame	责备	責備	zébèi	v.	7
active, voluntary	主动	動	zhǔdòng	adj.	8
adjust; adjustment	调整	調	tiáozhěng	v./n.	3
adopt, carry out	采取	採	cǎiqǔ	v.	3
adopt, use	采用	採	cǎiyòng	v.	3
advertise job offers, recruit employees	招聘	聘	zhāopìn	v.	6
afterwards, later	过后	過後	guòhòu	adv.	7
agitated, anxious	焦虑	慮	jiāolǜ	adj.	6
aisle	走道		zǒudào	n.	1
alarm bell	警钟	鐘	jǐngzhōng	n.	2
alarm clock	闹钟	鬧鐘	nàozhōng	n.	5
almost, nearly	几乎	幾	jīhū	adv.	6
along with, in the wake of	随着	隨著	suízhe	prep.	2
and	与	與	yǔ	conj.	1
annual salary	年薪		niánxīn	n.	9
anonymous, anonymity	匿名		nìmíng	attr.	9
answer, reply	答复	復	dáfù	v.	7
anticipate, expect	期待		qīdài	v.	5
apartment	公寓		gōngyù	n.	3
appear on the scene	出场	場	chūchǎng	v.o.	9
apply for a job	求职	職	qiúzhí	v.o.	6
architecture, building	建筑	築	jiànzhù	n.	6
area, square measure	面积	積	miànjī	n.	3
as follows	如下		rúxià	v.	6
as for	至于	於	zhìyú	prep.	3
ask (a question) in reply	反问	問	fǎnwèn	v.	9
at first, in the beginning	起初		qǐchū	adv.	7

英文	简体	繁体	拼音	词性	课数
attempt, try	尝试	嘗試	*chángshì*	v.	7
attract	吸引		*xīyǐn*	v.	9
authority	权威	權	*quánwēi*	n.	10
be born	出生		*chūshēng*	v.	2
be close to, approximate	接近		*jiējìn*	v.	8
be faced with	面临	臨	*miànlín*	v.	2
be faithful to one's husband (or be faithful to one's master)	从一而终	從 終	*cóng yī ér zhōng*	i.e.	8
be forced, be compelled	被迫		*bèipò*	v.	4
be full of	充满	滿	*chōngmǎn*	v.	6
be in charge of, administer	掌管		*zhǎngguǎn*	v.	10
be passionately in love	热恋	熱戀	*rèliàn*	v.	9
be rebuffed	碰壁		*pèngbì*	v.o.	7
be well-matched in social and economic status for marriage	门当户对	門當戶對	*mén dāng hù duì*	i.e.	8
be willing to, want to	愿	願	*yuàn*	v.	9
be worried, be concerned, worry	忧	憂	*yōu*	v.	2
be worth, deserve	值得		*zhídé*	v.	2
bead of sweat	汗珠		*hànzhū*	n.	9
begin, initiate, establish	创	創	*chuàng*	v.	7
belong to	归	歸	*guī*	v.	3
belong to	属于	屬於	*shǔyú*	v.	10
besides, in addition, furthermore	此外		*cǐwài*	conj.	2
Bible	圣经	聖經	*Shèngjīng*	p.n.	5
(of eyes) blink, wink	眨		*zhǎ*	v.	5
block, suffocate	堵		*dǔ*	v.	1
blush with shame or shyness	脸红心跳	臉紅	*liǎnhóng xīntiào*	v.p.	7
bookshelf	书架	書	*shūjià*	n.	5
bored, depressed	闷	悶	*mèn*	adj.	10
boss	老板	闆	*lǎobǎn*	n.	6
both sides, two parties	双方	雙	*shuāngfāng*	n.	8
box lunch	盒饭	飯	*héfàn*	n.	7
brave, courageous	勇敢		*yǒnggǎn*	adj.	8

英文	简体	繁体	拼音	词性	课数
break through	突破		tūpò	v.	7
breathe rapidly, gasp for air	喘		chuǎn	v.	5
bring about, cause	造成		zàochéng	v.	3
broad, numerous	广大	廣	guǎngdà	adj.	3
broaden, expand	扩大	擴	kuòdà	v.	3
build, construct	兴建	興	xīngjiàn	v.	3
bundle, bunch	束		shù	m.	8
burden; load	负担	負擔	fùdān	v./n.	3
bureau	局		jú	n.	3
business	业务	業務	yèwù	n.	7
campus, schoolyard	校园	園	xiàoyuán	n.	4
cannot stand; extremely	不堪		bùkān	v./adv.	1
can't help	不由得		bùyóude	adv.	5
capacity for liquor	酒量		jiǔliàng	n.	9
Car-Free Day	无车日	無車	wúchērì	n.	1
carriage, compartment	车厢	車廂	chēxiāng	n.	1
(have a son to) carry on the family name, continue the ancestral line	传宗接代	傳	chuán zōng jiē dài	i.e.	8
carry out, implement	实行	實	shíxíng	v.	2
carry out, implement	推行		tuīxíng	v.	5
castle	城堡		chéngbǎo	n.	10
century	世纪	紀	shìjì	n.	2
certificate, diploma	证书	証書	zhèngshū	n.	2
challenge	挑战	戰	tiǎozhàn	v./n.	2
change profession	转行	轉	zhuǎnháng	v.	4
check tickets	检票	檢	jiǎnpiào	v.o.	1
children and grandchildren, descendants	儿孙	兒孫	érsūn	n.	10
chocolate	巧克力		qiǎokèlì	n.	8
circulate, spread	流传	傳	liúchuán	v.	8
citizen	公民		gōngmín	n.	2
clan, family	家族		jiāzú	n.	8
classics; classical	经典	經	jīngdiǎn	n./adj.	8
client, customer	客户	戶	kèhù	n.	7

英文	简体	繁体	拼音	词性	课数
close to, almost	将近	將	*jiāngjìn*	adv.	1
collect, gather	收集		*shōují*	v.	7
collect to be recycled	回收		*huíshōu*	v.	6
college entrance examination	高考		*gāokǎo*	n.	4
colony, community, group	群体	體	*qúntǐ*	n.	10
(it) comes/originated from this (cause or source)	由此而来	來	*yóu cǐ ér lái*	i.e.	5
comfortable, cozy	舒适	適	*shūshì*	adj.	3
commodity, goods	商品		*shāngpǐn*	n.	3
companion, mate, partner	伴侣	侣	*bànlǚ*	n.	9
compete; competition	竞争	競爭	*jìngzhēng*	v./ n.	4
complete study	学成	學	*xuéchéng*	v.	4
complete, well-stocked	齐全	齊	*qíquán*	adj.	3
conflict, contradiction	矛盾		*máodùn*	n.	8
constrain, inhibit, depress	压抑	壓	*yāyì*	v.	5
construct, build	建造		*jiànzào*	v.	3
contribute; contribution	贡献	貢獻	*gòngxiàn*	v./n.	6
courage, guts, nerve	胆量	膽	*dǎnliàng*	n.	6
crawl	爬行		*páxíng*	v.	1
create	创造	創	*chuàngzào*	v.	5
crowded, jammed	拥堵	擁	*yōngdǔ*	adj.	1
crowded, packed	拥挤	擁擠	*yōngjǐ*	adj.	1
cupboard, cabinet	柜子	櫃	*guìzi*	n.	5
decade, time, era	年代		*niándài*	n.	2
deep sleep, slumber	睡梦	夢	*shuìmèng*	n.	5
definitely, undoubtedly	肯定		*kěndìng*	adv.	6
delivery	送餐	餐	*sòngcān*	n.	7
descend, drop, fall, decline	下降		*xiàjiàng*	v.	2
describe	描述		*miáoshù*	v.	6
detailed, elaborate	详细	詳細	*xiángxì*	adj.	7
developer	开发商	開發	*kāifāshāng*	n.	3
differentiation, difference	差异	異	*chāyì*	n.	6
distant, remote, far away	遥远	遙遠	*yáoyuǎn*	adj.	5
distribute, allocate	分配		*fēnpèi*	v.	3

英文	简体	繁体	拼音	词性	课数
divide (into)	分成		*fēnchéng*	v.	4
divorce	离婚	離	*líhūn*	v.o.	8
dizzy, feel one's head swimming	头昏脑胀	頭腦脹	*tóu hūn nǎo zhàng*	i.e.	5
do or manage with difficulty	勉强	強	*miǎnqiǎng*	v.	9
doubt, suspect, distrust	怀疑	懷	*huáiyí*	v.	7
draw or mark a line	划	劃	*huà*	v.	4
dusk	黄昏		*huánghūn*	n.	10
duty, obligation	义务	義務	*yìwù*	n.	4
duty, responsibility	责任	責	*zérèn*	n.	10
early morning	清晨		*qīngchén*	n.	5
earn, make a profit	赚取	賺	*zhuànqǔ*	v.	7
educational background	学历	學歷	*xuélì*	n.	4
elder generation, elders, seniors	长辈	長輩	*zhǎngbèi*	n.	10
emerge in response to the proper time or opportunity	应运而生	應運	*yìng yùn ér shēng*	i.e.	3
emit, give off, send out	冒		*mào*	v.	9
emotion, feeling	情感		*qínggǎn*	n.	8
emperor	皇帝		*huángdì*	n.	10
employ people	用人		*yòngrén*	v.o.	4
encourage, urge	鼓励	勵	*gǔlì*	v.	3
engineer	工程师	師	*gōngchéngshī*	n.	5
enjoy (rights, benefits, etc.)	享受		*xiǎngshòu*	v.	10
enter a higher school	升学	學	*shēngxué*	v.o.	5
enter a school, be enrolled in, matriculate	入学	學	*rùxué*	v.o.	4
entrepreneur	企业家	業	*qǐyèjiā*	n.	9
environmental protection	环保	環	*huánbǎo*	attr.	6
estimate, calculate in advance	预计	預計	*yùjì*	v.	2
ethnicity, race, a group of people with common features	族		*zú*	n.	4
even if, even though	即使		*jíshǐ*	conj.	8
exchange, communicate	交流		*jiāoliú*	v.	6
exhausted, worn out	精疲力尽	盡	*jīng pí lì jìn*	i.e.	5
expect, anticipate, predict	预期	預	*yùqī*	v.	2
explode; blast, explosion	爆炸		*bàozhà*	v./n.	1

英文	简体	繁体	拼音	词性	课数
express or state clearly	表白		*biǎobái*	v.	8
extent, level, standard, degree	程度		*chéngdù*	n.	4
face, be geared to the needs of, cater to	面向		*miànxiàng*	v.	3
fail, lose; failure, loss	失败	敗	*shībài*	v./n.	6
fast food	快餐		*kuàicān*	n.	7
favor, discount	优惠	優	*yōuhuì*	n.	7
feudal; feudalism	封建		*fēngjiàn*	adj./n.	8
fight a war	打仗		*dǎzhàng*	v.o.	1
finally, at last	最终	終	*zuìzhōng*	adv.	1
finance, banking	金融		*jīnróng*	n.	4
first choice	首选	選	*shǒuxuǎn*	n.	6
first, first of all	首先		*shǒuxiān*	adv.	2
fixed number of years	年限		*niánxiàn*	n.	2
florist	花店		*huādiàn*	n.	8
focus, focal point, central issue	焦点	點	*jiāodiǎn*	n.	2
food and drink	餐饮	飲	*cānyǐn*	n.	7
food made of wheat	面食	麵	*miànshí*	n.	7
form a complete set	配套		*pèitào*	v.	3
formal, official	正式		*zhèngshì*	adj.	2
fragrant and sweet, sound (sleep)	香甜		*xiāngtián*	adj.	5
free as the wind, light-hearted	自由自在		*zìyóuzìzài*	adj.	10
free of charge	免费	費	*miǎnfèi*	v.o.	4
full of zest or enthusiasm	兴致勃勃	興	*xìng zhì bó bó*	i.e.	9
function	功能		*gōngnéng*	n.	3
future	前途		*qiántú*	n.	4
gather, get together	聚集		*jùjí*	v.	1
gender	性别	別	*xìngbié*	n.	2
get angry, lose one's temper	发火	發	*fāhuǒ*	v.o.	5
get, receive, suffer	受		*shòu*	v	4
give birth to; childbearing	生育		*shēngyù*	v./n.	2
go all out in work	拼		*pīn*	v.	5
go up (in grade, etc.)	升级	級	*shēngjí*	v.o.	7
God	上帝		*Shàngdì*	p.n.	5

英文	简体	繁体	拼音	词性	课数
God's favored one, an unusually privileged person	天之骄子	驕	tiān zhī jiāo zǐ	i.e.	6
good luck, good fortune	福气	氣	fúqi	n.	10
govern, reign	统管	統	tǒngguǎn	v.	10
gradually	逐渐	漸	zhújiàn	adv.	4
graduate student	研究生		yánjiūshēng	n.	4
grandchildren (generation)	孙辈	孫輩	sūnbèi	n.	10
green light	绿灯	綠燈	lǜdēng	n.	1
(of water or clouds) gush, surge	涌	湧	yǒng	v./n.	6
hang or lower one's head	低头	頭	dītóu	v.o.	5
happy, joyous; happiness	喜悦		xǐyuè	adj./n.	2
harm, injure; damage	损害	損	sǔnhài	v./ n.	4
harmonious	融洽		róngqià	adj.	8
have a surplus; surplus	余	餘	yú	v./n.	9
have (a certain) accomplishment, accomplished, accomplished	有所作为	為	yǒu suǒ zuò wéi	i.e.	9
have and raise children	生养	養	shēngyǎng	v.	10
have many children and grandchildren	儿孙满堂	兒孫滿	ér sūn mǎn táng	i.e.	10
have the right/power to be entitled to	有权	權	yǒuquán	v.o.	10
head of the household	一家之主		yìjiāzhīzhǔ	n.	10
helpless	无奈	無	wúnài	adj.	5
hire	聘请	請	pìnqǐng	v.	7
honor, glory, credit	荣誉	榮譽	róngyù	n.	2
hope, expect; expectation	期望		qīwàng	v./n.	8
hundred million	亿	億	yì	num.	1
immediately, right after	紧接着	緊 著	jǐnjiēzhe	adv.	5
implicit, veiled, reserved	含蓄		hánxù	adj.	8
improve	改进	進	gǎijìn	v.	7
improve	改善		gǎishàn	v.	3
in advance, beforehand	事先		shìxiān	adv.	7
in one breath, without a break	一口气	氣	yìkǒuqì	adv.	5
income, revenue	收入		shōurù	n.	3
incomparably, unparalleled	无比	無	wúbǐ	adv.	2
indeed, as a matter of fact	实在	實	shízài	adv.	3
(become) independent	独立	獨	dúlì	v./adj.	10

英文	简体	繁体	拼音	词性	课数
industry and commerce	工商		gōngshāng	n.	4
infant, baby	婴	嬰	yīng	n.	2
information	信息		xìnxī	n.	7
innate quality	素质	質	sùzhì	n.	2
installation, facility	设施	設	shèshī	n.	3
intense, acute, fierce	激烈		jīliè	adj.	4
investigate; investigation, survey	调查	調	diàochá	v./n.	2
iron rice bowl, secure job	铁饭碗	鐵飯	tiěfànwǎn	n.	6
issue, award (certificate, medal)	颁发	頒發	bānfā	v.	2
issue, publish	颁布	頒	bānbù	v.	4
junior college, technical college	大专	專	dàzhuān	n.	4
junior high school	初中		chūzhōng	n.	4
junk, scrap	破烂	爛	pòlàn	n.	6
just, fair	公正		gōngzhèng	adj.	3
keep house, run one's household	持家		chíjiā	v.o.	10
knock, strike, beat	敲		qiāo	v.	2
land, disembark	登陆	陸	dēnglù	v.o.	8
large city in Sichuan Province	重庆	慶	Chóngqìng	p.n.	1
law	法律		fǎlǜ	n.	3
lawyer	律师	師	lǜshī	n.	5
lifetime	终身	終	zhōngshēn	n.	6
like, be fond of	喜好		xǐhào	v./n.	10
line up	排队	隊	páiduì	v.	1
loan, mortgage	贷款	貸	dàikuǎn	n./v.o.	3
lobby, hall	大厅	廳	dàtīng	n.	1
local	当地	當	dāngdì	n.	7
lock	锁	鎖	suǒ	n.	5
lonely, solitary, lonesome	孤独	獨	gūdú	adj.	10
look forward to	盼望		pànwàng	v.	9
look, sight, vision	目光		mùguāng	n.	5
lose balance; unbalanced	失调	調	shītiáo	v./adj.	2
lose, miss	失去		shīqù	v.	6
loss; damage	损失	損	sǔnshī	n./v.	1

英文	简体	繁体	拼音	词性	课数
lover, sweetheart	情人		qíngrén	n.	8
luxurious, extravagant	豪华	華	háohuá	adj.	3
maintain, repair	维修	維	wéixiū	v.	3
major, specialize	主修		zhǔxiū	v.	4
make a difficult situation even more difficult	难上加难	難	nán shàng jiā nán	i.e.	1
make do (with), passable, improvise	凑合	湊	còuhe	v.	8
make; system	制		zhì	v./n.	3
manage, administer; management, administration	管理		guǎnlǐ	v./n.	4
manage, run	经营	經營	jīngyíng	v.	10
marriage and courtship	婚恋	戀	hūnliàn	n.	8
marry (a man)	嫁		jià	v.	8
marry (a woman)	娶		qǔ	v.	8
master, master's degree	硕士	碩	shuòshì	n.	4
measure, step	措施		cuòshī	n.	3
mediate, reconcile	调和	調	tiáohé	v.	8
mention, speak of	谈起	談	tánqǐ	v.	10
menu	菜单	單	càidān	n.	7
meter	米		mǐ	n.	3
model; typical	典型		diǎnxíng	n./adj.	10
more and more	日益		rìyì	adv.	6
mostly	大多		dàduō	adv.	8
mountains and seas of people	人山人海		rén shān rén hǎi	i.e.	1
move, touch (emotionally)	感动	動	gǎndòng	v.	8
multi-storied building	楼房	樓	lóufáng	n.	9
mysterious, mystical	神秘		shénmì	adj.	9
name of a store	店名		diànmíng	n.	7
(computer) network	网络	網絡	wǎngluò	n.	6
newly built	新建		xīnjiàn	v.	3
nobleman, aristocrat	贵族	貴	guìzú	n.	10
not	未		wèi	adv.	1
(do) not care, be indifferent	无所谓	無 謂	wúsuǒwèi	i.e.	6
notice, announcement	启事	啟	qǐshì	n.	9
notion, thought, concept	观念	觀	guānniàn	n.	2

英文	简体	繁体	拼音	词性	课数
nowadays, now	如今		*rújīn*	adv.	10
nutrition	营养	營養	*yíngyǎng*	n.	7
obey, follow	服从	從	*fúcóng*	v.	10
obtain, acquire	获得	獲	*huòdé*	v.	6
obtain employment	就业	業	*jiùyè*	v.o.	6
of one's own will	自主		*zìzhǔ*	v.	6
office	机关	機關	*jīguān*	n.	6
office building	写字楼	寫 樓	*xiězìlóu*	n.	7
old age	老龄	齡	*lǎolíng*	attr.	2
old age, one's later years	晚年		*wǎnnián*	n.	10
one after another	纷纷	紛	*fēnfēn*	adv.	3
one by one	逐		*zhú*	adj.	4
only child	独生子女	獨	*dúshēngzǐnǚ*	n.	10
open-minded	开放	開	*kāifàng*	adj.	8
order (goods)	订购	訂購	*dìnggòu*	v.	7
order form	订单	訂單	*dìngdān*	n.	7
ordinary	平淡		*píngdàn*	adj.	9
ordinary people	老百姓		*lǎobǎixìng*	n.	3
outpatient service	门诊	門診	*ménzhěn*	n.	1
outside or external force	外力		*wàilì*	n.	8
outstanding, excellent	优秀	優	*yōuxiù*	adj.	5
overtime	超时	時	*chāoshí*	v.	1
pair, couple	对	對	*duì*	m.	2
parents, head of a family	家长	長	*jiāzhǎng*	n.	4
pass through	通行		*tōngxíng*	v.	1
pay attention to, strive for	讲究	講	*jiǎngjiu*	v.	8
pay close attention to	关注	關	*guānzhù*	v.	2
peak	高峰		*gāofēng*	n.	1
per capita, per person	人均		*rénjūn*	attr.	3
per household	户均	戶	*hùjūn*	attr.	3
period, duration	期间	間	*qījiān*	n.	1
period, full stop	句号	號	*jùhào*	n.	4
permit, allow, grant	允许	許	*yǔnxǔ*	v.	10

英文	简体	繁体	拼音	词性	课数
person with ability	人才		réncái	n.	4
personally, in person	亲自	親	qīnzì	adv.	7
person-time	人次		réncì	n.	1
Ph.D., doctoral degree	博士		bóshì	n.	4
pile up; pile, heap	堆		duī	v./n.	5
place (hope, feeling, etc.) on	寄托	託	jìtuō	v.	4
plastic	塑料		sùliào	n.	6
pleasant surprise	惊喜	驚	jīngxǐ	n.	8
pledge, guarantee, assure	保证	證	bǎozhèng	v.	7
policy	政策		zhèngcè	n.	2
poor people	穷人	窮	qióngrén	n.	8
popular, fashionable	流行		liúxíng	adj.	6
popular, hot	热门	熱門	rèmén	adj.	4
population	人口		rénkǒu	n.	2
position, status	地位		dìwèi	n.	4
positive, active, enthusiastic	积极	積極	jījí	adj.	10
power, authority	权力	權	quánlì	n.	10
power, rights	权	權	quán	n.	3
precious stone, gem	宝石	寶	bǎoshí	n.	5
press, push down	压	壓	yā	v.	5
price	价	價	jià	n.	7
price	价格	價	jiàgé	n.	3
price difference	差价	價	chājià	n.	7
price level	价位	價	jiàwèi	n.	7
privately owned house	私房		sīfáng	n.	3
profit, profit return	利润	潤	lìrùn	n.	6
promote (goods)	推销	銷	tuīxiāo	v.	7
promote, advance, accelerate	促进	進	cùjìn	v.	6
protect	保护	護	bǎohù	v.	10
protect, uphold, defend	维护	維護	wéihù	v.	10
proud	自豪		zìháo	adj.	10
psychology, mentality; mental	心理		xīnlǐ	n.	6
publish (in a newspaper or magazine)	登		dēng	v.	9

英文	简体	繁体	拼音	词性	课数
quantity, amount	数量	數	shùliàng	n.	2
range, scope, extent	幅度		fúdù	n.	2
rapid, speedy	迅速		xùnsù	adj.	3
rate, proportion, ratio	率		lǜ	n.	2
ratio, proportion	比例		bǐlì	n.	2
reach, achieve, attain	达到	達	dádào	v.	2
real estate, realty	房地产	達產	fángdìchǎn	n.	3
real man, true man	男子汉	漢	nánzǐhàn	n.	9
really, indeed, as expected	果然		guǒrán	conj.	7
recover, restore, reinstate	恢复	復	huīfù	v.	4
recruit students	招生		zhāoshēng	v.o.	6
register (at a hospital)	挂号	掛號	guàhào	v.	1
regrow, reproduce, recycle	再生		zàishēng	v./attr.	6
reside, dwell	居住		jūzhù	v.	3
residence, dwelling	住宅		zhùzhái	n.	3
resident, inhabitant	居民		jūmín	n.	3
resign, dismiss, decline	辞	辭	cí	v.	6
respond to an ad or solicitation	应征	應徵	yìngzhēng	v.	9
restrict, limit, confine	限制		xiànzhì	v.	3
résumé	简历	簡歷	jiǎnlì	n.	6
rice and other dishes, meal	饭菜	飯	fàncài	n.	7
ringing sound	叮吟吟		dīnglínglíng	ono.	5
rise, ascend	上升		shàngshēng	v.	2
rise, go up	上涨	漲	shàngzhǎng	v.	3
rise, spring up	兴起	興起	xīngqǐ	v.	4
RMB, Chinese currency	人民币	幣	rénmínbì	n.	1
road, journey	路途		lùtú	n.	5
romantic	浪漫		làngmàn	adj.	8
rose	玫瑰		méiguī	n.	8
sacrifice	牺牲	犧	xīshēng	v.	8
safeguard; protection, guarantee	保障		bǎozhàng	v./n.	6
salary, benefit, treatment	待遇		dàiyù	n.	4
salient feature, characteristic	特色		tèsè	n.	7

英文	简体	繁体	拼音	词性	课数
sample	抽样	樣	*chōuyàng*	v./n.	2
satisfy	满足	滿	*mǎnzú*	v.	7
scarf	围巾	圍	*wéijīn*	n.	9
school subject or course	科目		*kēmù*	n.	5
second time, once more	再次		*zàicì*	adv.	8
secretary	秘书	書	*mìshū*	n.	9
seek, pursue, court (a person)	追求		*zhuīqiú*	v.	8
select a career	择业	擇業	*zéyè*	v.o.	6
self-confident, confident	自信		*zìxìn*	adj.	9
senior	年长	長	*niánzhǎng*	adj.	10
series of	一系列		*yíxìliè*	attr.	4
series of, a chain of	一连串	連	*yìliánchuàn*	n.p.	9
serious	严重	嚴	*yánzhòng*	adj.	3
shake, wave, rock	摇	搖	*yáo*	v.	5
shed tears	流泪	淚	*liúlèi*	v.o.	7
shift to an earlier time	提前		*tíqián*	v.	1
shoot up, rise dramatically	飞涨	飛漲	*fēizhǎng*	v.	3
short message, text message	短信		*duǎnxìn*	n.	9
short period, a spell	阵	陣	*zhèn*	m.	5
shove, push; crowded	挤	擠	*jǐ*	v./adj.	1
sigh	唉		*ài*	intj.	5
sigh with emotion	感慨		*gǎnkǎi*	v./n.	6
Sina News website	新浪网	網	*Xīnlàngwǎng*	p.n.	6
single-plank bridge	独木桥	獨 橋	*dúmùqiáo*	n.	4
small particles	颗	顆	*kē*	m.(n.)	5
snacks	小吃		*xiǎochī*	n.	7
snail	蜗牛	蝸	*wōniú*	n.	1
so, such, like this	如此		*rúcǐ*	pron.	1
social intercourse	社交		*shèjiāo*	n.	9
solicit	征	徵	*zhēng*	v.	9
sons and daughters, children	儿女	兒	*érnǚ*	n.	10
spacious, roomy	宽敞	寬	*kuānchǎng*	adj.	3
special aptitude, specialty	特长	長	*tècháng*	n.	9

英文	简体	繁体	拼音	词性	课数
special flavor	风味	風	fēngwèi	n.	7
special, specialized	专门	專門	zhuānmén	adj.	7
speed, pace	速度		sùdù	n.	3
Spring Festival travel season	春运	運	chūnyùn	attr.	1
square	平方		píngfāng	n.	3
start an undertaking	创业	創業	chuàngyè	v.o.	6
state, condition	状态	狀態	zhuàngtài	n.	10
state-owned housing	公房		gōngfáng	n.	3
statistics, census; gather statistics	统计	統計	tǒngjì	n./v.	1
stress, emphasize	强调	強調	qiángdiào	v.	8
strive for	争取	爭	zhēngqǔ	v.	3
structure, composition	结构	結構	jiégòu	n.	2
study abroad	留学	學	liúxué	v.	4
style, manner	风格	風	fēnggé	n.	7
subsidize; subsidy	补助	補	bǔzhù	v./n.	3
subtract, reduce, decrease	减	減	jiǎn	v.	10
superior, advantageous	优越	優	yōuyuè	adj.	9
superior to, higher than	高于	於	gāoyú	i.e.	8
surpass, exceed	超过	過	chāoguò	v.	1
sustain, support, hold up	顶	頂	dǐng	v.	10
sweetheart, heart's desire	心上人		xīnshàngrén	n.	8
system	制度		zhìdù	n.	3
tai chi	太极拳	極	tàijíquán	n.	10
take an adventure, take a risk	冒险	險	màoxiǎn	v.o.	9
talent, ability, capacity	才能		cáinéng	n.	9
talk about, discuss; discussion	谈论	談論	tánlùn	v./n.	2
taste	口味		kǒuwèi	n.	7
teachers' college, normal school	师范	師範	shīfàn	n.	4
teaching staff	师资	師資	shīzī	n.	4
team, profession, troops, army	队伍	隊	duìwu	n.	4
temporary	临时	臨時	línshí	adj.	1
thin, fine, slender	细	細	xì	adj.	9
thousands of soldiers and horses (a big army)	千军万马	軍萬馬	qiān jūn wàn mǎ	i.e.	4

英文	简体	繁体	拼音	词性	课数
thousands of, millions of	成千上万	萬	*chéng qiān shàng wàn*	i.e.	1
thread	丝	絲	*sī*	m.	5
timely, prompt	及时	時	*jíshí*	adj.	7
together, jointly	共同		*gòngtóng*	adv.	9
topic, subject of conversation	话题	話題	*huàtí*	n.	9
trade, profession, industry	行业	業	*hángyè*	n.	6
tradition; traditional	传统	傳統	*chuántǒng*	n./adj.	2
traffic	交通		*jiāotōng*	n.	1
transfer, change hands	中转	轉	*zhōngzhuǎn*	v.	7
twilight romance, romance of the elderly	黄昏恋	戀	*huánghūnliàn*	n.	10
two-way, bidirectional	双向	雙	*shuāngxiàng*	adj.	4
unconsciously, unknowingly	不知不觉	覺	*bù zhī bù jué*	i.e.	5
undergraduate	本科		*běnkē*	n.	4
unmarried	未婚		*wèihūn*	attr.	9
unmarried, single	单身	單	*dānshēn*	adj.	10
Valentine's Day	情人节	節	*qíngrénjié*	p.n.	8
value	价值	價	*jiàzhí*	n.	7
value male more than female	重男轻女	輕	*zhòng nán qīng nǚ*	v.o.	2
value, worth	值		*zhí*	n.	8
vary, alternate	变换	變換	*biànhuàn*	v.	7
villa	别墅		*biéshù*	n.	3
volume of flow, rate of flow	流量		*liúliàng*	n.	1
wait, await	等候		*děnghòu*	v.	8
waiting room, waiting lounge	候车室	車	*hòuchēshì*	n.	1
waste	浪费	費	*làngfèi*	v.	6
waste product, reject	废品	廢	*fèipǐn*	n.	6
wealth	财富	財	*cáifù*	n.	6
wealth, money	钱财	錢財	*qiáncái*	n.	10
website	网站	網	*wǎngzhàn*	n.	6
well-known, famous	知名		*zhīmíng*	adj.	7
West, the Occident	西洋		*xīyáng*	adj.	8
white-collar (worker)	白领	領	*báilǐng*	n.	7

英文	简体	繁体	拼音	词性	课数
whole, complete	整		*zhěng*	adj.	10
whole, full	整整		*zhěngzhěng*	adj.	10
windowsill	窗台	臺	*chuāngtái*	n.	5
wish happiness to; blessing, benediction	祝福		*zhùfú*	v./n.	2
with great difficulty, finally	好不容易		*hǎobùróngyì*	adv.	1
woo, court	求爱	愛	*qiúài*	v.o.	8
yawn	哈欠		*hāqian*	n.	5
younger generation, juniors	晚辈	輩	*wǎnbèi*	n.	10
youth, teenager	青少年		*qīngshàonián*	n.	4